(Dis)ENTITLING
THE POOR

Elizabeth Bussiere

(DIS)ENTITLING THE POOR

The Warren Court, Welfare Rights, and the American Political Tradition

The Pennsylvania State University Press
University Park, Pennsylvania

Library of Congress Cataloging-in-Publication Data

Bussiere, Elizabeth.
    (Dis)entitling the poor : the Warren court, welfare rights, and the
    American political tradition / Elizabeth Bussiere.

        p.   cm.
    Includes bibliographical references and index.
    ISBN 0-271-01601-9 (cloth : alk. paper)
    ISBN 0-271-01602-7 (pbk. : alk. paper)
        1. Public welfare—Law and
    legislation—United States—History. I. Title.
    KF3720.B87   1997
    344.73′03—dc20
    [347.3043]   96-6451
                                                    CIP

It is the policy of The Pennsylvania State University Press to use acid-free
paper for the first printing of all clothbound books. Publications on uncoated
stock satisfy the minimum requirements of American National Standard for
Information Sciences—Permanence of Paper for Printed Library Materials,
ANSI Z39.48-1992.

Contents

In Memory of Choi

Acknowledgments

It is impossible to acknowledge all the people who have influenced my ideas or whose good company was especially beneficial when I hit an impasse in my work. But I trust that through face-to-face conversations or through letters, phone calls, and e-mail those people whose names do not appear here nevertheless understand the depth of my gratitude.

For their indispensable feedback dating back to drafts of dissertation proposals, Jeffrey B. Abramson, Jennifer L. Hochschild, and R. Shep Melnick deserve my deepest appreciation. They were sharp when I was muddled and kind when kindness mattered more than intellectual acumen. A measure of their grace as mentors is the room they have since created in our relationships for intellectual parity and friendship. In addition, I am grateful to Michael W. McCann, for although I fell short of his own high scholarly standards, his meticulous and insightful reader's reports enabled me to formulate my arguments with greater precision, persuasiveness, or punch. Bob Pepperman Taylor gave generously of his time and talent on an earlier version of the manuscript so that I might one day see it in print. Daniel A. Cohen helped me frame the book and keep the narrative and analytic lines in focus. His companionship has become equally valuable.

Other scholars and friends assisted on a variety of tasks. Even though I was a complete stranger, Rogers Smith gave me extensive comments on what subsequently became Chapters 5–7. Sidney Milkis's knowledge of American political development was especially illuminating as I reflected on the material for Chapters 4 and 8. And although I have not done justice to their complex and subtle ideas, Nancy J. Hirschmann and Elizabeth Wingrove each enriched my understanding of feminist theory, in addition to providing much-needed solace. Arthur (Rusty) Simonds and Kathe McCaffrey regularly welcomed me into their home and somehow managed to whip up veritable feasts while simultaneously tending to my intellectual or computer glitches. Marilyn Stelting helped prepare the manuscript for submission and became a good friend in the process.

The staff at Penn State Press could not have been more solicitous or patient. Director Sandy Thatcher sensed something of value in a conference paper I had presented and later deftly and efficiently guided the manuscript through the review process. Cherene Holland, managing editor, deserves recognition for the patience, flexibility, and unflappability she exhibited throughout the production process. Catherine Thatcher was a meticulous copyeditor.

I thank the Academy of Political Science for permission to use sections of my article, "The Failure of Constitutional Welfare Rights in the Warren Court," *Political Science Quarterly* 109 (Spring 1994): 105–31. I also thank the University Press of Virginia and my senior co-author, Jeffrey B. Abramson, for permission to use material from our article, "Free Speech and Free Press: A Communitarian Perspective," in *New Communitarian Thinking: Persons, Virtues, Institutions, and Communities,* edited by Amitai Etzioni (Charlottesville: University Press of Virginia, 1995): 218–19.

Several institutions deserve acknowledgment: the Women's Caucus for Political Science, for an Alice Paul Dissertation Award; the Bunting Institute of Radcliffe College, for a 1993–94 fellowship, which provided an oasis of stimulation, inspiration, and camaraderie; the University of Massachusetts–Boston, for several grants, a steady stream of engaging students, and department colleagues who genuinely care about one another's well-being; and the Center on Social Welfare Policy and Law, particularly Henry Freedman, for facilitating my research.

Closer to home, my parents, Norman and Ruth Bussiere, instilled in me a reverence for books, and then many years later they provided tangible help so that their daughter could write one herself. Jason Choi, my stepson, has given definition and meaning to my daily life for the past six years, providing the much-needed perspective that kids are uniquely capable of giving their parents. Finally, I dedicate this book to the memory of my late husband, Choi Sung-il, who was an indefatigable booster of my scholarly endeavors and who made my life enormously fulfilling. He remains present in so many ways, including in this book.

Abbreviations

ADC	Aid to Dependent Children
AFDC	Aid to Families with Dependent Children
CES	Committee on Economic Security
CSWPL	Center on Social Welfare Policy and Law
ERA	Equal Rights Amendment
FERA	Federal Emergency Relief Agency
GTU	General Trades Union
LSP	Legal Services Program
NAACP	National Association for the Advancement of Colored People
NCM	National Congress of Mothers
NOW	National Organization for Women
NTU	National Trades Union
NWP	National Woman's Party
NWRO	National Welfare Rights Organization
PTA	Parent-Teacher Association

Chapter One

Subsistence Rights and the Warren Court

In 1989 the United States Supreme Court addressed the question of state liability for the severe beating of a four-year-old child, Joshua DeShaney, at the hands of his father.[1] So traumatic were Joshua's injuries that they left him profoundly mentally retarded, requiring full-time institutional care. Mr. Randy DeShaney had been the subject of a Department of Social Services investigation into allegations of child abuse. He was eventually convicted and imprisoned for the abuse of his son.

Mrs. Melody DeShaney sued the county's Department of Social Services, a state agency, for "extreme misconduct" in failing to remove Joshua from his father's custody when evidence had accumulated suggesting that his father was beating the child. Donald Sullivan, Mrs. DeShaney's lawyer, argued that the Due Process Clause of the Fourteenth Amendment guarantees all individuals a "constitutionally

---

1. *DeShaney v. Winnebago County Department of Social Services*, 489 U.S. 189 (1989).

protected right to physical integrity, to bodily protection."[2] At stake, in Sullivan's view, was the deprivation of Joshua DeShaney's "right that arises out of the Constitution to remain alive."[3]

In *DeShaney v. Winnebago County Department of Social Services* the Supreme Court ruled that the state was not liable under the Fourteenth Amendment for Joshua's injuries. Mr. Sullivan's understanding of the scope of Fourteenth Amendment rights received a skeptical hearing during the oral argument. Chief Justice Rehnquist, the author of the six-member majority opinion, questioned Mr. Sullivan's characterization of the state's duties under the Fourteenth Amendment. The chief justice explained: "Certainly we've held in many cases that the state may not deprive someone of life, but we've never held that provision protects, in the constitutional sense, a private attack on another person."[4] Here Chief Justice Rehnquist was referring to the distinction between public and private action embedded in the Fourteenth Amendment, which reads in part, "nor shall any State deprive any person of life, liberty, or property, without due process of law." Since the amendment mentions only state action, the Department of Social Services could not be held constitutionally responsible for the abuse perpetrated by a private individual, Mr. DeShaney. Further, Chief Justice Rehnquist went on, the Fourteenth Amendment proscribes state action that trammels upon due process of law, but it does not impose "affirmative government duties."

The skeptical remarks aimed at Attorney Sullivan during the oral argument prefigured the final majority opinion, in which the chief justice once again emphasized that the Fourteenth Amendment functions as a limit on state action and is not a source of constitutional duties or substantive constitutional rights for the individual. To interpret the amendment as requiring government to furnish the assistance necessary to sustain life, liberty, or property would be, in the majority's assessment, an "expansive reading of the constitutional text" unhinged from the language and history of the Fourteenth Amend-

---

2. Transcript of oral argument, reprinted in *May It Please the Court: The Most Significant Oral Arguments Made Before the Supreme Court*, ed. Peter Irons and Stephanie Guitton (New York: The New Press, 1993), p. 42. For a more complete collection of documents regarding the *DeShaney* case, see *Landmark Briefs and Arguments of the United States Supreme Court: Constitutional Law* (1988 Term Supplement), vol. 184, ed. Philip B. Kurland and Gerhard Casper (Arlington, Va., and Bethesda, Md.: University Publications of America, 1990).

3. Irons and Guitton, eds., *May It Please the Court*, p. 42.

4. Ibid.

ment.[5] The majority was unmoved by Attorney Sullivan's claim that
the state's action of returning Joshua to his father after holding the
bruised boy in protective custody for three days was negligent and a
violation of the Due Process Clause. Chief Justice Rehnquist responded: ". . . when [the State] returned [Joshua] to his father's
custody, it placed him in no worse a position than that in which he
would have been had it not acted at all; the State does not become the
permanent guarantor of an individual's safety by having once offered
him shelter."[6] Although recognizing the "natural sympathy" elicited
by Joshua's fate, Chief Justice Rehnquist cautioned against letting
emotion distort constitutional judgment.[7]

   In a dissenting opinion that Justices Marshall and Blackmun joined,
Justice Brennan criticized the philosophical framework that guided
the majority's reasoning. At the heart of the majority's analysis lay
the distinction between negative and positive liberty—a distinction
that Justice Brennan found generally appropriate but not applicable
in this case. Negative liberty is the individual's right to be free of
government restraints on his or her liberty; positive liberty is the
individual's right to the means and resources to exercise liberty. The
Fourteenth Amendment, Chief Justice Rehnquist repeated, embodies
a negative liberty, shielding the individual from government actions
that fall short of Due Process standards. Justice Brennan explained
that this formula led the majority mistakenly to construe the state's
fault as mere "inaction" (i.e., not removing Joshua from his father's
custody). But to the dissents, the majority miscast the issue. "No one,"
Justice Brennan asserted, "has asked the Court to proclaim that, as a
general matter, the Constitution safeguards positive as well as negative liberties."[8] Rather the claim was staked on the actions that the
Department of Social Services had taken in Joshua's case.

   Justice Brennan recounted Wisconsin's procedures for investigating
suspected child abuse and its handling of Joshua's case in particular.
In chronicling the facts of Joshua's case Justice Brennan highlighted
the social worker's detailed reports on the boy and her suspicion that
the father continued to abuse his son. The dissents also called attention to the social worker's failure to insist on seeing Joshua on a visit
to the DeShaney home shortly before the boy sustained his crippling
injuries, when the father said his son was "too ill" to have contact.

   5. *DeShaney v. Winnebago County Department of Social Services*, 489 U.S. 189 (1989),
at 195.
   6. Ibid. at 201.
   7. Ibid. at 202–3.
   8. Ibid. at 204.

This lack of follow-through was bone-chilling, Justice Brennan remarked, in that the social worker herself had expressed a dreadful
foreboding: "I just knew the phone would ring some day. Joshua would
be dead."[9] To the dissents, the social worker's lack of persistence may
have amounted to reckless behavior forbidden by the Fourteenth
Amendment. At the very least, Justice Brennan submitted, Mrs.
DeShaney ought to have been given the chance to demonstrate that
the state's failure to help Joshua was the result not of the "sound
exercise of professional judgment that we recognized . . . as sufficient
to preclude liability, . . . but [of] the kind of arbitrariness that we have
in the past condemned."[10]

At the heart of the dissents' analysis was the argument that "inaction can be every bit as abusive of power as action, that oppression can
result when a State undertakes a vital duty and then ignores it."[11] In
the dissents' eyes the majority drew far too rigid a distinction between
state and private action and between action and inaction. But this
approach, Justice Brennan pointed out, blinded the majority to the
ways in which the state becomes involved in private action and
thereby assumes a certain level of responsibility for what happens
behind closed doors. The dissents believed that the county Department
of Social Services had some responsibility for Joshua's welfare as a
result of its prior measures investigating the abuse and therefore
acquired a constitutional obligation to follow through.

In a particularly vitriolic dissent Justice Blackmun attacked the
majority's "sterile formalism" as having "no place in the interpretation of the broad and stirring Clauses of the Fourteenth Amendment."[12] Moreover, in examining the relevant precedents Justice
Blackmun wished the whole Court had taken a " 'sympathetic'
reading, one which comports with dictates of fundamental justice
and recognizes that compassion need not be exiled from the province
of judging."[13]

The *DeShaney* case illustrates a way of thinking about constitutional interpretation and political obligation to meet human needs
that has had remarkable staying power. Interestingly, neither the
conservative majority nor the liberal dissenting opinion contended
that the Fourteenth Amendment as a general principle encapsulates
affirmative government obligations to ensure the protection of life or

9. Ibid. at 209.
10. Ibid. at 210.
11. Ibid. at 212.
12. Ibid.
13. Ibid. at 213.

liberty. Notice how Justice Brennan went out of his way attempting to show that the finding of state liability in Joshua's case would not be at all inconsistent with the Court's rulings in past cases rejecting claims of constitutionally based subsistence rights: "The cases that I have cited tell us that *Goldberg v. Kelly* . . . can stand side by side with *Dandridge v. Williams.* . . ."[14] Justice Brennan's juxtaposition of *Goldberg* and *Dandridge* was telling.[15] Within two weeks of each other the Court handed down the two decisions in 1970. In *Goldberg* the Court ruled that welfare assistance is a statutory entitlement that had to be administered in accordance with Due Process standards. That meant that a welfare recipient had to be given a fair hearing before his or her benefits could be terminated. In *Dandridge* the Court stated explicitly that the Fourteenth Amendment confers no *substantive* right to welfare but simply imposes *procedural* safeguards to ensure the fair implementation of state policy.

The dissenting justices perceived the *DeShaney* case in procedural terms: the social worker's passivity in the face of growing evidence of child abuse raised the possibility of gross misapplication of established investigatory procedures. The difference between the majority and dissenting opinions was not over the distinction between negative versus positive liberties under the Fourteenth Amendment. Justice Brennan conceded that the Due Process Clause functions as a bridle on arbitrary state action rather than as a source of positive, substantive rights. But he also argued that this philosophical distinction was misplaced in the *DeShaney* case. The disagreement between the majority and the dissents lay in their authors' characterizations of the county's handling of Joshua's case. They split on whether the social worker's decision to leave Joshua in his father's care, despite accumulating evidence of abuse, amounted to mere inaction or, possibly, negligent behavior.[16] As we have seen, the social worker's departure from the DeShaney home on one of her last visits without demanding to see Joshua seemed especially egregious conduct to the dissents, in light of the caseworker's past contact with Joshua's battered body and her suspicion that the father was the abuser. In the end, Mr. DeShaney's success in turning away the social worker because his son was "too ill" to see her allowed the father to turn that assertion into an irreversible, horrifying reality.

14. Ibid. at 207.
15. 397 U.S. 254 (1970); 397 U.S. 471 (1970).
16. Justice Brennan did not conclude that the social worker had in fact acted negligently: "I emphasize only that we do not know whether or not [irrationality was at work]." 489 U.S. 189 (1989), at 211.

The distinctions between public and private, negative and positive liberty, and procedural and substantive justice have shaped the Supreme Court's understanding of political obligation, of what citizens acting through their governments owe one another. The majority's dispassionate approach to the Fourteenth Amendment in the *DeShaney* case sent shivers up many people's spines because of the tragic hand dealt young Joshua. But strikingly, the majority and the dissenting justices actually *agreed* that the Due Process Clause contains no substantive right to "remain alive." In fact, when a constitutional right to life was first presented, the liberal Warren Court rejected it.

The Warren Court rebuffed the claim of a constitutional right to subsistence even though the justices had shown a long-standing commitment to shoring up poor people's legal rights through decisions that had helped the welfare rights movement reach its peak by the late 1960s. Unlike the Rehnquist Court, the Warren Court had given its approval to expansive readings of the Due Process and Equal Protection Clauses of the Fourteenth Amendment. Repeatedly, the Court had insisted that the open-ended clauses of the Constitution not be straitjacketed by the founding fathers' original intent. Rather, the justices sought to interpret them in light of changing social conditions and values.

Why, then, did the Warren Court refuse to accept the claim of constitutional welfare rights? Scholars of differing political perspectives typically respond that guaranteed welfare rights are fundamentally at odds with the individualist American political tradition. But this explanation assumes a unidimensional and an ahistorical view of American political thought. More specifically, it ignores the many moments in American history when business and government had to reckon with populist movements that challenged the individualist, market-oriented idea of freedom associated with John Locke and Adam Smith. A central theme of this book is that there were two potential intellectual sources for welfare rights in America. One was a natural-law tradition that found powerful expression in Revolutionary thought and that was revived by the radical artisan movements of the 1830s, when Workingmen created a powerful proto-welfare-rights philosophy out of deeply rooted natural-law and civic-republican principles. The second, "maternalism," dated back to the Jacksonian era and found its most potent political expression in the Progressive-era movement for mothers' pensions. The former grounded civic responsibilities toward the poor as a whole in the natural right to self-preservation. The latter stressed the civic obligation toward mothers, especially impoverished mothers, on account of the fundamental role they play in the moral development of children—the nation's future citizens. In short, the American political tradition was far more eclectic than often acknowledged by late twentieth-century political scientists.

In addition to the richness of the American political tradition there were more immediate developments that suggested the strong possibility of the Warren Court incorporating a right to welfare into the Constitution. Several developments in particular led one to have expected the Court to identify welfare as a right under the Fourteenth Amendment: (1) the Court perceived the Constitution as an evolving document, not shackled by its origins; (2) it fairly consistently handed important victories to Legal Services lawyers representing poor people; (3) more specifically, it gave encouraging nods to the welfare rights movement itself; and, (4) it rendered constitutional judgments at a time when a right to a guaranteed minimum income was at the top of the political agenda of a *Republican* president, Richard Nixon.

In light of these factors it is puzzling that the liberal Warren Court majority ultimately sounded so much like the conservative *DeShaney* majority on the issue of constitutional welfare rights. Surprisingly, Chief Justice Rehnquist's admonition to his colleagues not to be swayed by "natural sympathy" for Joshua's plight echoed that of his liberal predecessor, Chief Justice Earl Warren, in another famous welfare case. In 1968 Chief Justice Warren sounded an alarm at the idea of constitutionally based welfare rights, issuing this warning: "The plight of the poor has pricked the nation's conscience. To the extent that [Legal Services lawyers expose] . . . the handicaps upon the poor of the Nation, they appeal to the right instincts of all men. However, instinct cannot be our guide. . . ."[17]

The constitutional and philosophical issues regarding political obligation and individual rights to security have been of fleeting concern to the Rehnquist Court, which confronted them in the tragic, but isolated, context of an abused boy. But those issues were repeatedly brought into high relief and were argued with great zeal before the Warren Court throughout the 1960s. The explosion of poverty litigation, set off by the establishment of the Legal Services Program, regularly forced the Warren Court to confront questions pertaining to the proper relationship between reason and emotion, between constitu-

17. Draft, Opinion of the Court, *Shapiro v. Thompson*, June 3, 1968. The Earl Warren Papers, filed in container number 566, Library of Congress. This case was reargued the following year, and Chief Justice Warren was unable to maintain the majority coalition he had pieced together. As such, the opinion cited here did not carry the day, and in his official dissenting opinion in 1969 Chief Justice Warren did not include this passage.

tional judgment and human compassion. Poverty-related was launched by social reformers inside and outside the federal government.

Troubled by the coexistence of extreme affluence and poverty in American society, the administration of President Lyndon Johnson in 1965 fashioned a set of programs collectively known as the War on Poverty. One of the most successful antipoverty programs was the Legal Services Program (LSP), housed in the Office of Economic Opportunity. Johnson's advisors had urged the president to propose a federally funded program to provide free legal counsel to poor people. Although Legal Aid societies already existed in urban areas, critics contended that the societies were ineffective in rooting out the legal supports to discrimination against the poor. Legal Aid attorneys could, and did, for instance, save an indigent client from being evicted at the eleventh hour, but they left unchanged the laws that empowered slum lords to act with reckless disregard for the needs of destitute tenants. When President Johnson and Congress established the LSP in 1965, program leaders immediately set about soliciting and funding proposed programs. Leaders bandied about different philosophies and goals for the LSP, and eventually "law reform" became the program's priority. The idea here was to use vigorous advocacy on behalf of the poor to change statutes and regulations that hurt them.[18]

The LSP set up thirteen national backup centers to provide litigation information and support in various areas of poverty law. The most visible was the Center on Social Welfare Policy and Law (CSWPL), located initially at the Columbia University School of Social Work in New York City. There the law center was smack in the middle of intellectual ferment and community organizing for a poor people's movement. Richard Cloward and Frances Fox Piven, two prominent Columbia sociologists, developed a "crisis theory," which anticipated that poor people would flood the welfare system with eligibility claims and put so much strain on the system as to cause its collapse.[19] Then, as now, the welfare system allocated benefits to all Americans who fell into certain limited "categories," such as the elderly, the blind, and the single mother with dependent children. Piven and Cloward's expectation was that the system's collapse would provide the impetus for government to restructure welfare policy so as to guarantee *all* people a minimum income. Reformers looked to the day when a

18. For a comprehensive treatment of the LSP by one of its early leaders see Earl Johnson, Jr., *Justice and Reform: The Formative Years of the Legal Services Program* (New York: Russell Sage Foundation, 1974).

19. Martha F. Davis, *Brutal Need: Lawyers and the Welfare Rights Movement, 1960–1973* (New Haven, Conn.: Yale University Press, 1993), p. 45.

uniform guaranteed income would supplant the category-based welfare system.

The LSP supplied the institutional mechanism for putting Piven and Cloward's crisis theory into practice. LSP lawyers educated indigents about their eligibility for welfare assistance and helped them to assert their legal rights in court. In winning court victories that added poor people to the welfare rolls, especially to the much maligned Aid to Families with Dependent Children (AFDC) program, the hope was that government would experience a fiscal crisis. In addition, by effectively challenging welfare eligibility restrictions on statutory and constitutional grounds, LSP lawyers sought to dismantle the "categorical" edifice of the welfare system itself.[20]

The LSP lawyers knew that to be successful at all they would have to generate a steady flow of indigent clients who would serve as parties to lawsuits against the federal and state governments. In the mid-1960s, borne of the agitation of the civil rights movement, social reformers joined poor people to launch a welfare rights movement.[21] Welfare-rights leaders, AFDC mothers, and other poor people allied themselves with LSP attorneys. The lawyers at the CSWPL formulated a litigation strategy that they hoped would culminate in the United States Supreme Court's reading a right to welfare into the Constitution. For its part the welfare rights movement provided a large pool of clients to file class-action suits. Taking its cue from the Legal Defense Fund of the National Association for the Advancement of Colored People (NAACP), the CSWPL devised a litigation strategy that would enable lawyers to build incrementally on principles favorable to the poor rather than to thrust wholesale social change at the courts.[22]

LSP lawyers were emboldened to attempt to bring their cases all the

20. Edward V. Sparer, "The Right to Welfare," in *The Rights of Americans: What They Are—What They Should Be,* ed. Norman Dorsen (New York: Random House, 1971), pp. 65–93; see also *Law in Action* 3 (May 5, 1968).

21. For a comprehensive treatment of the welfare rights movement see Guida West, *The National Welfare Rights Movement: The Social Protest of Poor Women* (New York: Praeger Publishers, 1981). See also Neil Bailis, *Bread or Justice: Grassroots Organizing in the Welfare Rights Movement* (Lexington, Mass.: Lexington Books, 1974); Susan Handley Hertz, *The Welfare Mothers Movement: A Decade of Change for Poor Women?* (Lanham, Md.: University Press of America, 1981); and Nick Kotz and Mary Lynn Kotz, *A Passion for Equality: George A. Wiley and the Movement* (New York: W.W. Norton, 1977).

22. For an excellent study of the overall success of the LSP attorneys before the Supreme Court see Susan E. Lawrence, *The Poor in Court: The Legal Services Program and Supreme Court Decision Making* (Princeton, N.J.: Princeton University Press, 1990).

way to the Supreme Court because since 1938 the justices had an avowed stance of according heightened judicial solicitude to "discrete and insular minorities." Ninety-eight percent of the National Welfare Rights Organization (NWRO), the institutional base of the movement, were poor African-American mothers whose starkly vulnerable political status seemed to call out for judicial protection in welfare litigation.

Apart from the generally sympathetic posture of the Court toward minorities, there were specific reasons pertaining to constitutional doctrine that made LSP attorneys believe that the Warren Court might incorporate a right to welfare into the Constitution. Throughout the 1950s and 1960s the Court had come to identify wealth (or poverty) as a "suspect classification" eliciting "strict scrutiny" under the Fourteenth Amendment's Equal Protection Clause. The Equal Protection Clause states: ". . . nor [shall any state] deny to any person within its jurisdiction the equal protection of the laws." The original purpose of the Fourteenth Amendment was to protect the newly freed slaves following the Civil War; thus, it is not surprising that the Supreme Court came to identify race as a "suspect classification" under the Equal Protection Clause. Any law containing a racial classification aroused the Court's suspicion that discrimination lay behind it, and the Warren Court placed the burden on the states to prove otherwise. Significantly, during the 1950s and 1960s the Court extended the scope of "suspect classification" to include economic class. In a series of decisions the Warren Court ruled that classifications amounting to "wealth discrimination" violate the Fourteenth Amendment's Equal Protection Clause. LSP attorneys regarded the wealth-discrimination doctrine as a powerful tool to challenge laws and institutional practices that were biased against the poor.

Another specific development in Equal Protection doctrine during the Warren Court years encouraged LSP attorneys. In a few landmark decisions the Court determined that there are certain "fundamental rights" under the Fourteenth Amendment even though they have no express textual basis in the Constitution. For example, in 1964 the Court decided that, although not listed in the Constitution, voting in a state election is a "fundamental right" because it makes possible the exercise of "other basic civil and political rights."[23] If voting in a state election is a "fundamental right," welfare-rights advocates thought, surely material subsistence must also be deemed "fundamental." Con-

23. *Reynolds v. Sims*, 377 U.S. 533 (1964).

stitutional rights, they reasoned, are not very meaningful when a person lacks the very means to survive.

Those positive developments in Equal Protection review—what came to be called the "new Equal Protection"—led welfare-rights advocates to target the Warren Court as the political institution most amenable to the poor's need-claims. Of course, the legislative and executive branches had created antipoverty programs, but they had made political compromises so as to appease southern Democrats and others who were wary of broadening welfare eligibility. The progressive orientation of the Warren Court justices and lower-court federal judges, as well as their relative insulation from political pressure, made the courts an attractive forum to express the poor's grievances and to seek redress. Moreover, intellectual innovations in legal theory gave some welfare-rights strategists a heady feeling that substantial changes on behalf of the poor were finally feasible.

By the mid-1960s, then, the legal landscape seemed fertile ground for planting constitutional welfare rights. Once reserved for the affluent, litigation held the promise of being a powerful weapon in the War on Poverty. No longer were the courts an intimidating place where the state stripped poor people of their apartments, issued orders to garnish their wages to pay creditors, and acted in myriad other ways that made the lives of poor people more precarious. Instead, social reformers and the poor themselves perceived the courts as offering a haven from "lives on the edge."

LSP lawyers did achieve some early and important victories in the Supreme Court; however, in 1970 the Supreme Court declined to "constitutionalize" a right to subsistence, and soon afterward, under the Burger Court, the justices abandoned the wealth-discrimination doctrine.[24] The Court's adverse decisions crippled the welfare rights movement, which ultimately collapsed in 1975.

Why did the Warren Court decline to establish welfare assistance as a Fourteenth Amendment right? The Court, after all, had earned a reputation for protecting the disadvantaged. In fact, political scientists wrote about the tangible benefits that the Warren Court's decisions allocated to the "underdog" constituents who comprised the New Deal coalition.[25] Furthermore, the other branches of the federal government endeavoring to improve the poor's circumstances—first through John-

24. Susan E. Lawrence concludes that LSP attorneys had a 62 percent success rate before the Supreme Court. See *The Poor in Court*, p. 151.

25. Martin Shapiro, "The Supreme Court: From Warren to Burger," in *The New American Political System*, ed. Anthony King (Washington, D.C.: American Enterprise Institute, 1978), p. 193.

son's War on Poverty and then through Nixon's guaranteed income proposal, the Family Assistance Plan—had shown concern about the poor's unmet subsistence needs and thus did not appear to be an external restraint on the Warren Court. Nevertheless, the Warren Court refused to treat welfare assistance like voting in a state election, as a "fundamental right" that was a prerequisite to the meaningful exercise of the enumerated constitutional rights. So in what constitutional and philosophical language did the Warren Court adjudicate welfare cases and others affecting the poor? How did legal doctrines and norms influence the Court's approach to human needs and to the scope of political obligation? What impact did the Warren Court have on the American social contract? Those questions are addressed in this book.

Political scientists themselves have generally offered two theoretical approaches to studying law and society—"pluralism" and the "new institutionalism"[26]—that are widely regarded as improvements on the traditional "public-law" model. Practitioners of the public-law model, mostly law school professors, tended to examine the intricacies of legal doctrines in a political vacuum and implicitly cast the federal courts as disinterested actors within the American political system. The pluralist model, which still prevails in much of the scholarly literature, focuses on the intersection of law and social forces and was an important advance over the then dominant public-law model of judicial decision making.

Seeking to understand the political dimensions of judicial behavior, political scientists began to use pluralist frameworks to explain, for example, the influence of political party affiliation, religion, and other attitudinal factors on judges' value choices and decision making.[27]

26. For good assessments of the theoretical approaches to studying law and the courts see the following: David M. O'Brien, "Reconsidering Whence and Whither Political Jurisprudence," *Western Political Quarterly* 36 (December 1983): 558–63; Austin Sarat, "The Maturation of Political Jurisprudence," *Western Political Quarterly* 36 (December 1983): 551–58; Martin M. Shapiro, "Recent Developments in Political Jurisprudence," *Western Political Quarterly* 36 (December 1983): 541–48; and Rogers M. Smith, "Political Jurisprudence, the 'New Institutionalism,' and the Future of Public Law," *American Political Science Review* 82 (March 1988): 89–108.

27. C. Neal Tate, "Personal Attribute Models of the Voting Behavior of U.S. Supreme Court Justices," *American Political Science Review* 75 (1981): 355–67; Sheldon Goldman, "Voting Behavior on the U.S. Court of Appeals Revisited," *American Political Science Review* 69 (June 1975): 491–506; J. Woodford Howard, Jr., "Role Perceptions and Behavior in Three U.S. Courts of Appeals," *Journal of Politics* 39 (1977): 916–38; Herbert M. Kritzer, "Political Correlates of the Behavior of Federal District Judges: A 'Best Case' Analysis," *Journal of Politics* 40 (1978): 25–58; Stuart Nagel, "Political Party Affiliations and Judges' Decisions," *American Political Science Review* 55 (Decem-

Political scientists also started to treat litigation as a form of interest-group behavior or a tool of social reform;[28] to relate judicial decision making to broader forces in the local political system, such as the influence of business groups, as well as to forces in the wider national political system, such as party realignment and dealignment;[29] and to analyze the implementation and impact of judicial decisions by focusing on the courts' relations with other governmental institutions.[30] Those conceptual and methodological developments helped to explain judicial behavior with greater analytical sophistication than the older public-law model.

But, as Rogers Smith observed a few years ago in an important article, pluralism has had its deficiencies as an analytical model.[31] As pluralism got swept up in the behavioral revolution, political scientists tended to banish normative issues from their studies of the courts, except to treat values as thinly veiled political interests. The fact-value distinction that affected all subfields of political science made values seem irrelevant or tangential to the "real" forces that were said to drive judicial decision making. Consequently, court scholars who were interested in the normative dimension of judicial behavior tended to part company with empirically oriented pluralists. As Smith pointed out, the two sides of the divide spoke past one another,

ber 1961): 843–51; and Glendon Schubert, ed., *Judicial Decision-Making* (New York: The Free Press, 1963).

28. For a comprehensive evaluation of Legal Services and other public-interest lawyers see Joel F. Handler and Ellen Jane Hollingsworth, *Lawyers and the Pursuit of Legal Rights* (New York: Academic Press, 1978). See also Jack Katz, *Poor People's Lawyers in Transition* (New Brunswick, N.J.: Rutgers University Press, 1982), which is an incisive sociological inquiry into lawyers' values; review of Katz's book in Stuart A. Scheingold, "The Dilemma of Legal Services," 36 *Stanford Law Review* 879 (February 1984); Karen Orren, "Standing to Sue: Interest Group Conflict in the Federal Courts," *American Political Science Review* 70 (1976): 723–41; Jonathan D. Casper, *Lawyers Before the Warren Court: Civil Liberties and Civil Rights, 1957–1966* (Urbana: University of Illinois Press, 1972); and Stuart A. Scheingold, *The Politics of Rights: Lawyers, Public Policy, and Political Change* (New Haven, Conn.: Yale University Press, 1974).

29. An excellent look at the interaction between Legal Services programs and the local or national political environment may be found in Mark Kessler, *A Comparative and Contemporary Analysis of Interorganizational Politics* (Westport, Conn.: Greenwood Press, 1987); Richard Funston, "The Supreme Court in Critical Elections," *American Political Science Review* 69 (September 1979): 795–811; Shapiro, "The Supreme Court: From Warren to Burger," pp. 179-211.

30. See, for example, Jennifer L. Hochschild, *The New American Dilemma: School Desegregation and Liberal Democracy* (New Haven, Conn.: Yale University Press, 1984); and R. Shep Melnick, *Regulation and the Courts: The Case of the Clean Air Act* (Washington, D.C.: The Brookings Institution, 1983).

31. Smith, "Political Jurisprudence."

perceiving no common theoretical or methodological ground. Behaviorally minded pluralists chided normatively minded legal scholars for being out of touch with the actual factors impinging on judicial decision making. The latter regarded behavioralist paradigms, including the pluralist's, as ill-suited to capturing the often subtle influences of legal doctrines on judicial reasoning and decision making.

Exacerbating the scholarly divisions were the ideological battles taking place in the law schools. The split was primarily between the more traditional public-law scholars and the neo-Marxist critical-legal studies proponents. The acrimony between the two groups often threatened to obscure commonalities among the competing schools of thought. For example, critical-legal scholars shared the political scientists' goal of elucidating the political nature of judicial behavior. But unlike most political scientists, critical-legal scholars treated judicial values not as the personal predilections of the individual justices but rather as constituting a legal ideology that rationalized unequal power relations in society.[32] Yet, the critical-legal perspective itself has spawned postmodern critiques that emphasize the cultural meanings of law and not just the relation between law and economic structures. They stress that there are "multiple realities" represented by different groups and that "outsider" marginalized groups do not necessarily share the meanings ascribed to law by "insider" privileged groups. Such multiple perspectives on law create cracks in the "hegemonic" ideology emphasized by critical-legal scholars.[33] Thus, even within the academic Left there are theoretical cleavages.

With deep splits in the field producing mostly bitterness among scholars of different theoretical persuasions, Rogers Smith proposed a research strategy that has helped to foster communication across the different perspectives. Smith's carefully hewn research agenda was inspired by the "new institutionalism" models that have become prominent in political science. Reacting against the pale and unidimensional account of political life found in most pluralist analyses, the new institutionalism places institutional processes at the center of political life.[34] Whereas pluralists conceptualize institutional behavior as the by-product of "exogenous forces," such as power-seeking politi-

32. For a good overview of critical-legal studies scholarship see Robert W. Gordon, "Critical Legal Histories," 36 *Stanford Law Review* 57 (January 1984); and Mark Kelman, *A Guide to Critical-Legal Studies* (Cambridge, Mass.: Harvard University Press, 1987).

33. The "Amherst" School is most closely associated with postmodern critiques of the legal system. See especially Austin Sarat and Thomas R. Kearns, eds., *The Fate of Law* (Ann Arbor: University of Michigan Press, 1993).

34. In particular, Smith found theoretical guidance in James G. March and John P.

cal parties, interest groups, and social classes, the new institutional-
ists highlight moments in public policymaking when the "state" acts
independently of societal pressures. Describing political institutions
as "more than simply mirrors of social forces," Smith attributes to
political institutions "a kind of life of their own, . . . influenc[ing] the
self-conception of those who occupy roles . . . in ways that can give
those persons distinctively 'institutional perspectives.' "[35]

Drawing on the work of other scholars, Smith defined institutions
broadly so as to encompass patterns of political and legal discourse.
He suggested reconceiving them as "key mental or rhetorical structures" that might be independent influences in their own right.[36]
His research proposals were gleaned from the new institutionalist
scholarship that was already beginning to affect other subfields of
political science. Dissatisfied with pluralist approaches, some scholars
during the 1980s urged "bringing the state back in" as a focus of
political analysis. In fact, this plea became the title of a widely read
collection of essays edited by Peter Evans, Dietrich Rueschemeyer,
and Theda Skocpol. In *Bringing the State Back In* and other books
Skocpol and her colleagues have performed yeoman work, unearthing
the institutional antecedents and foundations of the modern welfare
state.[37] They have meticulously traced the substantial part that state
actors have played in setting and sometimes contesting the institutional and ideological parameters of the welfare state.

Yet, with respect to American welfare policy the new institutionalism has had two problems. First, the literature published to date has
paid relatively scant attention to the place of legal discourse and the
courts in the American welfare state.[38] The overall neglect of the
courts in the new institutionalism literature may be due to the fact
that so much of the work has focused on Western European welfare

---

Olsen, "The New Institutionalism: Organizational Factors in Political Life," *American
Political Science Review* 78 (1984): 734–49. Since the publication of Smith's article John
Brigham has treated legal doctrines, including the "double standard" examined in this
book, as "institutional practices." See Brigham, *Property and the Politics of Entitlement*
(Philadelphia: Temple University Press, 1990).

35. Smith, "Political Jurisprudence," p. 95.

36. Ibid., p. 102.

37. Peter R. Evans, Dietrich Rueschemeyer, and Theda Skocpol, eds., *Bringing the
State Back In* (New York: Cambridge University Press, 1985). See also Margaret Weir,
Ann Shola Orloff, and Theda Skocpol, eds., *The Politics of Social Policy in the United
States* (Princeton, N.J.: Princeton University Press, 1988).

38. Notable exceptions are R. Shep Melnick's *Reading Between the Lines: Interpreting
Welfare Rights* (Washington, D.C.: The Brookings Institution, 1994); and Theda Skocpol,
*Protecting Soldiers and Mothers: The Political Origins of Social Policy in the United
States* (Cambridge, Mass.: Harvard University Press, 1992).

states, where the courts are much less prominent policymakers than they are in the United States. The relative absence of the courts in scholarship on the United States is regrettable because of the ubiquity of legal processes in American politics, as contrasted with Western Europe. As Mary Ann Glendon has pointed out, "law language" has become a striking feature of American political discourse as other sources of consensual values, such as religion and community life, have withered in our increasingly heterogeneous and fragmented society.[39] In America, law language shapes the very way in which grievances are expressed, and whether they are conceived at all. In this book I show how legal discourse shaped not only the Warren Court's but also poor people's understandings of constitutional and political obligations to the most needy members of society.

A second and related weakness of the new institutionalism approach is that its concentration on governments' administrative capacities has tended to shift attention away from the very people whom government programs serve. As Barbara Nelson speculates: "Perhaps because the main thrust of the new state-building literature is comparing state formation among and between nations, the literature has not turned its own comparative methodology toward the consequences of gender and race on questions of welfare state formation within one country."[40] Yet the very identity of many AFDC recipients—African-American and female—is essential to understanding the ideological conflicts that the welfare rights movement unleashed and even the very language in which lawyers conceptualized the welfare mothers' claims. Indeed, serious gender divisions within the welfare rights movement resulted from the disagreements between AFDC mothers and the primarily white, male LSP attorneys and welfare-rights leaders over the ideological meaning and the constituent base of "welfare rights."

In short, the existing literature largely slights the role of the American judiciary and the particular racial and gender identities of AFDC recipients. Yet in the late 1960s and early 1970s the Supreme Court and federal appeals courts played an important role in welfare policy, largely in response to grievances brought by members of the

39. Mary Ann Glendon, *Rights Talk: The Impoverishment of Political Discourse* (New York: The Free Press, 1991).

40. Barbara J. Nelson, "The Origins of the Two-Channel Welfare State: Workmen's Compensation and Mothers' Aid," in *Women, the State, and Welfare*, ed. Linda Gordon (Madison: University of Wisconsin Press, 1990), p. 129. A recent exception is Jill Quadagno's *The Color of Welfare: How Racism Undermined the War on Poverty* (New York: Oxford University Press, 1994).

welfare rights movement who received free legal representation from LSP attorneys.[41] AFDC mothers and other indigent clients, for their part, were the conduits through which legal thinkers could test new ideas about constitutional obligation and welfare entitlement.

Three recently published books make valuable contributions to the scholarly literature on judicial policymaking in welfare: Susan Lawrence's *The Poor in Court*, Martha Davis's *Brutal Need*, and R. Shep Melnick's *Reading Between the Lines.* [42] Susan Lawrence analyzes the effect of litigation brought by Legal Services Program lawyers on Supreme Court policymaking. Mindful of the weaknesses of the classical pluralist approach, Lawrence argues that "who litigates" is a critical independent variable in Supreme Court policymaking because it is the litigants who shape the Court's agenda in the first place. With the creation of the Legal Services Program in 1965 a torrent of legal claims on behalf of poor people swept through the Supreme Court. The result was that public policies comprising the heart of the American welfare state were suddenly the objects of Supreme Court decision making. Remarkably, Lawrence reports, LSP attorneys won close to two-thirds of their cases in the Supreme Court between 1965 and 1974 and had an important influence on judicial policymaking.

Lawrence is right on the mark that LSP attorneys had a considerable effect on the Court's docket and policy agenda; in this regard she disarms both traditional "pressure group" proponents and their critics. Without the free legal counsel provided by LSP attorneys it is doubtful that an entire area of "poverty law" would have been created. The private bar, after all, was not known for aggressive lawyering on behalf of the poor. In addition, Lawrence's quantitative analysis, which manipulates different "input" variables correlating them with judicial outputs, is like a kaleidoscope illuminating different dimensions that are constantly in flux and providing a more complicated and complete whole.

But in magnifying the pivotal role of litigants, Lawrence diminishes the importance of institutional pressures, such as the role of legal doctrines in Supreme Court decision making. For the other side of the question of "who litigates" is the question of what effect judicial doctrines have on litigants' strategic calculations about the specific legal claims that are or are not worth pursuing in the first place. As I argue in this book, the Warren Court's wealth-discrimination and

41. Melnick, *Reading Between the Lines.*

42. See Lawrence, *The Poor in Court*; Davis, *Brutal Need*; and Melnick, *Reading Between the Lines.*

fundamental-rights doctrines, which began to take shape in the late 1950s, subsequently emboldened LSP attorneys to engage in vigorous advocacy. Without those doctrinal innovations the LSP attorneys would have been far less successful and would have had a diminished impact on Supreme Court decision making. Yet, had the Warren Court not been so faithful to a doctrine that dichotomized the domains of individual rights and economics, its responses to poor people's constitutional claims might have been more favorable to the indigent across the board.

Without sketching a fuller picture of the doctrinal, ideological, or institutional setting within which the Supreme Court decided its cases, Lawrence is unable to explain why the poor's access dramatically affected some areas of poverty law (Food Stamps) and only modestly affected other areas (AFDC). She assigns great weight to the external political environment, noting that the justices live within "the beltway" and share the same values and attitudes as other government officials. Furthermore, she attributes the Court's refusal to "constitutionalize" a right to welfare to the justices' reluctance to circumvent the political branches of government at a time when the Nixon administration and Congress were wrestling over welfare reform. But explaining the Court's actions in terms of the external political environment is not wholly convincing because the Warren Court *did*, in fact, enter the "political thicket" of welfare policy. Through its statutory interpretations of AFDC the Court actually *rebuffed* legislative intent by invalidating eligibility restrictions that Congress had permitted through a fairly broad grant of discretion to state policymakers.

Martha Davis, an attorney for the National Organization for Women (NOW) Legal Defense and Education Fund, brings a lawyer's acute sensitivity to the nuances of legal doctrines and a heightened appreciation of the promises and pitfalls of litigation as an instrument of social reform. Whereas Lawrence provides a macroview of the LSP and poverty law, Davis focuses on the role of Legal Services attorneys in the welfare rights movement and in the reform of AFDC. *Brutal Need* is distinguished by Davis's personal access to key legal players in the welfare rights movement, by her eye for relevant detail, and by her elegant prose and talent for storytelling—all of which have been lacking in the political science literature. But part of what makes her book such a good story is also its weakness: the lack of a fully developed analytical structure.[43]

43. I should add, however, that I do not believe it is fair to criticize Davis too

Davis shares Lawrence's belief that the Court's refusal to constitutionalize a right to welfare was due primarily to external political
pressures and to ambivalent or even hostile public attitudes toward
the poor. Had politicians and the public mood not turned on welfare
mothers, she suggests, LSP attorneys might have had the time to
pursue the kind of deliberate litigation strategy that the NAACP had
employed so effectively during the 1940s and 1950s. The external
political pressures exerted on the Supreme Court gave LSP lawyers a
very small window of opportunity to "achieve perhaps even more
revolutionary victories between 1965 and 1970" than the NAACP had
pursued over the course of twenty-five years.[44] But as with Lawrence's
explanation, the influence that Davis assigns to "political climate"
dwarfs the serious barriers to constitutional welfare rights that the
liberal Warren Court *itself* had erected and glosses over the complicated relationship between legal doctrine and political ideology in
judicial decision making.

Finally, R. Shep Melnick's *Reading Between the Lines* is a comprehensive and lucid analysis of the federal courts' position in the American welfare state. He casts his policy net broadly, encompassing
judicial rulings in cases involving AFDC, Food Stamps, and education
for handicapped children. Melnick's account of judicial policymaking
is exemplary for the analytical sharpness of his institutionalist perspective. He meticulously traces the changing institutional relations
among the courts, congressional committees, and social reformers,
explaining how the configurations of power in each of the three policy
areas account for different outcomes in judicial decision making.

With regard to AFDC, Melnick argues that, although the Supreme
Court refused to read a right to welfare into the Constitution, it freely
read "between the lines" of the Social Security Act to divine a statutory entitlement to welfare assistance. The overall thrust of the
Court's sometimes twisted and tortuous decisions was to enshrine
"need" as the only relevant factor in distributing AFDC, despite the
fact that Congress had repeatedly shown its willingness to use federal
monies to control recipients' behavior, even if needy children were
punished because of the actions of a wayward adult.

---

strenuously for this general lack of analytical structure. For one thing, she did not set
out to explain the victories and defeats of the welfare rights movement. Furthermore,
as a practicing attorney, one should not expect Davis to be a master of the political
science literature. Her book provides a wealth of information and a lawyer's insider
insights that are invaluable to political scientists, and her clear prose makes legal ideas
accessible to the nonexpert.

44. Davis, *Brutal Need*, p. 143.

Thus, whereas Lawrence and Davis underscore the external pressure on the Court to keep "welfare rights" at bay, Melnick perceives
the justices' behavior as relatively unfettered. He contends that despite congressional hostility to the Court's statutory rulings, it was
not until the Reagan era that the elected branches of government
reined in the Court. The ultimate demise of the Court's need-based
approach to statutory welfare cases, Melnick argues, owed to the
subjective nature of "welfare rights," the public visibility of rising
welfare costs, and the enduring value of individual responsibility in
the American political culture.

Melnick's explanation for the different outcomes in statutory cases
across the three policy areas is persuasive, but his treatment of
constitutional doctrine as the political plaything of judges seems less
plausible. While the Supreme Court did make liberal use of statutory
interpretation, the Warren Court was far more constrained by constitutional doctrines and legal conventions than Melnick allows. On
Melnick's own terms the Warren Court should have "constitutional-
ized" a right to welfare since, as he himself amplifies, Chief Justice
Warren was the one who offered the "need-only" interpretation of Title
IV of the Social Security Act. Yet it was Chief Justice Warren who, in
response to the assertion of a constitutional welfare right, admonished
his colleagues: "Instinct cannot be our guide." In other words, the
liberal chief justice refrained from reading a right to welfare into
the Constitution precisely because he perceived it as a subjective
interpretation, akin to the discredited "liberty of conduct" doctrine
fashioned by an earlier Supreme Court, that went beyond the purview
of established constitutional principles. In short, judges' own role
conceptions and what one might call the "paradoxes of politics" impede
the kind of bald instrumental calculations that Melnick imputes to
liberal judges.

In this book I make use of the insights of the new institutionalism
perspective while keeping in full view the political significance of
the social identity of those who joined the National Welfare Rights
Organization: black AFDC mothers. I argue that the Warren Court
inherited a doctrinal construct called a "double standard" that shaped
the justices' understanding of the Equal Protection Clause. Within the
doctrinal parameters bequeathed to it by the Harlan F. Stone Court,
the Warren Court formulated constitutional doctrines under the Equal
Protection Clause that, while encouraging the poor to seek justice in
the federal judiciary, appear to have made a downwardly redistributive welfare state harder to promote even through the liberal, activist
Supreme Court.

As will become clear, I do not contend that the Warren Court's refusal to "constitutionalize" a right to welfare was inevitable. On the contrary, there were actually *two* long-standing traditions in American political thought that *might* have established the government's obligation to satisfy the subsistence needs of society's most vulnerable members. The first was the venerable Anglo-American tradition of natural law. One strain of that natural-law tradition made the property rights of the wealthy contingent on meeting the basic subsistence needs of the poor. The second tradition was maternalism, according to which the government could properly pursue policies that recognized the particular vulnerabilities of mothers and their children and offered them special protections from hardship or abuse. In regard to indigent single mothers in particular, exponents of maternalism often argued that because such women were struggling to raise responsible future citizens under the most daunting of circumstances, they deserved direct material assistance from the state.

Those two long-standing traditions *might* have sustained a constitutional right to welfare—one on the basis of a universalistic natural right to subsistence, the other on the basis of a particularistic concern for the special needs and vulnerabilities of children. And yet neither tradition ultimately prevailed in the liberal Warren Court. This book seeks to explain that failure not in terms of some enduring "fatal flaw" in America's liberal political tradition, and not primarily in terms of underlying shifts in the balance of political power and public opinion after 1968 (although those shifts almost certainly played a role), but rather in terms of the intellectual and institutional dynamics of legal doctrines and judicial decision making. Indeed, far from pursuing their liberal "instincts" or "sympathies" without regard to doctrinal consistency, the judges of the Warren Court were ultimately *so* inhibited by their fidelity to legal doctrines and precedents that, during an admittedly brief "window of opportunity" at the end of the 1960s, the justices turned decisively *against* those very "instincts" and "sympathies"—and doomed the notion of a constitutionally based right to welfare to oblivion.

In order to demonstrate that American political culture was capable of accommodating the idea of a right to subsistence, Chapters 2 and 3 take a look at the earlier efforts of the Workingmen's movement of the 1830s and of the "maternalist" movement for mothers' pensions launched in the first decade of the twentieth century. More specifically, focusing on Jacksonian-era New York City, Chapter 2 examines the Workingmen's use of natural-law principles to privilege human needs over property rights, at least when subsistence was jeopardized. As in other parts of the country, New York City leaders were compelled to take the Workingmen's movement seriously because of the strength of their ideas (if not their specific political program). Chapter 3 illuminates how women leaders during the Progressive era articulated an ethic of maternalism that proved to be so popular that well over half the states established mothers' pensions. Chapter 4 analyzes the roots of the national welfare state in President Franklin Roosevelt's New Deal, with most attention focusing on Aid to Dependent Children. Although, on the one hand, embracing a natural-law–based conception of constitutional subsistence rights and, on the other hand, incorporating mothers' pensions into the Social Security Act, paradoxically, Roosevelt made it difficult for a later generation of social reformers to persuade the Supreme Court of a Fourteenth Amendment right to welfare, and his administration shunned the original maternalist justification for Aid to Dependent Children. Chapter 5 analyzes the potential of the Warren Court's "new Equal Protection" doctrines to encompass a constitutional right to subsistence, while Chapter 6 lays bare the doctrinal barriers to the notion of such a constitutional right. Chapter 7 considers the intellectual or ideological ramifications of the Warren Court's Equal Protection doctrines. The final chapter revisits the question of why neither the natural-law nor the maternalist tradition proved to be viable for the cause of *constitutional* welfare rights—notwithstanding the Warren Court justices' "natural sympathies" toward impoverished single mothers and their children. Although rendered nearly twenty years ago, the Warren Court's decision to reject the claim of a constitutional right to welfare looms large, as of this writing, in the aftermath of President Bill Clinton's approval of a Republican-crafted welfare bill in August 1996, terminating the federal *statutory* entitlement to AFDC.[45]

---

45. I regard *Dandridge* as the culmination of the Warren Court's position regarding a constitutional right to welfare, despite the fact that Warren Burger had replaced Earl Warren as Chief Justice. Since Chief Justice Warren himself opposed the idea of a *constitutional* right to welfare, the outcome in *Dandridge* was probably unaffected by Chief Justice Burger's arrival on the Court. The 6-3 vote in *Dandridge* also suggests that the outcome was unaffected by Justice Abe Fortas's resignation.

Chapter Two

Artisan Republicanism and Natural Rights in Jacksonian America

Most scholarly accounts of welfare in early American history highlight the stingy and repressive nature of the institutions that dispensed assistance to the poor.[1] Ideologically, such policies are explained by reference to the thin theory of obligation that is said to have underpinned classical liberalism, with its emphasis on protecting private property, encouraging acquisitiveness, and demanding self-sufficiency.[2] The New Deal thus marked a turning point in American welfare history because, *finally*, the poor's subsistence needs and the nonpoor's property rights were reconciled in a new social contract that recognized the ethical demands entailed by widespread economic insecurity.

This account of the trajectory of American welfare policy is not so

1. See, for example, Michael B. Katz, *In the Shadow of the Poorhouse: A Social History of Welfare in America* (New York: Basic Books, 1986); and Raymond A. Mohl, *Poverty in New York, 1783–1825* (New York: Oxford University Press, 1971).
2. For a good description of this theory see C. B. MacPherson, *The Political Theory of Possessive Individualism: Hobbes to Locke* (New York: Oxford University Press, 1962).

much wrong as oversimplified. The notion that the poor's needs "trump" the nonpoor's property rights actually has deep roots in American political culture. Scholars who confine their retrospective focus to the actions of governmental agencies and charitable institutions are apt to miss the rich political vocabulary in which many Americans have debated community obligations to the less fortunate during earlier historical periods.

The Jacksonian-era artisan movements dramatically illustrate a more communal natural-law tradition and a more egalitarian civic-republican tradition than are described in the seminal works by Louis Hartz and J.G.A. Pocock.[3] More specifically, those artisans protesting against the economic changes that subordinated their needs to the profit interests of their superiors proceeded from a natural-law premise of shared natural resources to which all individuals always retained access in order to meet subsistence needs. Moreover, unlike the antilabor thrust of classical civic republicanism, which disqualified laborers from citizenship, those artisans whose needs were threatened emphasized that their rights flowed from the indispensable contribution of their labor to the well-being of the republic. That the artisans ultimately failed to gain (or hold) political power beyond the local level does not negate their ideological significance. The very fact that their opponents struggled to fend off the Workingmen's evolving critique of market relations attests to the resilience of more communal, less individualistic, ideas about obligation in a society experiencing capitalist development.

This chapter will show how conceptions of natural rights and civic republicanism converged and galvanized artisan movements for economic justice during the 1830s. Based on the writings of artisan leaders and on the newspapers and conference proceedings that craft organizations circulated in the late 1820s and early 1830s, it describes how the protest movements imported a welfare-rights philosophy from

3. See especially Louis Hartz, *The Liberal Tradition in America* (New York: Harcourt, Brace and World, 1955), which characterizes American political culture as derived from the natural-rights philosophy of John Locke; and J.G.A. Pocock, *The Machiavellian Moment: Florentine Political Thought and the Atlantic Republican Tradition* (Princeton, N.J.: Princeton University Press, 1975). See also John P. Diggins, *The Lost Soul of American Politics: Virtue, Self-Interest, and the Foundations of Liberalism* (New York: Basic Books, 1984); Gordon S. Wood, *The Creation of the American Republic, 1776–1787* (New York: W.W. Norton, 1979); and Wood, *The Radicalization of the American Revolution* (New York: Alfred A. Knopf, 1992). For the most comprehensive and insightful treatment of the New York Workingmen see Sean Wilentz, *Chants Democratic: New York City and the Rise of the American Working Class, 1788–1850* (New York: Oxford University Press, 1984).

abroad and adapted it to their own particular circumstances. The result was an eclectic political ethos that melded natural rights and civic republicanism to denounce unbridled economic accumulation.[4] The leaders of the economically ailing artisans insisted that subsistence needs take priority over business profits, especially during economic crises. We will see that notions of private property in the Anglo-American natural-rights tradition were not a monolithic bul-

4. See, for example, Michael Leinesch, *New Order of the Ages: Time, the Constitution, and the Making of Modern Political Thought* (Princeton, N.J.: Princeton University Press, 1988); Christopher Lasch, *The True and Only Heaven: Progress and Its Critics* (New York: W.W. Norton, 1991); and James Kloppenberg, "The Virtues of Liberalism: Christianity, Republicanism, and Ethics in the Early American Political Discourse," *Journal of American History* 74 (June 1987): 9–33. Christian and Scottish Enlightenment traditions pose alternatives to the natural-rights liberalism and civic-republicanism traditions as formative influences on the Workingmen. Recent scholarship has noted the allure of the Bible for political thinkers in the late eighteenth and early nineteenth centuries; see Daniel Walker Howe, "The Evangelical Movement and Political Culture in the Second Party System," *Journal of American History* 77 (March 1991): 1216–39, and Jama Lazerow, "Spokesmen for the Working Class: Protestant Clergy and the Labor Movement in Antebellum New England," *Journal of the Early Republic* 13 (Fall 1993): 323–54. Although the leaders of religious sects and of the Workingmen's movements communicated, I believe that the influence of pietistic religion was less manifest in the Workingmen's political theory than the more secular doctrines of natural rights and republican virtue in the heavily invoked imagery of the American Revolution. Furthermore, the Workingmen's leaders mistrusted ecumenical authority. Thomas Paine, the Workingmen's hero, was branded an "infidel" for his "deist" views, as was Thomas Skidmore, who helped to found the New York City Workingmen's movement. Robert Owens and his son were likewise known for their deist views, while Langston Byllesby took issue with thinkers who injected their political thought with Christian principles. The Workingmen's membership, moreover, was very diverse in its religious affiliations. See Howe, "Evangelical Movement and Political Culture," p. 1228; and Wilentz, *Chants Democratic*, p. 86. Regarding the relation between master artisans and the temperance movement see Amy Bridges, *A City in the Republic: Antebellum New York and the Origins of Machine Politics* (Ithaca, N.Y.: Cornell University Press, 1984), pp. 89–90. Finally, perhaps because alarmed at religious ferment in some quarters, many of the Workingmen seem to have supported wholeheartedly the separation of church and state. See Lee Benson, *The Concept of Jacksonian Democracy* (Princeton, N.J.: Princeton University Press, 1961).

Recent scholarship has also explored the influence of the Scottish Enlightenment on American political thought. See Gary Wills, *Explaining America: The Federalist* (New York: Penguin Books, 1981), and Kloppenberg, "Virtues of Liberalism." For reasons made clearer later in this chapter I do not preclude Scottish influence, but I also do not see it as exerting a sufficiently independent force to use it as a separate analytic category. I prefer to subsume it under natural-rights liberalism, as Kloppenberg does.

Finally, natural-rights liberalism as used here is not meant to represent the whole of the American liberal tradition. It is one version of liberalism, with utilitarianism being the main competitor that was suspicious of natural-rights terminology—"nonsense on stilts," the British philosopher Jeremy Bentham quipped.

wark protecting the accumulated wealth of capitalists against the raids of the poor. Jacksonian craftworkers and others who experienced a threat to their livelihood invoked the labor theory of value and the natural right to property to justify the nonpoor's responsibility to meet the subsistence needs of fellow citizens.

The chapter's first two sections provide a rough sketch of the natural-law and civic-republican theories as the artisans appropriated them. Sections three and four examine the political thought of two influential reformers and the efforts to organize a "Workingmen's movement" in Jacksonian New York City. The fifth section looks at the master artisans' response to the Workingmen's protests.

I.

The ideal of a positive community of goods, found in the ancient and medieval writings of Aristotle and Aquinas, was a central assumption in early modern natural-law theory, according to which God bequeathed to man a common earth to remake in His image. Early modern natural-law philosophers, such as Hugo Grotius, Samuel Pufendorf, and John Locke, made their own deductions from the premise of an original "common" of shared natural resources, but they all inquired into the conditions necessary for citizens' consent to the division of God's dominion. Although most natural-law philosophers defended private property on moral grounds, the specter of poverty figured into their conjectural histories and typically led them to acknowledge subsistence rights.[5]

Political theorists have identified two strands in the modern natural-law tradition. In one strand, as Thomas Horne explains, welfare rights were a "side-constraint" on the rich's property rights, the poor's needs being elevated to the rich's rights only in times of famine or depression. In the other strand welfare rights were an institutional prerequisite of property rights.[6] Whatever the status accorded to subsistence needs, all natural-law philosophers grappled with the

5. Thomas Horne, "Welfare Rights as Property Rights," in *Rights, Responsibilities, and Welfare: The Theory of the Welfare State*, ed. J. Donald Moon (Boulder, Colo.: Westview Press, 1988), pp. 107–32; Istvan Hont and Michael Ignatieff, "Needs and Justice in the *Wealth of Nations*: An Introductory Essay," in *Wealth and Virtue: The Shaping of Political Economy in the Scottish Enlightenment*, ed. Hont and Ignatieff (Cambridge, Eng.: Cambridge University Press, 1983), pp. 1–44.

6. Horne, "Welfare Rights as Property Rights."

question of how the poor could be said to be bound to a polity that neglects their basic needs.

Scholars disagree over the position of subsistence rights in Locke's political philosophy, since he treated them alternately as legally binding and as mere objects of private benevolence.[7] What is important for our purposes is how the Jacksonian Workingmen culled from Locke's theory and from the natural-law tradition more generally a political language to protest against large disparities between rich and poor. Specifically, the Lockean provisos limiting private accumulation to what is necessary to satisfy subsistence needs (so that others have guaranteed access to nature's bounty) were fraught with egalitarian implications. Locke's provisos opened the door for subsequent arguments that "land rightfully reverted to common ownership and cooperative shares precisely when that individual ownership became . . . monopolistic, or as soon as it led to exclusive scarcity and to exploited people."[8] Indeed, the artisan movements' leaders used Locke's provisos and the labor theory of value to fight the displacement of human labor by machines and the exclusion of craftworkers and mechanics from the profits thereby generated. How to square the well-off's property rights with the poor's need-claims was not simply a philosopher's conundrum; it was a subject of passionate political discussion and struggle in Jacksonian America.

II.

A glimpse of the Jacksonian artisan movements reveals a more egalitarian civic republicanism than Pocock showcases in *The Machiavellian Moment*. The preoccupation with civic virtue in "artisan republicanism," to borrow Sean Wilentz's term—the concern with advancing

7. See the contradictory passages in Locke's "First Treatise on Government," in John Locke, *The Two Treatises of Government*, ed. Peter Laslett (New York: New American Library, 1965), pp. 205–6.

8. Paul Conkin, *Prophets of Prosperity: America's First Political Economists* (Bloomington: Indiana University Press, 1980), p. 228. Locke's limits on accumulation drop out once money is introduced. But, given that the system of property for Locke ultimately rests on God's intentions, tacit consent does not appear to obliterate the poor's need-claims. It appears that the natural-law injunction against allowing another human being to starve takes effect if the poor's needs are jeopardized: "But we know that God hath not left one Man so to the mercy of another, that he may starve if he please. . . . [God] has given his needy . . . a right to the Surplusage of his goods." Locke, "First Treatise on Government," p. 205.

a common good and with warding off enslaving and corrupting foreign
influences—certainly resonated with civic republicanism.[9] Artisan
republicanism, however, encapsulated an economic vision that was at
odds with classical-republican understandings of production.[10]
Whereas classical republicanism disparaged production, relegating it
to the private, inferior domain of the household—the domain staffed
by noncitizens—artisan republicanism made the producer the centerpiece of its economic and political theory. For the producers, whose
labor supplied the community with subsistence and other goods, provided the material foundation for both individual liberty and the
republic's independence.

Transported to America during the colonial period, artisan republicanism went through several metamorphoses as relations between
master artisans and craftworkers became strained during the first half
of the nineteenth century.

The writings of Thomas Paine, in whom artisans found a commin-
gling of natural-law and civic-republican assumptions, roused those
artisans whose livelihood faltered in a nascent industrial economy.
Paine became a hero and an icon to the Workingmen's movement;
artisans injected his name into political debate at every turn. Paine
started with a civic-republican tenet: "Every government . . . that does
not make the *res publica* its whole and sole object, is not a good
government."[11] He highlighted the social basis of individual wealth
and the communal obligations embedded in the social contract: "Separate an individual from society . . . and he cannot acquire personal
property. . . . All accumulation, therefore, of personal property, beyond
what a man's own hands produce, is derived to him by living in
society; and he owes on every principle of justice . . . a part of that
accumulation back again to society from whence the whole came."[12]

Chastising the rich for paying the laborer a meager wage, Paine
was alarmed at the coexistence of "depredation" and "splendor," the
latter both the result and fuel of private passions, which the artisans
negatively contrasted with civic virtue. Paine advocated policies re-
storing the poor's "birthright" to nature's resources. For example, he

9. Wilentz, *Chants Democratic.*

10. Ibid., pp. 87–101.

11. Thomas Paine, *The Rights of Man, Part Second*, printed in *The Complete Writings
of Thomas Paine*, ed. Philip S. Foner (New York: Citadel Press, 1945), 1: 370. Paine's
philosophy lacked the hostility to commerce found in classical civic republicanism. His
particular mix of natural-rights liberalism and civic republicanism shaped Workingmen's thinking.

12. Thomas Paine, *Agrarian Justice*, reprinted in ibid., p. 620.

proposed the creation of a "national fund" to give to each person at the age of twenty-one a cash benefit to compensate for the "loss of his natural inheritance" that occurred when property fell into private hands. The elderly were to be assured an annual sum to weather the difficulties associated with old age, while widows, the disabled, and poor children were to be entitled to supplementary benefits for their particular needs.[13]

To Paine, providing government relief as a right would alleviate the poor's suffering and restore civic virtue to a system run amok by self-interest.[14] Paine's artisan heirs decried the triumph of mercenary interest over community welfare. Their writings and political pamphlets were interspersed with appeals to civic virtue and to the common good; dire warnings about the descent into corruption when passions prevail were also plentiful in the artisans' publications and speeches. The application of republican categories to economic relations—for example, the equation of wealthy master artisans and manufacturers with "kings" and "tyrants" bent on "enslaving" journeymen—mimicked civic republicanism insofar as the latter also depicted the merchant as so absorbed in material pursuits as to lose the qualities and disposition necessary for citizenship.

In short, natural law and civic republicanism offered the Jacksonian artisans a moral vocabulary to unite individual rights and communal responsibility in a political theory that cast the producer as the virtuous citizen. The artisans' use of those two traditions grew out of the reciprocal relations that had characterized the craftshop, but always their rallying cry and frame of reference was the American Revolution. The Revolution represented the victory of freedom and independence over a corrupt, tyrannical monarchy. A staple in artisan protest, then, was an admonition against betraying the principles of the Revolution. In the artisan struggles waged in Lynn and Lowell, Albany, New York City, and Philadelphia, craftsmen whose livelihoods were threatened by capitalist development fashioned a political ethic out of the natural-rights and civic-republican traditions.[15]

13. Ibid., pp. 612, 617.

14. Paine was disturbed not by self-interest per se but by the unchecked pursuit of it, which divided society between "the rich" and "the great mass of the poor" who are like a "hereditary race." Ibid., p. 619.

15. See, for example, Alan Dawley, *Class and Community: The Industrial Revolution in Lynn* (Cambridge, Mass.: Harvard University Press, 1976); Paul G. Faler, *Mechanics and Manufacturers in the Early Industrial Revolution: Lynn, Massachusetts, 1780–1800* (Albany: State University of New York Press, 1981).

III.

The political theory of artisan protest can be gleaned from the writings and speeches of the most influential thinkers, many of whom were activists in the Workingmen's movements. Thomas Skidmore and Robert Dale Owen organized the New York City Workingmen's movement in 1829, and the latter's famous father founded several communitarian experiments between 1825 and 1840. Equally important, although far less noticed by scholars, were Cornelius Blatchly and Langston Byllesby. Blatchly concentrated on the depredations of landlords, while Byllesby exposed the role of bankers, lawyers, moneylenders, and sycophantic politicians in what he perceived as the subjugation of laborers by capitalists and "middlemen."

Cornelius Blatchly, a Quaker physician affiliated with Columbia University, was appalled by the economic misery he saw engulf some New York City neighborhoods. Blatchly's essay "Some Causes of Popular Poverty" (1817) manifests the blending of natural-rights and civic-republican traditions in artisan protests.[16] Although ensconced in urban problems, Blatchly's eye gravitated toward agrarian ills. Interests and rents on farmland symbolized to Blatchly the injustice of economic arrangements because some individuals were allowed to reap the benefits of other people's labor and to accumulate property and wealth. Artificial sources of wealth, such as interest and rent, were "very unjust in their nature" because they flouted the labor theory of value. Nonlaboring landlords "extorted" wealth from working people by buying up large tracts of land and renting them at exorbitant rates. According to Blatchly, the "destitute and industrious men" who are the "sources of social wealth" suffer at the hands of absentee landlords.[17]

Excessive concentration of wealth, Blatchly argued, was a perversion of natural law. After all, "Man . . . had *dominion* given to him (not in his individual but in his aggregate capacity) over every living thing. . . . If individuals usurp, what is the divine right only of the aggregate, they deprive *man* . . . of his rights and privileges granted him in the beginning by God, his creator. . . ."[18] The hoarding of wealth contravened the communitarian foundation of the social contract: "All men should . . . esteem themselves as deriving their titles from [God],

---

16. Cornelius Blatchly, "Some Causes of Popular Poverty," printed in *The Pleasures of Contemplation*, by Thomas Branagan (Philadelphia: Eastwick and Stacy, 1817).

17. Ibid., p. 202.

18. Ibid., p. 199, emphases in original.

for general use and benefit, and not for individual aggrandizement and oppression."[19]

Like Paine, Blatchly underlined the social origins of property as "the result and fruits of social protection, policy, assistance, and of individual care." But Blatchly went farther than Paine in his policy proposals. Whereas Paine called for a 10 percent inheritance tax on the deceased person's personal property, Blatchly urged the abolition of inheritance. "How can a man who is dead," Blatchly queried, "be said to will? . . . To whom can [the deceased person's property] more naturally and rationally revert than to its most immediate source, to the community . . . whence his property was derived? It is the commonwealth's."[20] Since property issued from God and was passed to the political community, property ought to return to the community upon an individual's death.

In addition to natural law, Blatchly appealed to civic-republican principles to criticize the growing chasm between rich and poor. The "wretched" condition of the poor signaled a "radical defect of virtue and a potent principle of vice. . . . And vices in the great, beget inequalities in the poor."[21] Oppression sprung from a "selfish love" of power and indulgences, and the law legitimated such selfishness. Repeating the civic-republican refrain that economic self-interest threatens the moral pillars of a polity, Blatchly advised returning to a simpler economy. His idea was to limit commercial intercourse to necessary and useful items, as luxuries preyed upon people's vanities and thus ought to be barred from the exchange economy. Blatchly's was a politics oriented to communal needs, not artificially induced desires, as he saw them.

In 1819 Blatchly put his vision into practice by organizing the New York Society for Promoting Communities. His plan was to form small-scale communities in which civic virtue would flourish. Some such communities were actually established, though they never attracted a mass following.[22] Years after creating the New York Society for Promoting Communities, Blatchly ran on a Workingmen's ticket fielded in the 1829 city election. His greatest impact, however, was through his writing, which informed the politics of artisan protest in the late 1820s and early 1830s. Some thinkers, however, found Blatchly's

19. Ibid.
20. Ibid., pp. 205–6.
21. Ibid., p. 213.
22. Arthur Bestor, *Backwoods Utopias: The Sectarian Origins and the Owenite Phases of Communitarian Socialism in America, 1663–1829*, 2d ed. (Philadelphia: University of Pennsylvania Press, 1970).

agrarian vision to be too nostalgic. Langston Byllesby operated with a sharper edge in his analysis of journeymen's deteriorating economic circumstances.

Byllesby believed that Blatchly's theory was wedded to a past when face-to-face market transactions were the order of the day. Those disgruntled artisans looking for a diagnosis of urban ills found one in Byllesby's writings. Byllesby's *Observations on the Sources and Effects of Unequal Wealth* (1826) was the "first systematic American treatise" critical of capitalist development.[23] As economic conditions worsened in 1826, Byllesby's book tapped into the rising discontent and intellectual ferment that catapulted the Workingmen's movement to political prominence in New York City, Philadelphia, and other places.

Like most reformers, Byllesby turned to the Declaration of Independence for moral guidance. He felt that the grand purpose of the Revolution had been circumvented because an aristocratic class of merchants who never produced anything was free to amass wealth and to block craftworkers' pursuit of happiness. Echoing Blatchly, Byllesby argued that capitalists' extraction of the fruits of artisans' and mechanics' labor mocked the labor theory of value. Further, in likening workers' "bondage" to slavery, Byllesby called attention to the legal apparatus and the "parasitic middlemen" who sustained economic inequality. By his estimate nine-tenths of the laws were "directed to the service and defense of that superabundance which the . . . existing system generates for the few."[24] Byllesby was more reluctant than Blatchly to identify unscrupulous landlords and selfish merchants as the principal causes of the poor's oppression, perceiving economic inequality as far more entrenched, locked in through the legal system.

Byllesby offered an account of how society, passing through four stages, deviated from natural-law principles. In stage one the harmony of the state of nature was shattered when men fended off hostile neighbors. In phase two a "fixed property in the soil" was instituted.[25] The introduction of money in the third stage eroded the labor theory of value, and in the final stage "trafficking" altogether displaced the simple exchange of basic necessities.

To Byllesby the establishment of absolute property rights in the

23. Langston Byllesby, *Observations on the Sources and Effects of Unequal Wealth* (New York: Russell and Russell, 1961), p. 9. The quote is from Joseph Dorfman, introductory essay in *A Documentary History of American Industrial Society*, ed. John R. Commons et al. (New York: Russell and Russell, 1958), 7: 9.

24. Byllesby, *Observations on the Sources and Effects of Unequal Wealth*, p. 68.

25. Ibid., p. 32.

second stage conflicted with natural law, according to which nature's bounty, a communal good, was to be distributed on the basis of need and labor: "For these 'dividers of the earth,' instead of setting bounds to what each individual might possess, and considering the portion allotted to their use as a part of the general whole which the Creator had given for the use of all . . . presently erected a claim of absolute property therein, that should affect its disposition perpetually and even after their death. . . . [The poor] thenceforth [are] exposed to the mercy . . . of their more prosperous fellows."[26] Thus, when the rich appropriated surplus labor value, they automatically put "restraints in the supply of [the craftsman's or farmer's] wants."[27] The denial of laborers' needs was the most insidious consequence of capitalist inequality because "(t)he necessity of food cannot cease; the comfort of shelter . . . cannot be forgone by a sane person. . . ."[28] Unmet subsistence needs meant the subversion of natural law.

When the rich fabricated means of generating money, such as requiring interest, they departed from the common understanding that "Labor alone is the source of all wealth."[29] Moreover, labor-saving technology exacerbated the poor's plight because craftsmen and farmers were suddenly unemployed and stripped of their "natural birthright" to the earth's resources. Unemployment not only induced desperation in those who lost the means to their livelihood but also, in Byllesby's view, emboldened capitalists to rebuff employed laborers' demands for higher wages—thereby pitting one group of poor people against another and continuously threatening their survival.

Byllesby expressed civic-republican disgust toward avaricious merchants who, instead of being grateful for their comforts, used their wealth to drive the less fortunate still harder for the rich's indulgence. He branded capitalists and professionals who live off others' labor as the "gang of nobility."[30] The poor's dependence on the rich's whims robbed the former of the independence necessary to exercise civic virtue, while the latter's pursuit of luxuries knew no bounds. Byllesby detested the sundering of communal ties wrought by commercial development, but he lacked Blatchly's optimism about the possibility of returning to a simpler economy. Instead of spurring the formation of utopian communities, Byllesby's political theory made artisan leaders aware of the gravity of economic divisions and prompted them to

26. Ibid., pp. 35–36.
27. Ibid., p. 51.
28. Ibid., p. 102.
29. Ibid., p. 52.
30. Ibid., p. 61.

reclaim the mantle of republicanism.[31] In 1829 angry artisans and mechanics were ready to rectify those divisions through concerted political action.

IV.

The Workingmen's movement emerged in 1829, when the New York City economy experienced runaway inflation and a short, but debilitating, depression. For already beleaguered artisans, especially journeymen, those economic shocks were like electric jolts. The egalitarian rhetoric and symbols that Jacksonian-occupied Tammany Hall employed were hollow in the face of the skewed pattern of wealth distribution in the city. The top 4 percent of the population owned roughly half of the wealth; 1 percent owned 35 percent of noncorporate wealth.[32]

An unusually bitter winter, combined with the recession of early 1829 that produced unemployment and bankruptcy, pushed many craftworkers to the brink. What precipitated the emergence of the Workingmen's movement, however, was not an uncontrollable act of nature but rumblings that some large employers intended to expand the workday from ten to eleven hours. In anticipation, a young machinist named Thomas Skidmore called a meeting of mechanics to devise a political plan that would force the employers to retreat. Skidmore published an inflammatory agrarian tract, *The Rights of Man to Property*, that, although drawing heavily on Blatchly's and Byllesby's ideas, offered an even more scathing critique of capitalism and more radical proposals than those of his predecessors.[33] At the meeting Skidmore and the mechanics issued resolutions, including the refusal to work more than ten hours daily. The mechanics agreed with him that the legitimacy of private property inheres in the consent of the political community and that laborers never consented to a system in which "the many" depend "for their daily subsistence upon a few [who are] . . . barbarously made enormously rich."[34]

31. Wilentz, *Chants Democratic*, p. 166.

32. Edward Pessen, *Riches, Class, and Power Before the Civil War* (Lexington, Mass.: D.C. Heath and Co., 1973), pp. 33–34.

33. Thomas Skidmore, *The Rights of Man to Property! Being a Proposition to Make it Equal among the Adults of the Present Generation: and to Provide for its Equal Transmission to Every Individual of Each Succeeding Generation* . . . (New York, 1829).

34. Quoted in Commons, ed., *Documentary History of American Industrial Society*, 4: 149, a reprint of part of Skidmore's book.

A few days after the resolutions passed, a meeting of about fifty-five hundred mechanics took place in the Bowery. Asserting the equal rights of all men, the mechanics stated that no person can alienate his original right to the soil without being guaranteed a comfortable life in return for his labor. They formed a Committee of Fifty to guide striking journeymen and to plunge artisans and mechanics into electoral politics. Skidmore wrote the Committee of Fifty's Report, the Workingmen's manifesto. Completed in October 1829, the report essentially outlined the main points of *The Rights of Man to Property*. It identified the "hereditary transmission of wealth" as the source of oppression and demanded the following: the equal education of all children in publicly funded schools; the passage of a lien law; and the abolition of banks, monopolies, imprisonment for debt, and the tax-exempt status of church property.[35] The committee's report did not, however, contain Skidmore's proposal for the equal division of property, which some Workingmen felt to be too extreme.

Despite disagreements among the Workingmen, they achieved impressive electoral gains in the 1829 election. Skidmore's critique of capitalist accumulation, couched in the language of natural law and civic republicanism, touched a raw nerve. The citywide election revealed a pattern of "class voting," with poorer wards voting for the Workingmen candidates rather than for the candidates of Tammany Hall.[36] Skidmore himself fell short of election by only twenty-three votes. In fact, the maverick Workingmen secured one-third of the total vote by making inroads into the Jacksonian-Democrat constituency.

The disagreements among some of the Workingmen's leaders, however, soon became deep, intractable schisms. Historians have already described how Skidmore's opponents, including Robert Dale Owen and Henry Evans, conspired to oust him from a leadership position, only to find the Workingmen taken over by entrepreneurial artisans who were hostile to the movement's interests. Skidmore continued to edit the labor newspaper *The Friends of Equal Rights*, and his colleagues claimed to be the true spokesmen of "those who live by the labor of their hand." Having been stamped a radical "agrarian," though, Skidmore lost his political leverage, and the Workingmen eventually splintered.

35. This proposal bore the stamp of the "free-thinkers," Robert Dale Owen and Frances Wright. See J.F.C. Harrison, *Robert Owen and the Owenites in Britain and America: The Quest for the New Moral Order* (London: Routledge and Kegan Paul, 1969); Robert Owen, *The Book of the New Moral World* (New York: Augustus M. Kelly Publishers, 1970).

36. Wilentz, *Chants Democratic*, p. 199.

Although a fleeting political presence, the Workingmen's movement is important because it was "the first modern American radical political movement—[the] first case study of a lower-class insurgency that emerged through the cracks in the party system. . . ."[37] Notwithstanding the co-optation of some Workingmen by politicians who parroted Workingmen's rhetoric, many artisans and mechanics felt that existing economic arrangements were unjust and threatened the republic. Their discontent simmered until some craftsmen organized the General Trades Union of New York City and Vicinity.

After the Workingmen's collapse in New York City craftworkers and mechanics became politically fractured. They distanced themselves from political action after having been courted and then abruptly dropped by Tammany Hall and other politicians. The General Trades Union (GTU) was formed in 1833 to coordinate strikes and to exert pressure on master artisans and manufacturers who were perceived as exploiting laborers.[38] The impetus for the GTU's creation was a carpenter's strike for higher wages that garnered the enthusiastic support of other trades. Shortly thereafter the printers called for a general convention of the trades and urged each trade to send several representatives. Ely Moore, of the Typographical Association, became the GTU's president and also won election to Congress. His moderate politics were unpalatable to some of the former Workingmen, however, and eventually John Commerford, a more radical labor activist, became Moore's successor at the GTU.

Under Commerford's stewardship the GTU sponsored and aided many strikes for higher wages and against rent and price increases. The following address to the Boston carpenters shows the confluence of natural-law and civic-republican principles in the GTU's resolutions:

> [The Boston House Wrights believe] that they have the right to sell their labor in such quantities at such prices as may to them appear necessary to their health and morals, and the adequate support of their families, therefore, be it resolved that this Committee highly approves of the . . . stand our fellow mechanics of Boston have taken . . . knowing it to be founded on justice and the rights of man. Resolved, that while we indignantly deprecate the cause which has forced them to strike, viz.—the hostile efforts of their aristocratic employers,

37. Ibid., p. 213.
38. Ibid., chap. 6.

> to keep them in a state of vassalage—. . . we will use our
> united exertions to sustain them in so . . . glorious a cause.[39]

The GTU berated the entrepreneurs who claimed to be the standard-bearers of natural law and civic republicanism. In strike after strike the GTU scoffed at the master artisans' hypocrisy in insisting on their right to set prices for consumer goods while denying workingmen's rights to determine the price of their own labor. For example, in support of striking journeymen tailors, the GTU condemned the master tailors for reducing wages during a time of economic hardship and for blacklisting GTU members: "[T]hese said masters are arrogantly attempting to coerce the independent spirited men who have taken upon themselves the unquestionable right of affixing a value to their own labor."[40] When the "Employing Leather Dressers" declined to hire a GTU member, the trade union denounced their "spirit of tyranny and dictatorial impudence [which was] unequaled in the annals of American mushroom democracy." Such blacklisting was a "violation of the constitutional and natural rights of American citizens," which the employees are duty bound to resist in this "boasted land of liberty." The craftworkers refused to give to an "ignorant and contemptible aristocracy the power to feed or starve us."[41]

The GTU and master artisans fought over more than higher wages and reasonable working hours. The masters' treatment of labor as a commodity aroused the ire of craftworkers. The masters' belief that "labor, like every other commodity, will seek its own level, its true value, in an open and unfettered market" showed, in the GTU's view, the debasement of labor.[42] This new view of labor as something to be bought and sold according to market forces conflicted with the craftsmen's conception of labor as their own "personal estate" and signaled an era of protracted battles between master artisans/manufacturers and journeymen.

Although the GTU generally acted like a trade union rather than a political movement or party, its members felt impelled to resume the political activity and organization they had abandoned in the wake of the Workingmen's demise because of the brutal suppression of a journeymen tailors' strike in 1836. The tailors had decided to strike to protest against a reduction in their wages that followed on the heels

39. *National Trades Union*, August 1, 1835; reprinted in Commons, ed., *Documentary History of American Industrial Society*, 5: 251–53.
40. Ibid., February 20, 1836; reprinted in ibid., p. 287.
41. Ibid., May 23, 1836; reprinted in ibid., p. 302.
42. *New York Enquirer*, March 26, 1836; reprinted in ibid., p. 310.

of an austere winter, during which the cost of basic necessities soared 20 percent. Instead of attempting to compromise with the journeymen tailors, the masters accused their employees of a conspiracy to restrain trade. A jury composed of businessmen found the journeymen guilty, and the GTU interpreted the verdict as a "concerted plan of the aristocracy" to rob laborers of their natural rights.[43] The GTU lambasted the judge for "manifesting his well-known partiality for the Rich, and his notorious injustice for the Poor."[44] The incident convinced the GTU that the entire political system was stacked against laborers; politicians heeded the "yells of wolves, 'learned in legal lore,'" while "crush[ing] the toil worn laborer."[45] Accordingly, labor activism shifted from the workshop to the streets and legislative assemblies. In September 1836 the Loco Foco, or "Equal Rights Party," was born.[46]

V.

Until the Jacksonian period, artisans regarded the craftshop as a microcosm of the republic, for there they nurtured the values of mutuality and cooperation in their day-to-day quest to secure the material foundation of the polity. As many scholars have remarked, in early industrializing America the spheres of family, work, and community life enfolded together; they were not separate and distinct spheres, as they are today in our complex postindustrial society. Whenever there was friction between the master artisans and their journeymen, each could turn to natural law and civic republicanism for a common language to resolve their differences.

The social harmony of the workshop evaporated as labor became displaced by machines and as artisan-laborers lost ground economically and socially. Gradually, the economic changes and the circulation of Adam Smith's free-market ideas made a new moral vocabulary available to the master artisans. The political economy of Adam Smith offered the master artisans a way to defend their profits in accordance with a revised version of natural law and republican virtue. This

43. *National Laborer*, June 18, 1836; reprinted in ibid., p. 319.
44. Ibid; reprinted in ibid.
45. Ibid; reprinted in ibid., p.320.
46. For a colorful insider's account of the rise and fall of the Equal Rights Party see Fitzwilliam Byrdsall, *The History of the Loco-Foco or Equal Rights Party: Its Movements, Conventions, and Proceedings* (New York: Burt Franklin, 1967; first published in 1842).

revision did not occur without resistance. We turn now to a brief look at Adam Smith's ideas and at the mix of Smithian and republican elements in the master artisans' reactions to journeymen's protests.

As the economy changed, master artisans found in Adam Smith's theory a defense of a laissez-faire market as the "natural" and "just" order of things. Smith elevated property rights above subsistence needs because he believed that the former provided incentives for production, the expansion of which would benefit all citizens even as it increased or accentuated relative inequality. He made no bones about the "invisible hand" accentuating economic disparities between rich and poor. But the moral linchpin of Smith's argument was that economic production and growth would make the poor's lives far less wretched because they would be better off in absolute terms.[47]

The market economy, then, would overcome the conflict between subsistence needs and property rights because the division of labor and high wages would yield "universal opulence which extends itself to the lowest ranks of the people, . . . a general plenty diffus[ing] itself through all the different ranks of society."[48] Confident that the market mechanism would guarantee the poor's needs, Smith proposed a ban on government regulations, including controls on food prices.

Smith self-consciously sought to undo civic republicanism because he felt it subordinated "the many" as the price for the support of a so-called virtuous, privileged elite.[49] The civic republicanism that Smith scorned was the hierarchical version described in Pocock's work—a political theory that stigmatized "the many" as unfit for citizenship. In this regard Smith's moral animus was absolutely genuine. But, as Istvan Hont and Michael Ignatieff argue, Smith's importance lay in his break with an earlier natural-law tradition in which subsistence needs took moral precedence over property rights. Smith "insisted on the all but absolute priority of the property rights of grain merchants and farmers over the claims of need made by poor laborers."[50] The legal protection of private property was a prerequisite to transcending nature's limits because without unconditional safeguards individuals would lack the motivation to make improvements.

The implication of Smith's theory was this: if property rights are absolute, the poor do not have a "perfect right" to the rich's bounty, as

47. Michael Ignatieff, *The Needs of Strangers: An Essay on Privacy, Solidarity, and the Politics of Being Human* (New York: Viking Penguin, 1985), chap. 4.

48. Adam Smith, *An Inquiry into the Nature and Causes of the Wealth of Nations*, ed. Edwin Cannan (New York: Random House, 1937), p. 11.

49. Ignatieff, *Needs of Strangers*, chap. 4.

50. Hont and Ignatieff, "Needs and Justice in the *Wealth of Nations*," p. 22.

earlier natural-law theorists had entitled the destitute. For Smith, society should not return to an "original positive community of goods," even in times of food shortages and other catastrophic events.

Apart from Smith's confidence in the market economy's ability to meet human needs, he had faith in man's innate capacity for sympathy. Man relished the pleasure of contributing to other people's well-being. Assisting others, in fact, was a form of self-interest in that one's self-estimation rises as it is reflected in the eyes of others. Moreover, Smith noted that the social conventions fostered by a market economy compel individuals to honor rules of propriety, one such rule being generosity toward those less fortunate than oneself.

Not only would increased economic productivity eliminate the "antinomy" between the poor's needs and the nonpoor's property rights, but human benevolence and conformity would increasingly inspire private charitable acts. However, in Smith's view the poor did *not* have a legally enforceable claim on the rich's assistance. Smith was unequivocal: "A beggar is an object of our charity and may be said to have a right to demand it—but when we use the word right in this way it is not in a proper but a metaphorical sense."[51] In this way Smith shifted the terms of the earlier natural-rights tradition from a "vocabulary of rights" to a "vocabulary of markets."[52]

51. Adam Smith, *Lectures on Jurisprudence*, ed. R. L. Meek et al. (Oxford: Oxford University Press, 1978), pp. (a)i and 14–16.

52. Hont and Ignatieff, "Needs and Justice in the *Wealth of Nations*," p. 26. As noted in footnote 4, some scholars place early American political thought in the context of Scottish "commonsense" philosophy. The Scottish influence is seen in the understanding of virtue and benevolence. See, for example, Kloppenberg, "Virtues of Liberalism", p. 17, where he claims that the Scottish impact blunted the sharp edges of a so-called Lockean material acquisitiveness. Certainly there are some similarities between the Workingmen's thinking and Scottish moral philosophy and political economy. The Workingmen's assumption that virtue and benevolence are the glue of a community found expression in Scottish moral philosophy. Similarly, the Workingmen's resort to conjectural histories to explain how economic arrangements had gone awry was common in Scottish works. See J.G.A. Pocock, "Cambridge Paradigms and Scotch Philosophers: A Study of the Relations Between the Civic Humanist and the Civil Jurisprudential Interpretation of Eighteenth-Century Social Thought," in *Wealth and Virtue: The Shaping of Political Economy in the Scottish Enlightenment*, p. 242. Such conjectural histories were displayed most vividly in Blatchly's and Byllesby's writings. Further, the Workingmen's concern with devising economic forms that would maintain virtue and not just create profits accorded with Scottish thinkers' efforts. It is undeniable, too, that Adam Smith, one of the most prominent Scottish thinkers, acquired "prestige in America." See Conkin, *Prophets of Prosperity*, p. 17.

The foregoing account of the way in which Smith dealt with the poor's need-claims via the language of the market sets the theoretical context for understanding the master artisans' defense of capital accumulation. But while Smith's own thinking was a reaction against an ancient *elitist* civic-republican ethos that sanctioned the destitution and exclusion of laborers from citizenship, American master artisans confronted an *egalitarian* artisan republicanism. According to the egalitarian version of republican thought, the rights to private property and accumulation of wealth were predicated on the prior satisfaction of all citizens' subsistence needs. That concern about human subsistence proved to be remarkably resilient during and after the antebellum period, notwithstanding the "prestige" of Smith's *The Wealth of Nations.* For example, Paul Faler's study of shoemakers in Lynn, Massachusetts, reveals that the Workingmen became hostile to what they perceived as "acquisitive corruption," to the growing gap between rich and poor and, later, to the wage system.[53] Thus the master artisans did not immediately embrace the ideas of Adam

---

Yet I am hesitant to ground the Workingmen's thought in the Scottish Enlightenment instead of the broader natural-law and civic-republican traditions as they had evolved in Great Britain and were imported and revised in America. The Workingmen's understanding of virtue was couched in overtly republican language, while the content derived from the indigenous ideals of "the Trade" and the craftshop as a minirepublic. Additionally, the Scots' generally optimistic view of "progress," of the moderation and social propriety that a market economy instills, seems at odds with the Workingmen's skepticism toward, and disillusionment with, a nascent industrial economy. The Workingmen were wary of market relations, which because of their impersonality allowed master artisans to evade moral responsibility for those under their stewardship.

Smith's influence on the master artisans was unmistakable, however. His thought enabled them to be both moralists and proponents of a free market. But to conclude from Smith's influence on the master artisans a more pervasive Scottish impact is risky since the claim depends on the assumption that Smith was representative of the Scottish Enlightenment. As some scholars have noted, this assumption is problematical. See, for example, Knud Haakensson, "Natural Law and Moral Realism: The Scottish Synthesis," in *Studies in the Philosophy of the Scottish Enlightenment,* ed. M. A. Stewart (Oxford: Clarendon Press, 1990), p. 60; Hont and Ignatieff, "Needs and Justice in the *Wealth of Nations,*" p. 2; and John Robertson, "The Scottish Enlightenment at the Limits of the Civic Tradition," in *Wealth and Virtue: The Shaping of the Political Economy in the Scottish Enlightenment,* pp. 137–78. These works contend that Smith's innovations set him at odds with his Scottish contemporaries. The moral tone of the master artisans' response to the Workingmen seems more akin to evangelical Christianity than to Scottish commonsense philosophy, with dramatic uses of civic republicanism as a way to battle their opponents on their own turf and to prevent them from claiming the mantle of republicanism and the status of heirs to the American Revolution.

53. Faler, *Mechanics and Manufacturers in the Early Industrial Revolution,* p. 173.

Smith; rather, they sought ideological support for laissez-faire doctrine by identifying masters' commercial prosperity with the republican concept of the public good.

Rowland Berthoff explains this strategy of appealing to civic-republican ideals so as to "seem to live by an older and far more honorific standard of individual rights than the laissez-faire theories of the Manchester economists."[54] In reworking the concept of the public good the masters gradually imbued it with individualistic, entrepreneurial values. These values embodied the experience of the commercially successful master artisan. The masters' desire to fundamentally alter republicanism by engrafting Smith's ideas onto the "common good" sprang from a conviction that the liberated individual, the entrepreneur, was someone to salute. There was, indeed, an alluring quality to this liberation; the economic fortunes of some artisans induced loyalty to the new economic regime and ethos even among some of the less prosperous artisans and journeymen.[55]

Feeling no such liberation in the transformation of labor into a commodity, most of the economically disadvantaged artisans and journeymen rebuffed Smithian principles. As protests became more disruptive, master artisans assailed trade unions, which they deemed to be unnecessary and unjust. Refusing to surrender the moral high ground to journeymen, master artisans used the language of natural law and civic republicanism to attack "combinations," especially trade unions: "[A]ccording to our notions of the obligations of society, all combinations to compel others to give a higher price or take a lower one, are not only inexpedient, but at war with the order of things which the Creator has established for the general good, and therefore wicked."[56] Master artisans also warned that labor unions weakened the work ethic by "taking from [workers'] hard-earned wages a portion to support the idle and unemployed members of the society [during labor strikes]."[57]

The masters/manufacturers also made use of the natural-law and

---

54. Rowland Berthoff, "Independence and Attachment, Virtue and Interest: From Republican Citizen to Free Enterpriser, 1787–1837," in *Uprooted Americans: Essays to Honor Oscar Handlin*, ed. Richard L. Bushman et al. (Boston: Little, Brown & Co., 1979), p. 119.

55. For a welcome reminder of just how alluring this vision of the liberated entrepreneur was see Joyce Appleby, *Liberalism and Republicanism in the Historical Imagination* (Cambridge, Mass.: Harvard University Press, 1992).

56. *New York Journal of Commerce*, June 1, 1833; reprinted in Commons, ed., *Documentary History of American Industrial Society*, 5: 209.

57. *New York Enquirer*, March 26, 1836; reprinted in ibid., p. 310.

civic-republican languages to oppose strikes, which were said to transgress "masters' market rights" and laborers' "own duty to the commonwealth."[58] In fact, masters/manufacturers relied heavily on the labor theory of value to defend their profits against craftworkers' attacks. Obviously, the masters put a different spin on the labor theory of value, observing that an entrepreneur's investment creates the worker's employment and livelihood in the first place.[59] Failing to convince journeymen of the injustice of strikes waged to eke out higher pay or shorter work hours, many master artisans organized associations resolved to withstand labor's "coercion."[60]

With their clashing interpretations of natural-law and civic-republican principles, master artisans and journeymen were increasingly at loggerheads. For those artisans who were excluded from economic progress and subjected to a faster, more impersonal rhythm of work, the masters' identification of commercial prosperity with the public good simply did not wash. Exerting pressure through trade union strikes was, in the journeymen's estimation, their only recourse. Many journeymen complained bitterly that they were unable to save a "competence," a nest of money to dip into in old age and one that master artisans had hitherto ensured through the regulation of wages. To the journeymen, economic security was elusive.

Consequently, the battles between masters and craftworkers became nastier and the rhetoric of resistance more acerbic. Advertising the formation of the Equal Rights Party in 1836, bedraggled craftworkers posted signs: "Bread, Meat, Rent and Fuel! The Prices Must Come Down!" Addressing a huge crowd of craftworkers and mechanics, a laborer proclaimed: "When in the course of human events it becomes necessary for the many to declare hostility against the rapacity of the few, who willfully impoverish and oppress them . . . those grievances should be recited which impel . . . the people to speak the sentiments . . . directed by the first law of nature—self-preservation."[61] Master artisans, in turn, became more recalcitrant. Hence, throughout the 1830s journeymen and masters in all trades became more aware of their separate and distinct interests even as both sides held out hope of reaching common ground. Neither the natural-law nor civic-republican traditions died as a result of the estrangement between

58. *New York Journal of Commerce*, June 1, 1833; reprinted in ibid., p. 209.

59. David Montgomery, *Beyond Equality: Labor and the Radical Republicans, 1862–1872* (New York: Alfred A. Knopf, 1967), p. 253.

60. *New York Enquirer*, March 26, 1836; reprinted in Commons, ed., *Documentary History of American Industrial Society*, 5: 310–12.

61. Quoted in Byrdsall, *History of the Loco-Foco or Equal Rights Party*, p. 101.

journeymen and masters. Instead, these languages spun off new dialects, which spawned new protest movements and political alliances throughout the nineteenth century.

VI.

This chapter examined a particular political discourse, "artisan republicanism," that informed the thinking of many working Americans during the Jacksonian period. Posing a challenge to the dominant strains of classical liberalism and classical republicanism, the artisan republicanism that inspired the Workingmen's movement construed property rights and human needs as mutually contingent rather than opposed to one another. In times of economic hardship the poor's claims to basic subsistence needs superseded the wealthy's property rights. Two assumptions drawn from the natural-law and civic-republican traditions lay behind this ordering of values: the natural-law assumption stipulating that no person could alienate his natural right to self-preservation and the civic-republican assumption positing reciprocal relations among persons that bind together a political community. The Workingmen melded natural rights and civic republicanism, fashioning a critique of government complicity in a developing commercial economy in which the pursuit of private profit for some meant the debasement of human needs for others. The Workingmen's protests thus articulated an ideological eclecticism that is absent in so many scholarly descriptions of early American political culture.

The case of the Jacksonian Workingmen also shows that the idea of a subsistence right has a long history, even in the "exceptional" United States. Subsistence rights did not first spring on the American scene in the 1930s or 1960s, nor were they restricted to philosophers' libraries. That the Jacksonian-era municipal governments did not take the Workingmen's road to justice does not negate the ideological appeal of a welfare-rights ethos for an earlier generation of American artisans.

Despite the existence of a welfare-rights tradition in America a full century before the New Deal, it is important not to overstate the case. The Workingmen's movement did not create large-scale agitation for government "entitlements" to aid the economically bereft. Although most Workingmen believed government should aid the poor, the target of their criticism was the economic conduct of master artisans and manufacturers. To the Workingmen and others who lived during the

Jacksonian period, an important mechanism of support for the poor was through the craftshop (and eventually the factory) itself. That does not mean, however, that the Workingmen had a strictly private conception of a duty to assist the poor, akin to the "welfare capitalism" that many businesses adopted in the early twentieth century. Rather, the Workingmen's understanding of the economy and of citizens' obligations was decisively more communitarian than that of capitalists—then or now.

Master artisans and manufacturers felt compelled to respond to the Workingmen's sense of injustice in 1829 precisely because of an enduring natural-rights ethic elevating the poor's needs above the rich's rights. To be sure, the masters' sense of obligation toward the needy was dwindling during the Jacksonian period. Entrepreneurs of that era fastened onto the belief, put forth by Adam Smith and other political economists, that the pursuit of economic profit unencumbered by public obligations would ultimately assure the poor a less miserable life than they would otherwise have. But the triumph of Adam Smith's ideas did not occur without political resistance, and since the resistance was ongoing in industrializing America, the triumph was always tentative. Indeed, as we will see in Chapter 4, President Franklin Roosevelt himself sometimes employed a rhetoric of class and community in order to contrast the wealth and greed of "economic royalists" with the bleak plight of ordinary citizens during the Great Depression.

Before turning to the first wave of *nationwide* reform on behalf of the poor—the movement for mothers' pensions—let us briefly look at the place of gender in the Workingmen's ideology. The Workingmen in the National Trades Union (NTU) regarded women as important members of the community of labor, but they identified domestic labor as women's principal contribution. As Christine Stansell notes, delegates to the NTU "implicitly acknowledged women's domestic labor to be central to the welfare of all, so much so that the material interests of the class as a whole were served when men supported women at home."[62] When cheap female labor displaced male workers, Workingmen felt that the entire class suffered. Yet, the Workingmen's belief in a gender-based division of labor was not exactly an emulation of the middle-class ideal of "separate spheres" for men and women. Through economic and political changes promising to restore the independence and dignity of the working-class family, whose labor was devalued through the wage system, Workingmen sought to carve

62. Christine Stansell, *City of Women: Sex and Class in New York, 1789–1860* (Urbana: University of Illinois Press, 1982), p. 138.

out a safe haven for their families from the exploitative forces of a burgeoning capitalist economy.

Jacksonian Workingmen, then, embraced the "family wage" as a bulwark against the economic and social dislocations of the time. To their mind, the family wage was secured when men earned sufficient wages to meet their wife's and children's *material* needs, while women attended to their husband's and children's *emotional* needs. During the Progressive era that idea of a "family wage" would remain central to social reform efforts. The Workingmen's belief that women's domestic labor helped to promote the well-being of the political community, not just of the family unit, found expression in the movement for mothers' pensions in early twentieth-century America. That movement would culminate in Progressive-era mothers' pension laws and in the New Deal's Aid to Dependent Children.

Chapter Three

The "Maternalist" Movement for Mothers' Pensions in the Progressive Era

The educated and economically privileged women who crusaded for mothers' pension laws during the Progressive period were a breed apart from the scruffy Jacksonian-era Workingmen; nevertheless, they were both committed to the ideal of a family wage. The family wage symbolized economic security in a male-dominated labor market and emotional security in the home provided by a full-time wife and mother. Most female advocates of mothers' pensions were quite certain that women could not be good workers and mothers simultaneously, for women exhausted by work would presumably compromise their care to dependent children. Mothers' pension activists used the family wage as a model for public assistance to indigent single mothers and their children.

Drawing on recent historical scholarship, this chapter examines the "maternalist" thinking behind the women-led movement for mothers' pension laws, which were the precursors to the Aid to Dependent Children program enacted as part of the Social Security Act in 1935. The effort to garner political support for mothers' pensions illuminates the origins of the American welfare state and provides a hint of the gender conflicts that were to surface in the welfare rights movement of the 1960s and 1970s.

I.

In the late nineteenth century women reformers shaped their own independent philanthropic and professional organizations alongside the political sphere. Denied the right to vote, women created organizations that became respected for their expertise and their innovative policy ideas. Some female reformers dedicated themselves to promoting protective labor legislation for women workers, including minimum-wage and maximum-hours laws. Other women reformers, queasy about stereotypes of feminine fragility, vehemently opposed protective legislation for women. Convinced that gender-based laws undermined women's pursuit of equal citizenship, those critics worked tirelessly on behalf of women's suffrage and an Equal Rights Amendment (ERA) during the 1910s and 1920s.

The ERA movement's concern about gender stereotyping did not, however, derail the movement for mothers' pensions. Quite the contrary, according to one scholar, mothers' pension laws were "one of the most successful reforms of the early twentieth-century United States" precisely because in many ways these laws legitimized traditional gender relations.[1] Female leaders of the mothers' pension movement deployed conventional ideas about gender in order to obtain public

1. Molly Ladd-Taylor, *Mother-Work: Women, Child Welfare, and the State, 1890–1930* (Urbana: University of Illinois Press, 1994), p. 135. As Theda Skocpol points out, women wielded heavy influence in the mothers' pension movement because of three additional factors. First, in the eyes of the very conservative U.S. Supreme Court of the time protectionist laws aimed at male workers smacked too much of "socialism," whereas similar legislation for women rested on the comforting premise that women needed men's protection, especially to perform their natural duties as mothers. Second, women were able to step into a vacuum that was created by the paucity of leadership on behalf of male workers, who were too weak as a class to exert significant influence over government policy. Third, the negative images associated with Civil War pensions due to the sway of patronage politics and the multiplication of beneficiaries hurt the chances of similar legislation being enacted for male workers. Since women lacked the right to vote, any program they advocated lacked the taint of "politics." After all, Progressive-era reformers had utter disdain for patronage politics and sought to take the politics out of policymaking. See Theda Skocpol, *Protecting Soldiers and Mothers: The Political Origins of Social Policy in the United States* (Cambridge, Mass.: Harvard University Press, 1992), pp. 261–67, 530, and 533.

assistance for society's most vulnerable members: husbandless women and their fatherless children. Women activists succeeded in expanding the scope of public obligation to the poor at a time when the most politically powerful men celebrated life as a fierce social Darwinian struggle between economic classes. Yet paradoxically, the female leaders of the mothers' pension movement appealed to traditional gender norms while turning their own backs on the very realm that their vision romanticized—the private domain of family. As biographical narratives reveal, many women leaders of the mothers' pension movement did not practice what they preached, for they were unmarried and childless. Those leaders' claims to expertise derived from social science knowledge rather than from personal experience, and social science evidence persuaded them that women's maternal instincts uniquely qualified them to care for children.

The ideology of maternalism encompassed a broad range of women's organizations, ideas, and policy interests, but according to historian Molly Ladd-Taylor, there were essentially four shared tenets:

1. There is a uniquely feminine value system based on care and "nurturance";
2. Mothers perform a service to the state by raising citizen-workers;
3. Women are united across class, race, and nation by their common capacity for motherhood and therefore share a responsibility for the world's children;
4. Ideally men should earn a family wage to support their "dependent" wives and children at home.[2]

Within this framework, Ladd-Taylor demonstrates, there were three strains of maternalist thinking, each with its own organizational base and policy agenda: "sentimental maternalism," "progressive maternalism," and "feminism."[3] Progressive maternalism dominated the mothers' pension movement, although sentimental maternalism was influential in its early years. Feminist ideas about mothers' rights also found expression in the political debates over mothers' pension legislation.

As historians Ladd-Taylor and Linda Gordon chronicle, sentimental maternalism characterized the thinking of the National Congress of Mothers (NCM) and its progeny, the Parent-Teacher Association (PTA). The NCM was instrumental in the passage of mothers' pension

2. Ladd-Taylor, *Mother-Work*, p. 3.
3. Ibid.

laws during the 1910s.[4] Ladd-Taylor describes the maternalism of those organizations as "sentimental" because their members relied exclusively on idealized conceptions of "mother-love" and traditional understandings of gender relations. Although NCM and PTA leaders came largely from middle-class or privileged backgrounds, they generally did not attend college because they believed that women's primary duty was toward their husbands and children. In fact, NCM and PTA members were critical of working women; they assumed that working women not only provided inferior care to dependent children but also displaced male workers in the labor market.[5] Sentimental maternalists did not fret over women's dependence on husbands and/or fathers for economic support, but saw that dependence as "natural" and desirable. And since NCM and PTA activists themselves depended on men for financial security, they empathized with single mothers who had no husband to provide them with economic assistance and who frequently had to endure the added anguish of relinquishing dependent children to public or private orphanages.

Progressive maternalism characterized the thinking of female activists in the Children's Bureau, which agitated for and eventually helped to administer protective labor laws for women, maternal and child health care programs, and mothers' pension laws.[6] Unlike their counterparts in the National Congress of Mothers, Children's Bureau leaders tended to be unmarried and childless, attached instead to a "family" of like-minded female reformers. Moreover, Children's Bureau women generally were privileged economically *and* educationally, and they relished their independence from men and their freedom to crusade for social reform. Although they believed that women ought to have the choice to pursue careers in public service, they felt that women could not, and ought not, to combine work with motherhood. While Children's Bureau reformers opted for careers and gravitated toward the public sphere of social reform, they regarded women generally as naturally inclined toward motherhood and the private sphere of home and family.

While the NCM extolled the virtues of motherhood using soft and sentimental language about maternal instincts, the Children's Bureau looked to "hard" social science research in order to develop professional standards for "mother-work." The bureau sought improvements in the

---

4. Ibid., p. 139; Skocpol, *Protecting Soldiers and Mothers*, pp. 445–56; and Linda Gordon, *Pitied But Not Entitled: Single Mothers and the History of Welfare, 1890–1935* (New York: The Free Press, 1994), p. 61.

5. Ladd-Taylor, *Mother-Work*, p. 8.

6. Ibid.

economic and social conditions that made child rearing so daunting and exhausting to women living on the edge of poverty. Eventually, bureau leaders hoped that the enactment of mothers' pensions would spawn more extensive laws incorporating public assistance for male workers.[7]

In contrast to sentimental and progressive maternalists, feminists were largely uninterested in maternal–child welfare reform. Many feminist activists in the National Woman's Party's (NWP) struggle for an Equal Rights Amendment actually opposed protective legislation for mothers and children because they felt such legislation presupposed gender inequality and women's dependence on men. Nevertheless, as Wendy Sarvasy reveals, feminists in the NWP employed the language of motherhood subversively in order to *challenge* male authority in the domestic sphere. For example, they argued that child rearing was a job like any other and that mothers ought to be paid a wage for their labor. Once women won the right to vote, however, many feminists shunned the imagery and rhetoric of motherhood because they perceived maternalism as a threat to the independence and parity inherent in equal citizenship. In her study of postsuffrage female reformers Sarvasy argues that feminists sought the "creation of a feminist, not a maternalist, welfare state."[8]

While Progressive-era female reformers split over the wisdom of protective labor laws for women, they came together on the issue of mothers' pensions.[9] For even though feminists like Helen Todd were leery of the political use of motherhood images, they believed that mothers' pensions would increase poor women's autonomy and might even be a stepping stone toward more comprehensive legislation, such as universal entitlements for workers. The convergence of female support for mothers' pensions, then, lent such proposals a legitimacy that helped to ensure their passage in many states.

Scholars agree that the rapidity with which states passed mothers' pension laws owed in large part to the resonance of idealized images of motherhood in American culture at large. In the first quarter of the twentieth century purveyors of popular culture endowed home and motherhood with particular reverence. Amidst the turmoil of World War I and the frothing xenophobia churned up by immigration it is

7. Ibid.

8. Wendy Sarvasy, "Beyond the Difference Versus Equality Policy Debate: Postsuffrage Feminism, Citizenship, and the Quest for a Feminist Welfare State," *Signs* 17 (Winter 1992): 332. See Sarvasy for an insightful analysis of the splits between the progressive maternalists and the feminists.

9. Ibid., p. 333.

not surprising that many Americans wanted to believe that good mothering and proper home lives could eradicate social problems like pauperism and juvenile delinquency. Tapping into the culture's respect for motherhood, advocates of mothers' pensions were able to arouse a sense of collective shame about the fact that conditions for real-life mothers and their children often brutally contradicted the rosy images found in popular magazines and advertising.

Arguing that child rearing is a service to the state, progressive maternalists, including Jane Addams, Julia Lathrop, and Grace Abbot, recast the "private" responsibilities of mothering as a public role.[10] After all, good mothering produced virtuous citizens, and although no price tag could be attached to women's indispensable service to the state, advocates could rightly trumpet that mothers' pensions would actually *save* the state money by sharply reducing the number of children placed in custodial care. Given press accounts of the deplorable conditions in some orphanages, the idea of home care appealed to politicians and public alike.

II.

A vigorous women's movement spearheaded the campaign for women's pensions. In 1909 the White House spotlighted the plight of single mothers and children in a conference on the "Care of Dependent Children." Although the conference endorsed private charity rather than government-funded mothers' pensions, it transformed an assumed private role, that of mother, into a topic of political debate. More important, the conference proclaimed that, whenever possible, impoverished children should be raised in the home rather than in an institution: "Home life is the highest and finest product of civilization. . . . Except in unusual circumstances, the home should not be broken up for reasons of poverty, but only for considerations of inefficiency or immorality."[11]

10. A similar political understanding of motherhood was popularized during the post-Revolutionary period; see Linda K. Kerber, *Women of the Republic: Intellect and Ideology in Revolutionary America* (Chapel Hill: University of North Carolina Press, 1980), pp. 283–88 and passim; Mary Beth Norton, *Liberty's Daughters: The Revolutionary Experience of American Women, 1750–1800* (Boston: Little, Brown & Co., 1980), pp. 242–50 and passim.

11. Roy Lubove, *The Struggle for Social Security, 1900–1935* (Cambridge, Mass.: Harvard University Press, 1968), p. 98.

The exposure and legitimacy that the White House conference gave to mothers' pensions helped to galvanize the movement for mothers' pension legislation. For example, the National Congress of Mothers devoted its attention to the plight of indigent single mothers and clamored for mothers' pension legislation.[12] The organization's sentimental maternalism was evident in a speech given by the president of the Tennessee NCM, Mrs. G. Harris Robertson: "We cannot let a mother, one who has divided her body by creating other lives for the good of the State, one who has contributed to citizenship, be classed as a pauper, a dependent. She must be given value received by her nation, and stand as one honored."[13]

However, it was not a sentimental maternalist but a hard-headed juvenile court judge who started the first mothers' aid program in Kansas City, Missouri, in 1909, in the belief that poverty and poor mothering created a breeding ground for juvenile delinquency. That same year a Chicago juvenile court judge played a key role in the passage of an Illinois mothers' pension law. Emphasizing the importance of good mothering to child development, Judge Merritt W. Pinckney asserted: "My chief endeavor has been to keep the home intact." But when circumstances prevented him from preserving a family unit, the judge lamented, "I have sought to substitute . . . the maternal love and care of some other good woman."[14] When a critic of maternalist reform efforts disparaged mothers' pensions as "not American" and "not virile,"[15] mothers' pension advocates responded by calling the policy of separating children from their destitute mothers "criminal."[16] The broad base of support for mothers' pensions led thirty-nine states to pass laws between 1911 and 1919.[17]

The enthusiasm for mothers' pensions remained steady among diverse women's organizations even after such pensions became policy. Once mothers' pensions were enacted into law, both sentimental maternalists and progressive maternalists paid close attention to the administration of benefits. As Ladd-Taylor discusses, sentimental maternalists continued to devote energy to mothers' pensions because,

12. Ladd-Taylor, *Mother-Work*, p. 158.
13. Quoted in ibid.
14. Quoted in Lubove, *Struggle for Social Security*, p. 100. See also Sonya Michel, "The Limits of Maternalism: Policies Toward Wage-Earning Mothers During the Progressive Era," in *Mothers of a New World: Maternalist Politics and the Origins of Welfare States*, ed. Seth Koven and Sonya Michel (New York: Routledge, Inc., 1993), p. 294.
15. Quoted in Lubove, *Struggle for Social Security*, p. 103.
16. Ibid., p. 106.
17. Ladd-Taylor, *Mother-Work*, p. 136.

lacking the educational backgrounds and the economic and personal independence of progressive maternalists, they felt a particularly strong personal stake in the laws. The sentimental-maternalist conviction that women belonged in the home, not the workplace, made them very vulnerable when their husbands' fortunes, or their marriages, deteriorated. Death and divorce were calamities for dependent women (although in some cases divorce was clearly preferable to maintaining a marriage). Antiquated child-custody laws placed custody of children in the hands of their fathers. The fear of losing custody of children thus reinforced the bond that sentimental maternalists felt toward indigent single mothers. Not surprisingly, as Ladd-Taylor explains, sentimental maternalists' support of mothers' pensions went hand in hand with their advocacy of changes in child-custody laws since both reforms were designed to keep children in the hands of nurturing mothers when fathers became ill, died, or divorced their wives.[18]

Reflecting the maternalist assumption that women are the proper stewards of home life and children, many state laws actually stipulated that women be members of mothers' pension investigating agencies. These requirements opened up opportunities for educated women to play a prominent role in public child welfare. Predictably, the better-educated and personally independent progressive maternalists came to dominate the administration of mothers' pensions, decisively eclipsing the role of sentimental maternalists and feminists.

The prominent role played by progressive maternalists in the administration of mothers' pension laws was largely exerted through the Children's Bureau. The Children's Bureau was established in 1912 in the federal Department of Labor, the work mainly of Progressive reformers Florence Kelly and Lillian Wald.[19] Wald and Kelly had used their connections to women's groups and reform organizations to promote the idea of mothers' pensions and to lay the political groundwork for the creation of a Children's Bureau in the federal government. Because legislators could hardly object to focusing government attention on child welfare, the sort of political resistance that had dogged other reform-oriented agencies did not afflict the Children's Bureau.

One consequence flowing from the Children's Bureau's administrative prominence was the dilution of the ideological fervor that had energized the mothers' pension movement in the first place. Ladd-Taylor and Gordon observe that maternalism became transformed into

18. Ibid., p. 141.
19. Linda Gordon, *Pitied But Not Entitled*, p. 89.

a professional discourse as social workers in the Children's Bureau attended to the details of policy administration.[20] To be sure, Children's Bureau leaders and staff continued to speak the language of maternalism, linking the rights of mothers to their service to the state. But their day-to-day jobs involved "case work," going to the homes of pensioners to inspect the quality of home life and to lend guidance and instruction to women in housekeeping, child supervision, nutrition, and budgeting. Linda Gordon states that case work became a "professionalized form of maternalism" as the Children's Bureau immersed itself in the details of policy administration.[21]

To some degree female solidarity was diminished once mothers' pensions were no longer a rallying cry of the women's movement but a bureaucratic puzzle to be worked out by experts. And as is so often the case in policy implementation, a gulf developed between the female administrators in the Children's Bureau and the clients of mothers' pensions. The gulf became pronounced because of the race and class differences separating the white women experts in the Children's Bureau from their indigent charges, some of whom were African-American and recent immigrants. The Children's Bureau exhibited a condescending attitude toward the poor and minority recipients of mothers' pensions, directing social workers in the field to prod clients to conform to Anglo-American standards of mothering. More perniciously, states sometimes pinned benefit levels to race or nationality, with white women of Western European descent receiving higher benefits than blacks and women perceived as foreigners.[22]

All in all, the bureaucratic language and orientation of social work—with its preoccupation with "standards of public aid"—eventually overshadowed the movement's original focus on "mother work and maternal dignity."[23] Ironically, as Ladd-Taylor and Gordon point out, the privileged women in the Children's Bureau flourished because of the bereft circumstances of their less fortunate sister-clients.

Gordon and Ladd-Taylor highlight the assumptions of gender inequality underlying the sentimental and progressive maternalist arguments for mothers' pensions. Advocates of mothers' pensions wished to increase indigent women's economic security, but they did not question the existing gender inequalities that exacerbated women's

20. Ibid., pp. 100–105; Ladd-Taylor, *Mother-Work*, p. 138.
21. Gordon, *Pitied But Not Entitled*, p. 103.
22. Ladd-Taylor, *Mother-Work*, pp. 142–43, 149.
23. Ibid., p. 138.

dependence on men. Their endorsement of the family wage presupposed a dominant husband and father, a subordinate wife and mother. Except for feminists occupying the left wing of the National Woman's Party, supporters of mothers' pensions regarded the pensions as a substitute for, not an escape from, paternal authority.[24] The women social workers who had the most contact with recipients of mothers' pensions regarded the state as a benevolent paternal figure providing the necessary economic support and supervision to a woman's fatherless children. In short, mothers' pensions were in no way intended to supplant male authority.

The disinterest of sentimental and progressive maternalists in gender equality was reflected in state eligibility conditions, administrative practices, and grant levels, which varied among the states. For example, some states limited mothers' pensions to widows, while others extended them to deserted and divorced women. But even in otherwise progressive states, divorced and abandoned women were frequently denied mothers' pensions because state officials feared that government benefits would provide an incentive to men to leave their wives and children when their families' financial circumstances became precarious. Similarly, the idea of giving public aid to families headed by able-bodied but financially faltering fathers did not sit well at all with most politicians. It was feared that such assistance would emasculate men by undermining their normative role as breadwinners.[25]

In time, government officials even became uneasy about providing public assistance to *fatherless* families. Politicians' ambivalence about mothers' pensions in some states put indigent single mothers in a bind. Some laws severely limited or prohibited paid labor altogether, on the assumption that mothers ought to stay at home and care for their children. And yet state benefits were so meager that they forced poor single mothers to get jobs on the sly if they couldn't do so openly.[26] Part of the disquietude about mothers' pensions was due to the more general concern about public assistance eroding recipients' moral values. As Ladd-Taylor points out, case workers scrutinized their clients' finances to make sure that mothers spent their pensions thriftily, and they were also zealous in trying to weed out any "cheaters" among the recipients of mothers' pensions.[27] The Children's Bu-

24. Ibid., pp. 145–46.
25. Ibid., p. 149.
26. Ibid., pp. 158–59.
27. Ibid., p. 151.

reau's vigilance in searching out fraud must, however, be placed in the proper historical context: administrators and case workers knew that the political success of mothers' pensions required the programs to be free of both administrative corruption *and* recipient fraud.

Throughout the 1910s and 1920s, as it developed close relations with state and municipal welfare agencies, the Children's Bureau increased its political stature by dispensing information and guidance to help improve administrative competence and efficiency. Furthermore, in the process of learning how to extract congressional appropriations the female leaders of the Children's Bureau honed their own political skills and advanced their bureaucratic interests. But at the same time that the Children's Bureau met with policy success, the women's movement became more fractured. As the 1920s approached, the Children's Bureau's belief that some women derived as much satisfaction from paid labor as from motherhood was drowned out by more conservative voices. Notwithstanding the control of the Children's Bureau by careerist women who subscribed to progressive-maternalist views, women's participation in the labor market was generally construed as a last resort to prevent an intact family from sinking into poverty. Even the Children's Bureau tended to define women's interests largely in terms of their role as mothers. Promoting *child* welfare, the Bureau proclaimed, also promoted *women's* welfare because a woman's primary identity and worth were bound up with motherhood, not wage work. The bifurcation of motherhood and work was more than an ideological construct; it was also starkly reflected in government structure, with the Children's Bureau having responsibility for child welfare and the Women's Bureau, established in the federal Department of Labor in 1918, having responsibility for employment issues relevant to women. The task of integrating motherhood with women's career interests would have to wait for a later time; the dominance of the family-wage model deterred women's organizations from formulating "proposals that recognized the whole lives of poor women, at home and in employment, with the family and with the market economy."[28]

28. Gordon, *Pitied But Not Entitled*, p. 99. Although historians tend to emphasize the postsuffrage splintering of the women's movement, a more nuanced perspective on women's political activism during the 1920s is emerging. For example, Sybil Lipschultz argues that during the 1920s women's advocacy of minimum wages and other laws targeted at female laborers became part of a more sophisticated and "feminist" theory than had been articulated in the earlier movements for "protective labor legislation." "Social feminism" of the 1920s, Lipschultz contends, broke from the paternalistic ideology underlying protective labor laws of the early twentieth century and constituted

Yet, as both Ladd-Taylor and Gordon explain, while women's fulfillment was defined principally as meeting children's needs, children's interests gradually became severed from women's interests. As economic necessity or educational opportunity pushed increasing numbers of women into the labor market, women's and children's interests began to part company—or so they were perceived.[29] For example, child-labor advocates contended that children should be spared employment whenever possible, thus putting pressure on economically straitened mothers to take jobs or to work longer hours if necessary.[30] Moreover, after gaining the right to vote and securing legal changes that fostered wives' independence from husbands, women were less likely to see themselves, or to be depicted by others, as victims. Children, by contrast, were looked upon as helpless and in need of society's care when their families could no longer meet their needs. But, as Gordon notes: "The problem was that the mother-child separation occurred not in a feminist discourse that would have validated women's needs and the work of parenting, but in a discourse that treated children, quite unrealistically, as a group with a unique claim on the state."[31] Therefore, one of the lasting consequences of mothers' pension laws was the gradual disjunction between mothers' interests and child welfare.

Another feature of mothers' pensions that would have an enduring impact on the United States welfare state was the classification of recipients according to particular categories. The "scientific charity" movement, launched in the late nineteenth century, sprang from the belief that public aid recipients required different treatment according to the source and nature of their impoverished circumstances. But implicit in the recognition of poverty's many faces was an assumption that not all poor people were equally *deserving* of public welfare.

---

a more egalitarian ideology concerned with fostering "industrial equality." Such equality, its supporters maintained, could come about only through laws that recognized the social and cultural inequality between men and women and that accorded different treatment to male and female workers. Lipschultz explores how the movement for industrial equality, although seemingly united, divided mainly along gender lines between male lawyers, whose support of protective labor laws was predicated on women's inferiority, and women reformers, who perceived labor laws as increasing gender equality. See Lipschultz, "Social Feminism and Legal Discourse, 1908–1923," in *At the Boundaries of Law: Feminism and Legal Theory* ed. Martha Albertson Fineman and Nancy Sweet Thomadsen (New York: Routledge, Chapman and Hall, Inc., 1991), pp. 209–25.

29. Ladd-Taylor, *Mother-Work*, p. 159.
30. Gordon, *Pitied But Not Entitled*, p. 99.
31. Ibid., p. 100.

Advocates of mothers' pensions were well aware that some categories of poor people were stigmatized because of culturally engrained beliefs about work, individual responsibility, and moral desert. For example, recipients of general relief were the objects of social disdain because they were regarded as able-bodied but as simply too lazy to hold a job.

The Children's Bureau was determined that indigent mothers, especially widows, be shielded from the contemptuous glare directed at general relief recipients. For good political reasons, then, the bureau sought to keep poor single mothers and their children off the general relief rolls and to nestle them in a separate, and sturdier, government program for women and children. Yet, as Gordon points out, in so doing the Children's Bureau magnified the distinction between the "deserving" and the "undeserving" poor.[32] Paradoxically, in trying to prevent its clientele from becoming stigmatized in the public mind, the Children's Bureau wound up opening a chasm between "worthy" and "unworthy" recipients that would prove so destructive in later years to the single-mother recipients of Aid to Families of Dependent Children.

An additional characteristic of mothers' pension laws that proved politically significant later was the Children's Bureau's preference for matching grants as a way to goad case workers outside the bureau to adhere to "professional" standards. States or municipalities that complied with the bureau's standards were rewarded with matching funds from the federal government, while states that failed to comply were denied such funds.

Due to the importance of case work and matching funds in the administration of mothers' pensions, then, the Children's Bureau ultimately put its weight behind federal *categorical* welfare programs rather than *universal entitlements*.[33] The endorsement of categorical programs owed, at least in part, to the bureau's fear of losing political influence under a regime of universal entitlements. But in putting its weight behind categorical programs the Children's Bureau lent momentum to an ideological transformation of mothers' pensions that undercut the progressive vision that had helped to ignite the movement from the start. Gordon explains that the bureau's approval of category-based public aid signified more than an ideological shift away from the original premise of mothers' pensions—that single mothers were *entitled* to public assistance by virtue of their maternal service to the state despite their adverse circumstances. It signified a wholesale

32. Ibid., p. 105.
33. Ibid., p. 106.

retreat to a conventional view about the institution of marriage itself: a wife and mother, as a party to a marriage contract, could expect a husband's financial security in exchange for ministering to the needs of children and of the household.[34] When a woman was deprived of her husband's support, the state stepped into his paternal shoes by providing economic support and discipline for the children.

Reflecting and accommodating those conservative changes, the Children's Bureau asserted in 1924 that mothers' pensions were a misnomer because "[a]id is being administered, not as a pension, but in accordance with the methods of case work."[35] In this remark the bureau was distinguishing between *unconditional* government entitlements and *means-tested* mothers' pensions. Thus, in a somewhat ironic twist, mothers' pensions for poor women were demoted at the hands of wealthy women whose actions enhanced their own professional status and political power. Although the beneficent intentions behind mothers' pensions were genuine, the female leaders of the Children's Bureau created for themselves a public space that paralleled and sometimes penetrated male authority over social policy, while ultimately reinforcing poor mothers' subordinate status.

III.

In conclusion, mothers' pensions were borne of a vigorous women's movement that culminated in 1920, when women gained the right to vote. The mothers' pension movement began as a presuffrage effort to connect mothers' aid to citizenship rights, on the grounds that poor single mothers were entitled to public assistance because of their contributions to the state in raising fatherless children. Once becoming law, however, mothers' pensions ended up accentuating the class and race differences between caretaker and client. And to the extent that mothers' pensions made the state a surrogate for an absent husband and father, the laws further institutionalized gender inequality.

Women at that time were aware of the many ways that mothers' pensions benefited poor women, who as a result were spared the added tragedy of having to surrender the care of their children to overburdened orphanages. Indeed, the progressive maternalists who

---

34. Ibid., p. 108.
35. Ladd-Taylor, *Mother-Work*, p. 159.

dominated the Children's Bureau witnessed the palpable ways that mothers' pension laws could alleviate the destructive effects of poverty on poor women's economic and psychological well-being. But the Children's Bureau also encountered some harsh words from feminists of their day. Feminists in the Women's Bureau, such as Assistant Director Agnes Petersen, were sharply attuned to the problems of all women, single or married, who tried desperately to juggle low-wage work and motherhood.[36] Lobbying for universal entitlements, feminists were disconcerted by the Children's Bureau's enthusiasm for case work, its support of categorical public assistance programs, and its reliance on conventional ideas about women's roles. As Sarvasy reveals, 1920s feminists in the United States looked to European models of public assistance, which embodied the concept of a universal family allowance. American feminists found this concept particularly promising, both politically and as a matter of sensible social policy.[37] From the perspective of feminists at the time, mothers' pensions lost their potentially radical edge once the Children's Bureau became the institutional center of the movement.

One of the ironies of the progressive maternalists' domination of the movement for mothers' pensions was that their ideology eventually undercut their special claim as the stewards of the nation's children. Since so many women reformers were unmarried and childless, they could not base their expertise about mothering on gender alone; after all, like male policymakers, these women did not have the direct personal experience of childbearing. They had no choice *but* to become knowledgeable about child welfare in order to command respect in a policy world inhabited by men. Yet, in appealing to social science and professional standards, rather than to the intuitions and maternal instincts of mothers themselves, women in the Children's Bureau made themselves dispensable as policymakers and administrators. After all, men could consult the latest social science on child development and welfare just as easily as could women.

During the New Deal period other reformers with different ideas and agendas overshadowed the Children's Bureau in the political process that resulted in the passage of the Social Security Act in 1935. Still, many of the broad questions with which Progressive-era maternalists had grappled were placed on President Franklin Roosevelt's policy agenda. Should gender-specific or gender-neutral norms be used in distributing public welfare? Should single mothers

36. Sarvasy, "Beyond the Difference Versus Equality Policy Debate," p. 341.
37. Ibid., p. 348.

with dependent children stay at home to care for their children or maintain a job? Did the experience of motherhood confer on women a unique competence to act upon children's needs and thus endow them with special privileges in the competition for government assistance? The welfare rights movement of the 1960s and 1970s also confronted those same questions, although in a different political environment. But for reasons to be explored in the next chapter, neither the natural-law tradition that had animated Jacksonian-era movements for economic justice nor the maternalist tradition that had inspired the Progressive-era women's movement found expression in Roosevelt's New Deal. The dissolution of natural law and maternalism during the 1930s has had profound consequences for the United States welfare state. One consequence, as Jean Bethke Elshtain has observed, is that contemporary public policy debates lack the vibrant democratic politics borne of a *union* of natural-law concepts of universalistic human rights and maternalist concepts of care and obligation.[38]

---

38. Jean Bethke Elshtain, *Public Man, Private Woman: Women in Social and Political Thought* (Princeton, N.J.: Princeton University Press, 1981), pp. 344–46.

Chapter Four

The New Deal
and Aid to
Dependent Children

The national economy was in a shambles when Franklin Roosevelt was elected president in 1932. The livelihoods of working- and middle-class families alike were profoundly threatened by the Great Depression. For example, between 1929 and 1932 iron and steel production plummeted 59 percent; the decline was so precipitous that the United States Steel Corporation had reduced its entire work force to *part-time* status by April 1933.[1] In 1932 one-half of all blacks living in southern cities were unemployed.[2] The poorest people were the eight million tenant and sharecropper families living in rural America, over a third of whom were black.[3] According to historian James Patterson, those

1. Anthony J. Badger, *The New Deal: The Depression Years, 1933–1940* (New York: Farrar, Straus, and Giroux, 1989), p. 22.
2. Ibid., p. 25.
3. As Jacqueline Jones points out, however, one should not over draw the distinction between urban and rural life in the South. Many sharecropper families worked the land during peak planting and harvesting seasons but migrated to cities in the off-seasons in an attempt to find factory and other jobs. Jacqueline Jones, *The Dispossessed: America's*

families "lived in two-to-three-room unpainted cabins without screens, doors, plumbing, electricity, running water, or sanitary wells."[4] Single mothers with children, totaling 3.8 million families in 1930, were among those trying to scrape by in the bleakest conditions. Although twenty-six states had mothers' pensions laws on the books, restrictive eligibility conditions and discriminatory practices toward women deemed "undeserving" reduced the number of poor families who actually received public aid. As late as 1937, four years into the New Deal, close to one-half of the United States population still lived in poverty.

The shocks to the nation inflicted by the Great Depression were not just economic; there were sharp political reverberations as well, with political leaders scrambling to respond to the biggest economic calamity to strike the United States in its history. Elected as president in 1932, Franklin Roosevelt proposed a new social contract, a "New Deal," that promised to relieve human want while stabilizing the faltering economy. As diverse scholars have observed, President Roosevelt explained the necessity of his New Deal programs in the language of liberalism, which was the dominant political ethos in the United States in the early 1930s.

I.

In 1932, facing the magnitude of unmet human need left by the Depression, presidential candidate Franklin Roosevelt called for an "economic declaration of rights." Again in the presidential campaign of 1944 he drafted an "Economic Bill of Rights"—a "second Constitution"—in order to guarantee security to all citizens, especially in times of economic crisis and acute human need. Perceiving the original Bill of Rights as a key institutional safeguard against the abuses of *government* power, Roosevelt stressed that it was incapable of inoculating citizens against uncontrollable *economic* forces. Unemployment, disability, old age, and the sudden death of a breadwinner, Roosevelt highlighted, posed serious threats to individual freedom. To put his point more philosophically, freedom entailed not only the *negative* liberties enumerated in the first ten amendments of the federal Consti-

---

Underclasses from the Civil War to the Present (New York: Basic Books, 1992), pp. 221–23.

4. James Patterson, *America's Struggle Against Poverty, 1900–1994* (Cambridge, Mass.: Harvard University Press, 1994), p. 38.

tution, but also *positive* economic liberties ensuring citizens "freedom from want."[5]

Roosevelt's proposal for an Economic Bill of Rights, although ultimately never codified, was probably the purest statement of his philosophy of government. Fifteen months after beginning his first term as president, Roosevelt explained the flurry of legislative activity during his first one hundred days in office as reflecting the New Deal's commitment to "the security of the men, women, and children of the Nation first."[6] At that time Roosevelt identified three essential elements of economic security: "People want decent homes to live in; they want to locate them where they can engage in productive work; and they want some safeguard against misfortunes which cannot be wholly eliminated in this man-made world of ours."[7]

In his 1943 State of the Union address and again during his 1944 election campaign Roosevelt drafted an expanded list of economic rights. Touted as a "second Constitution," Roosevelt's Economic Bill of Rights would enable "all persons, regardless of race, color, creed or place of birth, [to] live in peace, honor and *human dignity* . . . free from want—and free from fear."[8] Included in the economic charter were the rights to adequate food, clothing, housing, education, medical care, and security in times of sickness, accident, unemployment, and old age.[9] Those rights promised to meet citizens' physical and psychological needs by furnishing subsistence and thereby decreasing their fear of economic forces that no one individual could ever control.

Roosevelt's thinking "reflected the teaching of natural law, although he was probably most unaware of that teaching," noted Frances

5. David Hackett Fischer sees Roosevelt's understanding of liberty as harking back to the Puritans' notion of "freedom from the tyranny of circumstances." That ideal of freedom entailed a "collective obligation of the 'body politick' to protect individual members from the tyranny of circumstance." See his *Albion's Seed: Four British Folkways in America* (New York: Oxford University Press, 1989), pp. 204–5.

6. Franklin D. Roosevelt, "Message to Congress Reviewing the Broad Objectives and Accomplishments of the Administration," June 8, 1934; reprinted in *Fiftieth Anniversary Edition: The Report of the Committee on Economic Security of 1935 and Other Basic Documents Relating to the Development of the Social Security Act*, ed. Wilbur Cohen and Robert Ball (Washington, D.C.: National Conference on Social Welfare, 1985), p. 136.

7. Ibid.

8. Franklin D. Roosevelt, "Campaign Address on the 'Economic Bill of Rights,'" October 28, 1944; reprinted in *Fiftieth Anniversary Edition: The Report of the Committee on Economic Security of 1935 and Other Basic Documents Relating to the Development of the Social Security Act*, ed. Wilbur Cohen and Robert Ball (Washington, D.C.: National Conference on Social Welfare, 1985), p. 151.

9. Ibid.

Perkins, his secretary of labor.[10] In certain aspects Roosevelt's justification for national government involvement in the provision of basic
subsistence echoed that of natural-law philosophers John Locke and
Jean-Jacques Rousseau. For example, Roosevelt likened the historic
American frontier to a state of nature, in which the natural right to
life was secured through the individual's ready use and appropriation
of nature's "bounties": "In a simple and primitive civilization homes
were to be had for the building. The bounties of nature in a new land
provided crude but adequate food and shelter. When land failed, our
ancestors moved on to better land. It was always possible to push back
the frontiers."[11]

Roosevelt made clear that the settlers had retained access to the
means of subsistence when they began to organize themselves into
communities and to create town governments. The settlers had formed
communities in response to declining natural resources that had at
one time been so abundant. They met their subsistence needs through
the shared resources and cooperation of small communities. In Roosevelt's rendition of society's evolution, if any one individual proved
unable to procure his or her "right to life," he could count on the
pooled resources of "his neighbors" to meet subsistence needs.[12]

But industrialization put stress on communities, which decreased in
number and cohesion throughout the late nineteenth and early twentieth centuries. The modern industrial economy, Roosevelt believed,
was so interconnected that shocks to one sector often had reverberat-
ing effects on other sectors. The "hazards of life" were thus multiplied
at the very moment when individuals and families could no longer

10. Frances Perkins, *The Roosevelt I Knew* (New York: Viking Press, 1946), p. 143.
Perkins states that, to Roosevelt, "man's relation to God seemed based upon nature"
(p. 142).

11. Roosevelt, "Message to Congress Reviewing the Broad Objectives and Accomplishments of the Administration," p. 136. Locke and Rousseau had also offered an
account (albeit a conjectural history) of individuals first living in a state of nature,
eventually agreeing to enter civil society (the realm of nongovernmental associations),
and finally creating a "social contract" between government and citizens. Under the
social contract individuals' natural rights and liberties would be more secure than in
the state of nature, in which there was no neutral authority to adjudicate disputes
among individuals. Interestingly, in describing the state of nature Locke had once
compared it to the America of his time—a vast space with abundant natural resources
but untamed by civilization.

12. Franklin D. Roosevelt, "Radio Address on the Third Anniversary of the Social
Security Act," August 15, 1938, reprinted in *Fiftieth Anniversary Edition: The Report of
the Committee on Economic Security of 1935 and Other Basic Documents Relating to the
Development of the Social Security Act*, ed. Wilbur Cohen and Robert Ball (Washington,
D.C.: National Conference on Social Welfare, 1985), p. 147.

rely on their communities for assistance in satisfying basic needs. Hence, "[w]here heretofore men had turned to neighbors for help and advice," Roosevelt argued, "they now turned to Government."[13]

One consequence of industrialization was an exhaustion of natural resources, which, Roosevelt insisted, signaled a new task for the federal government: "Our new task is not discovery or exploitation of natural resources, or necessarily producing more goods. It is the soberer, less dramatic business of administering resources and plants already in hand."[14] Here, like Thomas Paine, Roosevelt's thinking reflected a basic natural-law assumption that individuals agree to a social contract in order to maximize their access to the means of subsistence. And since individuals could never alienate their natural right to self-preservation, their polity thus came to assume the primary obligation for meeting basic human needs. Government attended to subsistence needs while also pledging respect for the rights of private property.[15]

Roosevelt blamed the Herbert Hoover administration for privileging business's property rights over the human needs of ordinary Americans whose livelihoods were destroyed by the Depression. In Roosevelt's view Hoover resisted the necessary steps for effective government planning because he continually bowed to the will of the "financial titans" and "economic royalists" who fought hard to remain free of government restrictions. Indeed, at certain moments Roosevelt sounded not unlike the Jacksonian Workingmen, who had blended natural-law and civic-republican language to excoriate "moneylenders" and other "parasites" on productive labor. For example, in his first inaugural address Roosevelt harangued bankers and other businessmen:

> Plenty is at our doorstep, but a generous use of it languishes in the very sight of the supply. Primarily this is because rulers of the exchange of mankind's goods have failed through their own stubbornness and incompetence, . . . and have abdicated. . . . The money changers have fled from their high seats in the

13. Ibid.

14. Franklin Roosevelt, Commonwealth Club Address, 1932, quoted in Sidney M. Milkis, *The President and the Parties: The Transformation of the American Party System Since the New Deal* (New York: Oxford University Press, 1993), p. 41.

15. As will be recalled from Chapter 2, however, since (in one strand of natural-law philosophy) private property derived its legitimacy from citizens' use of it to satisfy subsistence needs, the rights of private property were to be subordinated to these needs, at least when people's livelihoods were jeopardized.

temple of our civilization. We may now restore that temple to the ancient truths.[16]

Roosevelt contended that if the Hoover administration had been willing to engage in effective planning, the federal government would not have been impotent to respond to the Depression's devastation. Absent some form of centralized planning, Roosevelt charged, the United States fell far short of the standards of administrative capacity and efficiency prevailing in the industrialized Western European countries:

> . . . economic circumstances and the forces of nature dictate the need of constant thought as the means by which a wise Government may help the necessary readjustment of the population. We cannot fail to act when hundreds of thousands of families live where there is no reasonable prospect of a living in the years to come. This is especially a national problem. *Unlike most of the leading Nations of the world*, we have so far failed to create a national policy for the development of our land and water resources and for their better use by those people who cannot make a living in their present positions. Only thus can we permanently eliminate many millions of people from the relief rolls on which their names are now found. *The extent of the usefulness of our great national inheritance of land and water depends on our mastery of it.*[17]

To Roosevelt's mind the absence of planning for a fair and efficient use of natural resources or for the relief of human needs resulted in a "rich man's security and a poor man's security," a disparity he found unjust.[18] Using natural-law rhetoric, he underscored his "administration's policy of conserving the enormous gifts with which an abundant Providence has blessed our country—our soil, our forests, our water."[19]

Roosevelt's most evocative use of the natural-law tradition was in his reference to the Declaration of Independence, which he viewed as

16. Franklin Roosevelt, Inaugural Address of 1933; quoted in William E. Leuchtenburg, *Franklin D. Roosevelt and the New Deal, 1932–1940* (New York: Harper & Row, 1963), p. 41.

17. Roosevelt, "Message to Congress Reviewing the Broad Objectives and Accomplishments of the Administration," p. 136; emphasis added.

18. Roosevelt, "Radio Address on the Third Anniversary of the Social Security Act," p. 148.

19. Roosevelt, "Campaign Address on the 'Economic Bill of Rights,' " p. 154.

embodying universalistic standards of justice. In drawing up the Democratic Party platform of 1936 Roosevelt set forth the rights to economic security and quoted from the Declaration: "We hold this truth to be self-evident—that government has certain inescapable obligations to its citizens. . . ."[20] Amplifying its historic roots, Roosevelt claimed that the Economic Bill of Rights would give the American people "a right . . . to the same security their forefathers sought."[21]

Through the use of natural-law language, then, Roosevelt linked positive economic rights with the negative rights contained in the Constitution's Bill of Rights. He skillfully interwove age-old natural-law principles with proposals for twentieth-century America. But the movement from general proposals to viable legislation was at times a formidable task, especially after the honeymoon periods following his elections to office. Even with his impressive electoral mandates, Roosevelt usually had to make compromises either in program conception or in specific policy details in order to muster the necessary votes to secure legislation.

II.

Franklin Roosevelt became president amidst a ferment of political activity among populist movements and social organizations that clamored for economic relief and, in some cases, for structural changes to bring about a more just society.[22] But although such populist groups got the attention of the Roosevelt administration, the prevailing scholarly view is that the New Deal did not usher in a new federal regime committed to income and wealth redistribution. Rather, the collection of programs known as the New Deal were principally aimed

20. Quoted in Milkis, *The President and the Parties*, p. 48.

21. Roosevelt, "Radio Address on the Third Anniversary of the Social Security Act," p. 148.

22. There was considerable agitation by labor groups across the political spectrum, from the older trade unions to the Communist Party. There was also a surge of populist movements and organizations, including: Huey Long's Share the Wealth organization, which boasted a huge popular following in parts of the South and Midwest; the elderly's vigorous Townsend Movement (named after its leader, Dr. Francis Townsend); the formidable presence of Father Coughlin, whose (often anti-Semitic) tirades against bankers, New Deal liberals, and others he accused of being in cahoots with a monied class reached millions of Americans over the radio and attracted a large membership in the National Union for Social Justice.

at alleviating human suffering while stimulating economic recovery by fostering an increased capacity for consumption.[23]

Among others, New Deal programs (1) provided unemployment compensation as well as public-works jobs for those thrown out of work, principally through the Federal Emergency Relief Administration and the Works Progress Administration; (2) established in the National Recovery Act "code authorities" allowing manufacturers to decide collectively on production and pricing policies free of antitrust restrictions while, in exchange, requiring companies to negotiate with labor unions on wage levels; (3) granted workers a *right* of collective bargaining in the Wagner Act and set minimum wage and maximum hours standards in the Fair Labor Standards Act; (4) introduced changes to the banking system by, for instance, placing control of the money market in the Federal Reserve Board through the Banking Act of 1935; and (5) set up rural electrification programs and federal farm subsidies through the Tennessee Valley Authority and the Agricultural Adjustment Act.[24]

The Social Security Act of 1935 was (and remains), however, the

23. Alan Brinkley, *The End of Reform: New Deal Liberalism in Recession and War* (New York: Alfred A. Knopf, 1995), p. 226.

24. Such classics by William E. Leuchtenberg and Arthur M. Schlesinger, Jr., are comprehensive and gracefully written treatments of the New Deal. For an equally informative book, a biography, see George McJimsey, *Harry Hopkins: Ally of the Poor and Defender of Democracy* (Cambridge, Mass.: Harvard University Press, 1987). There is, of course, a huge literature on the New Deal offering competing interpretations. For more recent work see, for example, Brinkley, *End of Reform;* and Colin Gordon, *New Deals: Business, Labor, and Politics in America, 1920–1935* (Cambridge, Eng.: Cambridge University Press, 1994) (both focusing on the political economy of the New Deal); Milkis, *The President and the Parties* (on the rise of the administrative state and its weakening of the party system); Steve Fraser and Gary Gerstle, eds., *The Rise and Fall of the New Deal Order, 1930–1980* (Princeton, N.J.: Princeton University Press, 1989) (essays focusing on the political origins and political economy of the New Deal); Margaret Weir, Ann Shola Orloff, and Theda Skocpol, eds., *The Politics of Social Policy in the United States* (Princeton, N.J.: Princeton University Press, 1988) (on the political economy and political origins of the New Deal). For a lively account of some of Roosevelt's more controversial actions, such as the Court-Packing Plan, see Kenneth S. Davis, *FDR: Into the Storm, 1937–1940, A History* (New York: Random House, 1993). For accounts emphasizing the gender dimensions of the New Deal see Linda Gordon, *Pitied But Not Entitled: Single Mothers and the History of Welfare, 1890–1935* (New York: The Free Press, 1994), chaps 7–10; Theda Skocpol, *Protecting Soldiers and Mothers: The Political Origins of Social Policy in the United States* (Cambridge, Mass.: Harvard University Press, 1992), especially the concluding chapter; Linda Gordon, ed., *Women, Welfare, and the State* (Madison: University of Wisconsin Press, 1990); and Susan Ware, *Beyond Suffrage: Women in the New Deal* (Cambridge, Mass.: Harvard University Press, 1981).

cornerstone of the welfare state in the United States. When Roosevelt first became president, there were different groups of experts jousting for power within his administration, each with its own ideas of social welfare. The most influential government body, which drafted the Social Security Act, was the Committee on Economic Security. Roosevelt had created and invested the Committee with the authority to make policy recommendations to ensure citizens' subsistence needs.

The three main government bodies that tried to put their stamp on the new national welfare state in the early 1930s were the Children's Bureau, the Federal Emergency and Relief Agency, and the Committee on Economic Security. The Children's Bureau envisioned a welfare state modeled on the mothers' pension laws already in existence in many states. Advocating a system of welfare involving joint federal-state administration and expenditures, the Bureau endorsed a categorically based welfare system that, along with distributing cash assistance, would send social workers into the homes of impoverished single mothers and their children. The women who led the Children's Bureau believed that indigent mothers, especially immigrants, needed advice and guidance in budgeting, housekeeping, and parenting. Well before the 1930s the Children's Bureau had abandoned its original commitment to promoting nonmeans tested universal entitlements for the poor and working class. The more conservative ideas that the Children's Bureau pushed by the late 1920s did receive a serious airing in the Roosevelt administration. As Susan Ware points out, although Roosevelt assigned the administration of Aid to Dependent Children (ADC) to a newly created Social Security Administration and the Bureau of Public Assistance, the Children's Bureau retained a strong advisory role and assumed direct responsibility for administering joint federal-state public health, nursing, and child health programs.[25] Yet, ironically, the political backlash against the women's movement of the Progressive era, fueled partly by male workers' frustration that women were displacing them, seems to have damaged the female leaders of the Children's Bureau.[26] Seeing educated and independent women in leadership positions within government, men assumed that they were elevating female over male employment opportunities. They overlooked the Bureau's support of women's tradi-

25. Ware, *Beyond Suffrage*, p. 101.
26. Badger, *The New Deal*, Also, as Linda Gordon points out, Harry Hopkins of the Federal Emergency Relief Administration belittled the importance of providing decent jobs for women. His "condescending" attitude brought him into conflict particularly with the Women's Bureau. Gordon, *Pitied But Not Entitled*, pp. 193–95.

tional roles as mothers.[27] In any event, by the late 1920s the distinctive maternalism that had informed the Children's Bureau reform efforts during the Progressive era had been lost. Although many women officials perceived the Roosevelt administration as receptive to women's participation in government policymaking, there was no strong maternalist voice that was heard within the administration.[28]

The second government agency that vied for power over public assistance was the Federal Emergency Relief Agency (FERA), led by Roosevelt's close advisor Harry Hopkins. Unlike the Children's Bureau, the FERA pressed for massive federal relief projects supplemented by noncontributory government assistance to the elderly and the unemployed.[29] A fervent believer in relief projects that kept the economically straitened at work, Roosevelt, however, was skeptical of noncontributory government assistance, which he disparaged as the "dole." Roosevelt dictated that "under no circumstances should any actual money be paid in the form of a dole . . . by the local welfare office to any unemployed man or his family."[30] If the number of relief projects was insufficient, then Roosevelt preferred to see government assistance provided in "kind" rather than in cash. Roosevelt put his own imprimatur on FERA relief projects, paying no heed to Hopkins's support of noncontributory public assistance.

The Committee on Economic Security (CES) was the government body that dominated the debate within the Roosevelt administration and played the largest role in drafting the Social Security Act, the cornerstone of the United States welfare state. It is not surprising that the CES commanded the most respect from Roosevelt. After all, it was composed largely of cabinet officials and a staff that was at ease with social science data and policy details. Secretary of Labor Frances Perkins headed up the CES, while Edwin Witte, a veteran Progressive-era reformer from Wisconsin, held the crucial post of executive director. As Ann Shola Orloff points out, Witte and other CES staff shared the Progressive-era commitment to fiscal responsibility and "good government."[31] Having had experience as administrators of

27. Gordon, *Pitied But Not Entitled*, pp. 195–96. This backlash was strikingly at work in 1930–31, when more than 75 percent of American school systems would not hire married women. Also, under the Economy Act, passed by Congress in 1932, fifteen hundred women were laid off under a provision stipulating that married employees with spouses employed in government be the first to be let go if dismissals were necessary. See Badger, *The New Deal*, p. 23.

28. Badger, *The New Deal*, p. 135.

29. Orloff, "The Political Origins of America's Belated Welfare State," in Weir et al., eds., *Politics of Social Policy in the United States*, p. 72.

30. Quoted in Badger, *The New Deal*, p. 70.

31. Orloff, "Political Origins of America's Belated Welfare State," p. 70.

state agencies responsible for labor and social legislation, Witte and other CES members were sensitive to the problem of public pressure expanding a program beyond its fiscal limits. Witte and his CES colleagues were determined to develop a set of programs that provided economic security within budgetary parameters but that kept it at a distance from the public's insatiable appetite for more benefits.[32] The CES's influence was almost guaranteed from the start, since Roosevelt as governor of New York had been intimately familiar with state-level social insurance programs.

The CES proposed a melange of programs—very different from the comprehensive, universalistic European-style entitlement programs— aimed at helping different groups of vulnerable citizens. The CES's proposals distinguished between two groups of people: those who were able to provide for themselves and those whose age or disability, such as blindness, prevented them from holding a job. Perhaps because of its popularity, what later became seen as the hallmark of the CES's multilayered "economic security" proposals was old-age insurance (or what we today call "social security"), benefits to individuals aged sixty-five or older to help ward against the infirmities that accompany old age. The CES assigned exclusive responsibility for administering old-age pensions to the federal government, which would then finance the program through employer and employee contributions, to be supplemented by subsidies from federal revenues thirty years later. Yet the real centerpiece of the CES's draft legislation was not old-age insurance but contributory unemployment insurance to be jointly administered by the national and state governments; Witte himself had been primarily interested in unemployment insurance while in Wisconsin, and over the objections of some of Roosevelt's other advisors he persuaded his CES colleagues to propose an unemployment plan that would preserve a significant role for the states. The contributory basis of both old-age and unemployment insurance soon gave them a higher status than the noncontributory public assistance programs for indigent persons who were incapable of working. With respect to the latter programs, the CES proposed three federal grants-in-aid to the states for fatherless, dependent children; for the indigent elderly who could not claim Social Security benefits; and for the blind. The CES also recommended universal, public health insurance, but that proved to be too controversial to be enacted into law.

The CES's draft legislation, as many scholars have argued, was carefully formulated so as to quell political opposition by appealing

32. Ibid.

ideologically to long-standing values and by accommodating powerful interests. The CES fixed upon social-insurance principles as the hallmark of its legislation for economic security. Such principles were easily accommodated to the language of contracts that was so familiar a part of American political thinking.

Part and parcel of the careful ideological packaging of the Social Security Act was the CES's pragmatic response to the political constraints faced by the Roosevelt administration. Anticipating some of those constraints, such as the pattern of Supreme Court decisions limiting federal power vis-à-vis the states and the political power that had already accrued to the state governments during the Progressive era, the CES was quick to preserve state political power in all titles of what eventually became the Social Security Act except old-age insurance. Regarding ADC, the prominent role that the CES gave to the states under Title IV was not done grudgingly. As governor of New York Roosevelt had not only acquired confidence in the capacity of states to administer welfare programs but also feared the citizenry becoming overly dependent on the federal government for relief. He felt that the states and not the national government were the proper dispensers of public assistance.

The CES's sensitivity to political factors was not always enough, however, to satisfy conservative southern congressmen, and so the CES was forced to make compromises in order to build the necessary support for the Social Security Act so as to secure its passage. Despite the CES's substantial grant of discretion to the states in the administration of public assistance programs, the committee had to omit the few federal standards it had established. For example, the CES was compelled to delete from old-age assistance the stipulation that states provide pensions that "when added to the income of the aged recipients" would provide "a reasonable subsistence compatible with decency and health."[33] In addition, the CES had to scuttle its broad definition of "eligible" children under ADC and abandon its requirement that states adopt a merit system for administrators in order to promote professionalism. But the most dramatic concession to the disproportionately large number of southern congressmen who chaired key committees was the CES's exclusion of agricultural workers and domestic servants from old-age and unemployment insurance, despite Roosevelt's own endorsement of universal coverage.[34] That

33. Ibid., p. 78.
34. Ibid., p. 77.

exclusion amounted to three-fifths of all African-American workers.[35] Conservative Democrats feared that the racial caste system in the South would be eroded by any government program that provided relief for unemployment since financial necessity kept African-Americans dependent on whites and enabled employers to keep wages low. They likewise wanted to ensure that black female recipients of ADC would remain financially dependent on white planters for labor during peak agricultural seasons. Yet, frequently, African-Americans were often denied ADC altogether. For example, although the proportion of need was far greater, only 14–17 percent of ADC recipients were black.[36]

The new welfare state codified in the Social Security Act, Barbara Nelson has argued, created a two-tiered system in which indigent and mostly female recipients were generally subordinate to middle-class and wealthy male recipients.[37] Women were heavily concentrated in means-tested public assistance programs, whereas men were the primary beneficiaries of social insurance. The gender inequality stemmed from the fact that men were paid workers who "earned" their right to old-age pensions as well as unemployment insurance and compensation, while women were dependent on the infamous "dole." The linkage of social insurance with the male-dominated marketplace and of public assistance with the "dole" reinforced gender biases.[38] A bifurcated welfare system thus arose in which male recipients were generally categorized as the "deserving poor" and female recipients as the "undeserving poor." Nelson shows how the gender inequality was played out in day-to-day policy administration: the procedures used in the programs associated with men tended to be quasi-judicial, universal, and public, whereas the procedures used in the programs associated with women tended to be informal, particularistic, discretionary, and "private."[39] Men were treated as rights-bearing citizens, ADC recipients as subjects to be molded into "good" mothers.

The degree of ambivalence aroused by ADC was determined in no

35. Jill Quadagno, "From Old-age Assistance to Supplemental Security Income," in Weir et al., eds., Politics of Social Policy in the United States, p. 238.

36. Gordon, Pitied But Not Entitled, p. 276.

37. Barbara J. Nelson, "The Origins of the Two-Channel Welfare State: Workmen's Compensation and Mothers' Aid," in Women, the State, and Welfare, ed. Linda Gordon (Madison: University of Wisconsin Press, 1990), pp. 123–51.

38. Ibid. See also Carole Pateman, "The Patriarchal Welfare State," in Democracy and the Welfare State, ed. Amy Gutmann (Princeton, N.J.: Princeton University Press, 1988), pp. 231–60.

39. Nelson, "Origins of the Two-Channel Welfare State," p. 133.

small part by the race or ethnicity of the recipients. On the one hand, there was a cultural image of the white, "helpless," "deserving" widow who, tragically, was suddenly deprived of the support of her husband and was thus unable to care for her children. On the other hand, deep-rooted prejudice against African-Americans and immigrants created stereotypes of women that mitigated sympathy in many locales. Yet political ambivalence seems to have gone beyond racial stereotypes in that sometimes white ADC recipients were perceived as challenging conventional gender relations because of their sexual entanglements (whether real or perceived) outside of marriage. Aside from the worries about recipient behavior, policymakers also were anxious that ADC would provide a financial incentive for married men to shirk their traditional role as head of their families by deserting their wives and children.

The gender unease stirred by ADC was especially manifested in the "suitable home" rules used in some states to deny ADC to women whose home lives were deemed "unsuitable" for children. Policy ad-ministrators used the "suitable home" rules to probe and often to call into question women's moral virtue and mothering skills. The "suit-able home" rules were fashioned in the context of a debate over how best to ensure that ADC recipients would be morally (sexually) virtuous and "fit" mothers in the absence of a male authority and breadwinner in the home. Thus ADC structurally resembled the mothers' pension programs, but insofar as it symbolized the "dole" rather than an "entitlement" in exchange for services rendered to the state, it lacked the ideological power of Progressive-era maternalism.

III.

The Social Security Act, with all its limits, thus established a national welfare state. But Roosevelt's political vision, at least at the level of rhetoric, went beyond the programmatic rights contained in that landmark legislation. Again, in his view "economic royalists" were trammeling upon the needs and rights of ordinary citizens. The Eco-nomic Bill of Rights promised to reverse that situation by guarantee-ing "security and Prosperity . . . for all—regardless of stratum, race or creed." But Roosevelt had an enemy in the United States Supreme Court, which employed natural-law reasoning for *conservative* ends. As a tactical, political move, Roosevelt linked his notion of economic rights to *statutory* law in order to promote *liberal* ends by maintaining control over the enforcement of such programmatic rights. He feared that the Supreme Court would simply dilute the content of economic entitlements (if they were upheld at all) if he failed to persuade the Congress to embody such rights in legislation—legislation that the executive branch, under his leadership, would have the authority to implement. Therefore, while relying on natural-law principles to justify his idea of liberty as incorporating a "right to life" as opposed to the Supreme Court's idea of liberty as "liberty of contract," Roosevelt ultimately proclaimed the need for a new social contract to be based on the national government's commitment to pursue the "general welfare." The "general welfare," as he understood it, referred to ordinary citizens' interests in economic security, which they registered at the ballot box. To Roosevelt, economic justice, although derived from natural law, was what the *people* and their president believed it to be and not what *elite* justices passed off as natural law. Roosevelt's populist rhetoric was aimed at gaining and solidifying the loyalty of the economically disadvantaged, many of whom were otherwise separated by differences of race, ethnicity, and religion.

By grounding individual rights to security and public obligations in statutory law, Roosevelt assured the presidency a central role in the evolution of the welfare state and national policymaking. Since the president alone was elected by all the people, he had a uniquely national constituency that increased his leverage vis-à-vis Congress. Although Roosevelt praised Congress for its "magnificent conception of . . . national needs," he clearly regarded the presidency and not the legislature as the engine of reform. Yet at the same time Roosevelt looked beyond the popular-democratic strain of the Constitution to the countermajoritarian strain, for he understood individual rights to economic security to be claims *against* majoritarian sentiment. Roosevelt's plan for reconciling the "democratic" and countermajoritarian elements of the Constitution envisioned a considerable expansion of the power of the modern presidency.

Roosevelt proposed changes in executive-branch organization that would have substantially strengthened and centralized the federal bureaucracy under his control. As Sidney Milkis persuasively argues, bureaucratic agencies were to be the guardians of the "programmatic rights" in the "second constitution."[40] Roosevelt envisioned his ap-

40. Milkis, *The President and the Parties*, p. 145. I do, however, disagree with Milkis's argument that Roosevelt's notion of economic rights was a marked departure from the natural-law tradition in America. It was a marked departure from *one strand* of natural-law thinking derived from Adam Smith (among others), according to which government ought to keep its hands off the market economy. But Chapters 2 and 3 of my book

pointed executive-branch policymakers standing above public and partisan interests (albeit not above his political vision!) and as relatively insulated from political pressure that threatened to undercut his policy goals. In gaining the trust and loyalty of the executive branch, Roosevelt felt confident that the programmatic rights contained in the Social Security Act would be protected from shifting political winds. In short, as Milkis makes clear, by utilizing executive agencies that were committed to his vision of economic and political reform, Roosevelt sought to consolidate his electoral coalition while simultaneously removing the presidency from direct partisan pressure and public opinion.

Roosevelt's landslide reelection in 1936 gave him good reason—or so he thought—for believing that a "second New Deal" and proposed reorganizations of the Executive Branch and Supreme Court would muster the necessary votes in Congress. Through executive-branch reorganization Roosevelt sought to "embed" economic rights to security in a social contract to be enforced by an administrative state rather than by elected officials. He believed he had leverage over Congress because of the enormous popularity of his conception of economic rights. How, Roosevelt wondered, could "the people" not help but support the increased expertise and efficiency of bureaucratic officials over pork-barrel politics? And since, in Roosevelt's view, the Supreme Court's interpretation of economic rights had made a mockery of natural law and of the Constitution itself, he felt an electoral mandate to rein in the justices. Roosevelt thought that his notion of economic rights eventually would triumph through the vigorous implementation of programmatic rights in the new administrative state, as well as through public humiliation of a Supreme Court that seemed completely bent on blocking his legislative agenda.

As indicated, Roosevelt believed that natural law entailed government's guarantee of human life, while the Supreme Court defined it as "liberty of contract" and thus sought to prohibit many government regulations. Not surprisingly, President Roosevelt had numerous and bitter clashes with the judiciary.[41] Although enormously frustrating to the president, Roosevelt's confrontations with the Supreme Court enabled him eventually to gain the upper hand by positioning himself

highlight that there were other powerful strands in the American political tradition than the laissez-faire natural-law strand.

41. See especially: *U.S. v. Schechter Poultry Co.*, 295 U.S. 495 (1935); *U.S. v. Butler*, 297 U.S. 1 (1936); *Carter v. Coal Co.*, 298 U.S. 238 (1936); but see also *National Labor Relations Board v. McLaughlin Steel Corp.*, 301 U.S. 1 (1937); and *U.S. v. Darby*, 312 U.S. 100 (1941), upholding federal regulations.

as the spokesman for "the people" pitted against the "nine old men" of the Court, whom he branded as the spokesmen of the "economic royalists." Until 1937 the Supreme Court rendered interpretations of the Constitution's Fourteenth Amendment to strike down "paternalist" labor and welfare regulations. The Fourteenth Amendment asserts, in part: ". . . nor shall any State deprive any person of life, liberty, or property, without due process of law. . . . " On its face, the amendment does not bar government from depriving an individual of liberty; it simply stipulates that *if* a state deprives an individual of liberty, it must do so in accordance with "due process of law." To the conservative bloc on the Court, however, the Fourteenth Amendment prohibited altogether laws that impinged on liberty of contract. The Court's "liberty of contract" rulings between 1890 and 1937 are known collectively as the *"Lochner-era"* decisions and have been widely stigmatized as a low point in Supreme Court jurisprudence.[42]

The Court's interpretation of the Fourteenth Amendment was extremely controversial, with critics highlighting the absence of any mention of "liberty of contract" in the Constitution. Mocking the Court's "horse-and-buggy" rulings, Roosevelt himself complained that its views of national government power were anachronistic, wholly oblivious to the needs of an advanced industrial society. In addition, opponents of the Court stressed that the authors of the Fourteenth Amendment were mainly concerned about strengthening the rights of the newly freed slaves and not the rights of corporations. They accused the justices of injecting their own conservative values into the Fourteenth Amendment's Due Process Clause and then using them as a standard by which to judge the substance of business regulations. But the criticisms of the Court carried no weight with a shifting majority of the justices. In their view liberty of contract needed no textual anchor because it was so obviously a "fundamental" principle of *natural law* that the Court had no choice but to prohibit regulations that "interfered with" the private relationship between employer and employee.

During the *Lochner* era the Supreme Court became a safe haven for corporations and smaller businesses in flight from state and federal regulations. Corporations usually found a sympathetic hearing in the Supreme Court, since many of the justices had practiced corporate law

42. The 1890–1937 cases take their name from the leading case of *Lochner v. N.Y.*, 198 U.S. 45 (1905), which came to represent all of the Court's declarations that the Fourteenth Amendment contains a "liberty of contract" prohibiting states from "unreasonably" regulating the private sphere of employer and employee relations.

earlier in their careers. In case after case the Supreme Court struck down minimum wage and maximum hours regulations along with numerous New Deal programs as violations of liberty of contract.[43] In treating employers and employees as legal equals the Court ignored the economic circumstances that forced so many workers to enter into labor contracts against their will. Roosevelt and many state and federal legislators were incredulous that the justices would ignore the starkly unequal bargaining power between employers and employees. They decried the Court's rulings, emphasizing that "liberty of contract" was a "sham" because "[a]n empty stomach can make no contracts."[44]

Elected officials and Progressive-era reformers were not the only ones to lambaste the *Lochner*-era Court. As early as 1905 Supreme Court Justice Oliver Wendell Holmes had chastised his colleagues for reading the Fourteenth Amendment through the lens of the Social Darwinian philosopher Herbert Spencer. Nonetheless, Holmes's critique of the "liberty of contract" rulings fell upon deaf ears, and the Court persisted in putting a laissez-faire gloss on the Fourteenth Amendment until its showdown with President Roosevelt in 1937.

The Court's many 5–4 rulings favoring businesses infuriated Roosevelt because he believed that government regulations of working conditions were necessary to safeguard the welfare of workers and general public alike. Roosevelt opposed not only the ideological content of the Court's rulings but also the justices' use of natural law to divine liberty of contract. To Roosevelt, the Court's appeal to natural law was disingenuous: a majority of the justices pretended to give voice to "the common understanding" of liberty and justice, but in reality, he fumed, their use of natural law was just a rhetorical ploy to deflect attention from the victories that they regularly handed to corporate interests over and above the needs of ordinary working people. After all, the Court's enemies wondered, wasn't natural law a repository of ethical principles that all reasonable people agree transcend and limit government action because of their intrinsic or "natural" justice? Roosevelt believed that the Court's views were a far cry from natural justice since they gave the economically strong *few* the *license* to pursue private profit and to amass wealth at the expense of the economically weak *multitude*. He was certain that the Court's

43. See for example: *Allgeyer v. Louisiana*, 165 U.S. 578 (1897); *Lochner v. N.Y.*, 198 U.S. 45 (1905); *Wolf Packing Co. v. Court of Industrial Relations*, 272 U.S. 522 (1923).

44. Quoted in David Montgomery, *Beyond Equality: Labor and the Radical Republicans, 1862–1872* (New York: Alfred A. Knopf, 1967), p. 252.

conservative conceptions of liberty and justice were not a part of "the common understanding," for if they were, he would not have won a landslide reelection to the presidency in 1936. So with his electoral mandate in hand, Roosevelt set out to show the Court just *which* branch of government had the most legitimacy in the public eye.

As events unfolded, the Supreme Court was not to have a monopoly on disingenuous behavior. Enormously frustrated and agitated by the justices' unrelenting assault on New Deal programs in cases brought by businesses, Roosevelt proposed to reorganize the Supreme Court. His proposal, which became known as the "Court-Packing" Plan, would have given the president the authority to appoint a Supreme Court justice for each one over the age of seventy and one-half years. The plan would have enabled Roosevelt to make six new appointments immediately, thus offsetting the votes of the entire conservative bloc. At first Roosevelt presented the reorganization plan as an antidote to the heavy work load befalling elderly justices. Additional justices were necessary, he said, "because the personnel of the Federal Judiciary is insufficient to meet the business before them."[45] Incredibly, Roosevelt spoke as if the justices' *ages*, not their politics, were the problem. The president's motivations were transparent, notwithstanding his solemn words: "I attach a carefully considered draft of a proposed bill, which, if enacted, would, I am confident, afford substantial relief" to the Court's personnel.[46]

It was plain to all, of course, that the proposed reorganization was nothing less than Roosevelt's desperate attempt to exert control over the Supreme Court by diluting the influence of the conservative justices. Even some of Roosevelt's advisors were uncomfortable with the Court-Packing Plan. For, in the wry words of Roosevelt biographer Kenneth S. Davis, the obvious question was: "How *could* the public become persuaded that the President's primary concern with the judiciary, which he had publicly castigated in the past for its 'horse-and-buggy' decisions, had now all at once become its 'inefficiency?' "[47] Nevertheless, Roosevelt persisted in the face of criticism and eventually tried to needle Congress into enacting the Court-Packing Plan into law.

Rebuffing Roosevelt, the Senate defeated the Court-Packing Plan in 1937. But as most commentators point out, although Roosevelt's plan failed to secure a congressional majority, he triumphed over the

45. Quoted in Davis, *FDR: Into the Storm, 1937–1940*, p. 49.
46. Ibid.
47. Ibid., p. 50.

conservative bloc that very same year. His victory was interpreted as a reflection of the Court's ignominy in the public eye and of the judicial liberals'/centrists' concern that the Supreme Court's legitimacy had been called into question, its authority badly tarnished. Henceforth, the Supreme Court took a deferential stance toward federal and state regulations of businesses, and the protracted conflict between the Court and presidency ceased. Roosevelt's victory was cemented with the appointment of nine additional justices over the course of his remaining eight years as president.

In failing to secure congressional passage of the Court-Packing Plan, scholars like to say that Roosevelt "lost the battle but won the war." The mere threat of presidential control of the Supreme Court amounted to a stern denunciation of the Court's conservative use of natural-law reasoning, which a majority of the justices themselves then repudiated the same year that his Court-Packing Plan went down in infamy. And in 1938, just one year after the defeat of the plan, the humbled Supreme Court gave voice to a "double standard" in constitutional interpretation.[48] In an otherwise innocuous case involving a business regulation, the Court steered clear of natural-law reasoning and applied the lax "reasonable basis" test associated with the theory of judicial restraint that had become so popular during the 1930s. In the fourth footnote of the opinion, however, Justice Harlan F. Stone hinted that henceforth the Court would apply the rigorous "strict scrutiny" test and engage in judicial activism in order to protect individual rights, the integrity of the democratic process, and minority groups.[49]

---

48. The term "double standard" does not have a pejorative connotation but simply refers to the contrasting standards of review the Court employs in "rights" versus "economics" cases. Yet some scholars argue that the Court's adherence to the "double standard" has sometimes been more symbolic than real and that in actual decision-making the Court has blurred the distinction between the realm of rights and the realm of economics. For example, Martin Shapiro argues that the Warren Court did not hesitate to give stricter scrutiny to labor practices if it would result in giving workers greater First Amendment protections to express their grievances. Shapiro, "The Supreme Court: From Warren to Burger," in *The New American Political System*, ed. Anthony King (Washington, D.C.: American Enterprise Institute, 1978), pp. 179–211. Although agreeing with Shapiro that the Supreme Court often muddies the boundary between economics and rights, Michael W. McCann traces the continuity between the conservatism of the *Lochner*-era decisions and the so-called liberal decisions of the Warren Court era. McCann, "Equal Protection for Social Inequality: Race and Class in Constitutional Ideology," in *Judging the Constitution: Critical Essays on Judicial Lawmaking*, ed. Michael W. McCann and Gerald L. Houseman (Boston: Scott, Foresman and Co., 1989), pp. 231–64.

49. *U.S. v. Carolene Products Co.*, 304 U.S. 144 (1938), n. 4.

Paradoxically, while using the natural-law tradition to justify government's responsibility to fulfill citizens' "right to life," President Roosevelt made it much harder for a later generation of social reformers to persuade the United States Supreme Court of a constitutional "right to live." Since *judicial* natural-law reasoning had been used for *conservative* political ends, Roosevelt and other liberals discredited it as a mode of constitutional interpretation. Unable to trust the Supreme Court, Roosevelt naturally sought to enshrine rights to economic security in statutory law, rather than through a constitutional amendment. After all, the post-*Lochner* Court would have no choice but to bow to the president's wishes, as reflected in statutory law and government programs, and allow the American welfare state to evolve (ideally, from Roosevelt's perspective) under the leadership of Democratic presidents.

Another irony disclosed in this chapter is that, although Roosevelt was known to have been very open and sensitive to the ideas of female leaders in government, his administration created a mothers' pension program—Aid to Dependent Children—that lacked the "entitlement" thrust of the earlier maternalist justification. Unlike state mothers' pension programs enacted during the Progressive era, ADC reflected an ambivalence about single mothers that essentially turned a maternalist "entitlement" into the much-reviled "dole." During the Progressive era mothers' pensions were separated from other programs in order to preserve and reward the single mother's unique status and claim upon the state. But during the New Deal period the separation of ADC from the male-dominated contributory, social-insurance programs reflected a *demotion* in the status of indigent single mothers. The political marginalization of ADC in the new national welfare state made life onerous for impoverished single mothers and their children. Yet, their hope for the future came in the 1960s, when Legal Services Program lawyers took up the cause of AFDC mothers for "welfare rights."

Chapter Five

The Warren Court's "New Equal Protection"

Opening the Court to Poor People

Just as the Supreme Court's decisions during the *Lochner* era constrained Franklin Roosevelt's efforts to legitimize a national welfare state, his administration's actions left an enduring legacy for the Supreme Court. The Warren Court's rulings, in turn, gave shape to the welfare rights movement launched in the mid-1960s, first by opening the courtroom to poor people's legal grievances and then by influencing the litigation strategy that welfare-rights advocates formulated in an attempt to convince the justices to establish a constitutionally protected right to subsistence. This chapter tells the first part of the story about the welfare rights movement's search for economic justice in court.

The National Welfare Rights Organization (NWRO) was formed in 1966. Ninety-eight percent of the membership were poor, black, female recipients of Aid to Families with Dependent Children (AFDC), the joint federal-state welfare program for indigent single mothers and their children that was formerly called Aid to Dependent Children. The NWRO leaders, by contrast, were mostly middle-class white men with professional experience in social reform. They worked with federally funded Legal Services Program (LSP) lawyers to try to revamp America's scattershot welfare system. Established in 1965 to provide free legal counsel for poor people in civil cases, the LSP was part of the Johnson administration's War on Poverty. The Center on Social Welfare Policy and Law (CSWPL), which was set up at Columbia University in New York City with foundation support, was an LSP-funded resource center for lawyers focusing on poor people's legal problems. Informed of the CSWPL's expertise in welfare law, NWRO leaders obtained litigation information and support from CSWPL lawyers. Based on the Warren Court's rulings defining "equal protection of the laws" under the Fourteenth Amendment, CSWPL attorneys and NWRO leaders identified the federal judiciary and especially the Supreme Court as the institutional forum most receptive to the poor's need-claims.

CSWPL litigation strategists and the top echelon of the NWRO worried about the precarious legal status of welfare recipients, particularly of AFDC beneficiaries whose poverty, race, and gender all tended to render them powerless in the political arena. With the help of NWRO leaders, CSWPL attorneys designed a litigation strategy aimed at securing procedural protections for welfare recipients, easing eligibility restrictions, and ultimately convincing the Supreme Court of a *constitutional* (not just statutory) basis for welfare rights.[1] In the lawyers' view the vagaries of welfare administration could not be eradicated until the courts treated welfare assistance as a constitutional right, shielded from the shifting and often chilly winds of budgetary politics.

I.

In seeking to establish a constitutional right to subsistence the LSP lawyers looked to the Fourteenth Amendment, which extends to all persons the "equal protection of the laws." Ratified after the Civil War, the amendment's original purpose was to protect the newly freed slaves. Yet the Supreme Court quickly abandoned blacks and instead

---

1. For a formal statement of the strategy see Edward V. Sparer, "The Right to Welfare," reprinted in *The Rights of Americans: What They Are—What They Should Be,* ed. Norman Dorsen (New York: Random House, 1971), pp. 65–93. See also Edward Sparer, "The Role of the Welfare Client's Lawyer," 12 *UCLA Law Review* 279 (January 1965).

used the Fourteenth Amendment's Due Process Clause to shelter businesses from government regulations. In case after case the Court contended that the Fourteenth Amendment's guarantee against the deprivation of "liberty" "without due process of law" actually protected "liberty of contract." From about 1890 until 1937 the Supreme Court's constitutional decisions allowed corporations and racists to behave with few constraints in the so-called private domain of individual liberty.

But then in the late 1930s in the context of President Roosevelt's assault upon the Supreme Court, the beleaguered justices signaled a new stance. In 1937 a bare majority of the Court upheld Washington state's minimum wage laws, asserting that in cases involving economic regulation the justices would henceforth defer to the judgment of the elected branches of government, since the Constitution made no mention of "freedom of contract." Lest people assume the Court would strike a uniform posture of judicial restraint in all types of cases, however, the justices indicated the very next year that they would subject to "strict scrutiny" those laws that threatened individual rights, impeded access to the democratic process, or were aimed at "discrete and insular minorities."[2] Blacks were foremost in the justices' minds as a minority that was particularly vulnerable to discrimination. The Warren Court turned the strict scrutiny test into a very exacting standard, one that was difficult for government to meet since the two strands of the test required proof that a law promoted a "compelling government interest" using the "least restrictive means" available. The solicitude that the Warren Court showed to blacks abetted the fledgling civil rights movement in the 1950s.

Starting in the late 1950s, however, the Warren Court indicated its willingness to cast the net of the Equal Protection Clause beyond racial categories. In a series of decisions known as the wealth-discrimination rulings, the Court expressed concern about the spillover effects of economic inequality on constitutionally guaranteed rights. Although the architects of the Fourteenth Amendment were principally aggrieved by the plight of African-Americans newly released from bondage, the Warren Court indicated that blacks were not the only

2. The first case refers to *West Coast Hotel v. Parrish*, 300 U.S. 379 (1937), and the second case to *U.S. v. Carolene Products Company*, 304 U.S. 144 (1938), n. 4. The *Carolene Products* ruling embodies what has become known as the "double standard" in constitutional law because, on the one hand, of the deference the Court states is appropriate for *economic* legislation and, on the other hand, the "more exacting" judicial scrutiny the Court states is appropriate when laws involve individual rights, government processes, and minority groups.

group at risk of discrimination. Indigent persons were also entitled to equal protection of the laws. Therefore, the Court noted in a series of cases, laws that established distinctions based on wealth were as "suspect" as those based on race.

Decided in 1956, *Griffin v. Illinois* was the first case in which the Warren Court exhibited queasiness over the unequal circumstances of poor and nonpoor.[3] The Court invalidated an Illinois law that required criminal defendants seeking appellate review to pay for a trial transcript. The Court's reason was that poverty, like race, is "constitutionally irrelevant," since a defendant's guilt or innocence is unrelated to the amount of money s/he possesses. Justice Black's plurality opinion stressed how wealth disparities distort the criminal-justice process: "There can be no equal justice where the kind of trial a man gets depends on the amount of money he has."[4]

Griffin was significant because for the first time in a nonrace case the Supreme Court declared unconstitutional a law that accorded *formal* equality to all persons (that is, the transcript fee applied to all equally). Prior to *Griffin* the Court had always upheld statutes that *resulted* in inequalities between rich and poor so long as they embodied neither discriminatory intent nor an arbitrary classification. Decrying the insufficiency of formal equality in criminal justice procedures, however, Justice Frankfurter noted sardonically in a concurring opinion that the Illinois transcript fee "would justify a latter-day Anatole France to add one more item to his ironic comments on the 'majesty equality' of the law. 'The law, in its "majestic equality," forbids the rich as well as the poor to sleep under bridges, to beg in the streets, and to steal bread.' "[5]

Justice Harlan, in dissent, responded that states are compelled only to ensure "numerically equal treatment" and since rich and poor alike were subject to the transcript fee, the Illinois statute satisfied the Equal Protection Clause. He insisted that states are not constitutionally obligated to offset the unequal position of indigent defendants.[6]

The egalitarianism of the *Griffin* ruling lay in the Court's implicit acknowledgment that wealth, like race, is a "suspect classification" because indigent persons, like racial, ethnic, and religious minority groups, faced discrimination at the hands of government officials. The Court contended that laws embodying a wealth-based classification

3. 351 U.S. 12 (1956).
4. Ibid. at 18–19.
5. Ibid. at 23.
6. Ibid. at 34–36.

and bearing on an important interest, such as appellate review in a criminal case, are tantamount to an "invidious discrimination" between rich and poor, in violation of the Equal Protection Clause. Not satisfied by what Justice Harlan characterized as a "uniform policy" applied to rich and poor equally, Justice Black's opinion for the Court deemed the differential impact of a law on persons with and without economic resources to be constitutionally suspect. *Griffin* laid the groundwork for judicial oversight of the effects of poverty on what the Court came to call "fundamental rights" or "fundamental interests."[7]

In 1963 the Court handed down two decisions that fortified constitutional protections of indigent criminal defendants. In *Douglas v. California* the Court declared unconstitutional a California procedure that authorized an appellate court to decide for itself whether an indigent criminal defendant would benefit from having appointed counsel on appeal. Writing for the majority, Justice Douglas insisted: ". . . where the merits of the *one and only appeal* an indigent has as of right are decided without benefit of counsel, we think an unconstitutional line has been drawn between rich and poor."[8] In the landmark *Gideon v. Wainwright* decision, Justice Black, for a unanimous Court, ruled that the Sixth and Fourteenth Amendments impose a constitutional duty on states to provide free legal counsel for criminal defendants unable to afford a lawyer. Justice Black explained: ". . . in our adversary system of criminal justice, any person haled into court, who is too poor to hire a lawyer, cannot be assured a fair trial unless counsel is provided for him. . . . Lawyers in criminal trials are necessities, not luxuries."[9]

During the 1960s the Warren Court applied the strict scrutiny test to a number of laws affecting democratic rights as well as criminal procedures. For example, in 1962, in *Baker v. Carr*, the Court for the first time ruled that state legislative malapportionment is an issue covered by the Equal Protection Clause rather than a "political question" involving substantive value judgments properly resolved in the federal and state legislatures.[10] Two years later, in *Reynolds v. Sims*, the Court defined voting in a state election as a "fundamental political right, because preservative of other basic political and civil rights."[11]

7. For a careful review of the Supreme Court's wealth-discrimination rulings see William H. Clune, III, "Wealth Discriminations Under the Fourteenth Amendment," 1975 *The Supreme Court Review* 289 (1975).

8. 372 U.S. 353 (1963), at 357 (emphasis in original).

9. 372 U.S. 335 (1963).

10. 369 U.S. 186 (1962).

11. 377 U.S. 533 (1964), at 568.

The Court went on to hold that the Equal Protection Clause mandates "equal state legislative representation for all citizens," or one person-one vote. *Harper v. Virginia Board of Election Commissioners*, decided in 1966, stands out because it was the first case in which the Court *explicitly* singled out indigence as a protected Equal Protection category.[12]

In *Harper* the Warren Court voided a Virginia poll tax because, according to Justice Douglas's majority opinion, a financial hurdle to voting creates an "invidious discrimination" between rich and poor. Justice Douglas explained that the "principle that denies the State the right to dilute a citizen's vote on account of his economic status or other such factors by analogy bars a system which excludes those unable to pay a fee to vote or who fail to pay."[13] Economic class is a "suspect classification" because it is wholly unrelated to a citizen's ability to vote intelligently. The poll tax merely perpetuated the anachronistic (and often racist) assumption that civic-mindedness is predicated on property ownership. In addition to flagging the wealth discrimination, the *Harper* majority reiterated its stance in *Reynolds* that voting in a state election is a "fundamental right." Although voting in a state election is not an enumerated constitutional right, the Court observed that it is a prerequisite to the exercise of the rights contained in the Bill of Rights. Far from finding either a compelling interest or a reasonable basis behind the poll tax, Justice Douglas's opinion branded the fee an affront to modern democratic sensibilities. The dissents, by contrast, believed it not unreasonable for legislators to assume that people who pay a poll tax value civic affairs more than those who do not pay. The dissenting justices, including Justice Black, the author of the *Griffin* opinion, castigated the majority for committing the same interpretive sins as the *Lochner*-era Court, whose reading of the Fourteenth Amendment lacked textual support in the Constitution.[14]

Harper signaled two important doctrinal innovations. First, the Court treated wealth distinctions as on a par with "invidious" racial discrimination, both running afoul of the Equal Protection Clause. Second, the Court described the right to vote in a state election as

12. 383 U.S. 663 (1966).

13. Ibid. at 668.

14. Justices Stewart and Harlan also dissented in *Harper*, contending that their personal aversion to the poll tax was beside the point. In their view it was not irrational to assume that "people with some property have a deeper stake in community affairs . . . and that the community and Nation would be better managed if the franchise were restricted to such citizens. . . ." Ibid. at 684–85.

a "fundamental right" even though no such right is listed in the Constitution. Since voting gives citizens the capacity to effectively exercise the rights safeguarded by the Bill of Rights, the Court considered it fundamental for Equal Protection purposes.

Even after the justices decided *Harper*, it was still unclear just how far the Warren Court would go toward equalizing the distribution of fundamental rights and goods. For poor people the promise of the wealth-discrimination rulings lay in the justices' apparent willingness to rectify economic inequalities that impinge on fundamental rights or interests. Still, as of 1967 the Court had not applied the strict scrutiny test outside the relatively familiar domains of criminal justice and political procedures.

Welfare-rights advocates thought that the Court's sensitivity to the unequal effects of statutes on rich and poor and the justices' incorporation of nonenumerated rights into the Constitution bode well for poor people. After all, reformers reasoned, if voting in a state election is a fundamental right because it makes possible the meaningful exercise of rights spelled out in the Bill of Rights, then surely welfare assistance must also be considered a fundamental right under the Equal Protection Clause. Welfare-rights supporters asked: "What good is the right to free speech or religious liberty if a person lacks the means to survive?"

A careful look at the Warren Court's Equal Protection decisions, however, revealed doctrinal obstacles to the establishment of constitutional welfare rights. The justices' ability to muster support for its wealth-discrimination opinions was due mainly to the Court's articulation of a shared belief in American political culture regarding the impropriety of inequality in the criminal justice and democratic processes. Since *Griffin* and *Harper* stood for the principle of equal access of rich and poor to the criminal justice and democratic processes, these rulings were seen as flowing from a procedural rather than a substantive conception of distributive justice. Yet the distinction between procedure and substance was murky in both opinions. Instead of issuing a categorical mandate to the states to supply a trial transcript or the vote in a state election, the Court held that *should* a state decide to provide these goods, it must do so in an evenhanded way. In other words, the wealth-discrimination decisions demanded the evenhanded distribution of what the *state* decided to furnish. But the question of *which* goods are so fundamental as to be distributed irrespective of wealth was ideologically charged and beleaguered the Warren Court.

Doctrinally, then, the Warren Court dealt with the value-laden question of which goods must be distributed in accordance with Equal Protection standards. Yet perceiving themselves as sticking to mere procedural issues, the justices assigned to the state legislatures the task of determining which goods were fundamental for Equal Protection purposes.[15] The procedure/substance distinction that the Warren Court tried to erect in its Equal Protection rulings could not, however, obscure the fact that the justices were making substantive judgments about distributive justice. This, predictably, troubled the Court because of the shadow cast by *Lochner*. After the *Lochner*-era debacle the consensus on and off the Supreme Court was that elected officials, who are accountable to the public, are responsible for hammering out distributive arrangements.

II.

To its credit, the Warren Court's attentiveness to the problem of economic inequality and its commitment to guaranteeing fair judicial and political processes and to safeguarding individual rights did help to alleviate some of the burdens that poor people shouldered in America. The Court's decisions, moreover, opened the door for other government institutions to respond to the poor's problems. President Lyndon Johnson agreed with an inner circle of legal reformers regarding the pressing need for a federally funded legal services program to ensure poor people's access to *civil* and not just criminal justice. The idea for a national legal services program had been germinating among legal reformers for years because of the inadequacies of private "legal aid" in responding to the poor's many legal grievances. Legal aid organizations were often underfunded and reluctant to represent poor people vigorously when local businesses or government agencies were the opposing party. While helpful to individual indigent clients, the "case work" that legal aid organizations performed usually had limited impact on the poor as a whole. As one early advocate of government-funded legal services explained: "Justice is not merchandise; it cannot be granted or withheld according to the purchasing

---

15. In the area of welfare policy the procedure/substance distinction was even more conceptually paramount than in other policy areas precisely because, as Nancy Hirschmann points out, "human need is varying, contextual, and highly substantive." Nancy J. Hirschmann, *Rethinking Obligation: A Feminist Method for Political Theory* (Ithaca, N.Y.: Cornell University Press, 1992), p. 99.

power of the applicant."[16] By 1964 there was growing concern among the Johnson administration's antipoverty warriors not only about the legal system's inaccessibility to the poor but also about the disaffection and distrust among indigents who perceived the laws as systematically stacked against them.

With those concerns in mind the Johnson administration won congressional approval in 1965 for a federally funded Legal Services Program, established under the auspices of the Office of Economic Opportunity. LSP leaders discussed different programmatic options, such as facilitating economic development in poor neighborhoods, community organizing, and law reform. Deciding upon law reform as the LSP's overriding goal, LSP leaders gave funding priority to projects that used test-case litigation to change bureaucratic regulations, statutes, and the constitutional obligations to the poor.

LSP leaders trumpeted several advantages to singling out law reform as the main goal. For starters, the use of test-case litigation to extract changes in statutory and constitutional duties toward the poor promised to help a large number of indigents whose neighborhoods had no legal services office. In addition, "vigorous lawyering" on behalf of the client squared with professional ideals and thus was more apt to garner political support than the more strident-sounding "community organizing" or "social reform."[17] LSP leaders quoted from the American Bar Association's Code of Professional Responsibility as proof of a lawyer's responsibility to pursue law reform on behalf of his or her client: "Rules of law are deficient if they are not just, understandable, and responsive to the needs of society. If a lawyer believes that the existence of a rule of law, substantive or procedural, causes or contributes to an unjust result, he should endeavor by lawful means to obtain appropriate changes in the law."[18]

In short, the redress of grievances through legal remedies was basic to the legal profession's role and helped to deflect political assaults on the LSP. Politicians who had protested against the reform-oriented legal services agencies found it "more difficult to challenge the right of lawyers to pursue their clients' interest in the appellate courts or legislative chambers than to dispute the merits of social revolution,

16. Reginald Heber Smith, *Justice and the Poor* (New York: Carnegie Foundation, 1919), p. 183.

17. Earl Johnson, Jr., *Justice and Reform: The Formative Years of the Legal Services Program* (New York: Russell Sage Foundation, 1974), p. 133.

18. *ABA Code of Professional Responsibility*, "Ethical Considerations," 8–1, 8–2; quoted in ibid., p. 131.

community organizing, and the like."[19] The second (and most influential) director of the LSP, Earl Johnson, Jr., liked to say that law reform was "neither liberal nor conservative" but represented nonpartisan "change within the system."[20]

Notwithstanding the support many expressed for law reform as a priority, an abundant literature attests to the fact that the LSP encountered ongoing conflicts between legal aid's narrow conception of justice for the poor and the reform orientation of the legal services movement. As Susan Lawrence states, "Legal aid attorneys showed little interest in the reformer role and appellate litigation."[21] While legal aid organizations focused on the individual case at hand and generally tried to avoid litigation altogether, reform-oriented LSPs were distinguished by their commitment to changing the "balance of rights between the poor and the government and the poor and the private sector."[22] Not surprisingly, the internal battle that the Warren Court waged over fair procedures vs. just outcomes, equal access vs. equal results, was reenacted within the Legal Services Program.

One of the staunchest supporters and practitioners of law reform was the Center on Social Welfare Policy and Law, which was one of the twelve national back-up centers that LSP leaders charged with developing expertise in assorted areas of poverty law. The centers offered training, information, and legal advice, and also engaged in national litigation and legislative/administrative advocacy. In addition, the CSWPL saw itself as a friend of the fledgling poor people's movements, providing expert knowledge and counsel to political activists and clients working to reform the welfare system.[23] The legal research that the CSWPL conducted was especially important because there had been no AFDC litigation in the federal courts prior to the center's opening. By all accounts the CSWPL was the most successful of the back-up centers. Its very success, however, ultimately embroiled it in political disputes. For some politicians it was one thing for LSP-funded agencies to represent a poor person in a bankruptcy hearing or a landlord-tenant conflict; it was quite another for lawyers to use

19. Johnson, *Justice and Reform*, p. 131.

20. Ibid., p. 133.

21. Susan E. Lawrence, *The Poor in Court: The Legal Services Program and Supreme Court Decision Making* (Princeton, N.J.: Princeton University Press, 1990), p. 21.

22. Eve Spangler, *Lawyers for Hire: Salaried Professionals at Work* (New Haven, Conn.: Yale University Press, 1986), p. 145.

23. Interview with Henry Freedman, Executive Director of the Center on Social Welfare Policy and Law, February 25, 1987. Freedman was an active staff attorney at the center in the early years of the Legal Services Program.

class-action suits as a means of bringing about a redistribution of income from the nonpoor to the poor, that is, to move from a procedural to a substantive, need-based understanding of justice.

The CSWPL received its first grant from the Office of Economic Opportunity in 1966. Immediately, Edward Sparer, the first executive director of the center and legal counsel for the NWRO, and his colleagues started to build a network of local Legal Services programs. Sparer's familiarity with academic theories of poverty and welfare rights, combined with the CSWPL staff's knowledge of the most arcane facets of welfare policy, enabled him to fuse the philosophy of welfare rights with the nuts and bolts of case law. The CSWPL monitored federal and state court decisions and gave practical advice on litigation to LSP attorneys committed to law reform. Most important, Sparer set out to work on devising a litigation strategy, the principal objective of which was to persuade the Warren Court to incorporate welfare into the Constitution's Equal Protection Clause.

III.

Rather than fashioning a wholly new doctrinal framework to present to the Warren Court, Edward Sparer and other welfare-rights lawyers tried to assimilate economic status into the category of "suspect classifications" and subsistence needs into the category of "fundamental rights." Like many LSP attorneys, Sparer believed in the emancipatory potential of law. He perceived in the Warren Court's Equal Protection decisions an opportunity to obtain greater constitutional protections for poor people. Starting from the liberal premises of the wealth-discrimination and fundamental-rights doctrines, Sparer developed a welfare-rights philosophy and litigation plan. He needed to respond to the various critics who grumbled about high taxes, wondering why their freedom and earnings were restricted so that the poor could collect government benefits. President Nixon's antiwelfare campaign rhetoric had rallied not only his own Republican troops but also blue-collar Democrats, once a strong constituency for progressive economic legislation. Privileged Republicans and wage-earner Democrats alike protested that *they* never agreed to federal government policies—funded with their taxes—giving "preferential treatment" to disadvantaged minority groups. Against the backdrop of simmering resentment, Nixon claimed to speak on behalf of the "silent majority" whose voices he said had fallen upon deaf ears in the "liberal" administrations of John F. Kennedy and Lyndon B. Johnson.

While most lawyers regarded issues of political philosophy as "impractical," Sparer was temperamentally inclined to wrestle with them. He appreciated that the law is, for better or worse, a polity's lived response to basic questions of political philosophy: On what basis does government claim authority and legitimacy? Are citizens obligated to obey the laws? What is the nature of rights?

Harking back to the natural-law tradition, which identified the guarantee of subsistence needs as a basic principle of justice, Sparer attempted to ground the "right to live" doctrine in an original social contract, arguing that government's legitimacy inheres in the consent of the citizenry. Turning the tables on welfare critics, he asked: "Upon what moral premise must the starving man or woman accept the majority's vote on whether he or she shall live or not?" To those insisting that the majority simply had not consented to their tax dollars being used to give "advantage" to minority groups, Sparer responded that citizen consent is first and foremost predicated on the fulfillment of subsistence needs. Government is obligated, in his words, to "do more than guarantee the right to persuade the majority; they must guarantee the right to live whatever the majority thinks. The right to live is a *sine qua non* of the social contract."[24] It is *the poor*, he argued, whose consent was systematically violated because of inadequate welfare policies.

Since human beings have an inalienable right to self-preservation, Sparer explained, government is obligated by the social contract to guarantee each person his or her subsistence needs. He noted that without the means of survival there is no life or liberty. Echoing President Franklin D. Roosevelt's justification of the New Deal, Sparer characterized the "right to live" as an age-old idea: "Ours is not a revolution in ideology, but in practice. It makes no new promises but demands that we fulfill the old ones."[25] But whereas Roosevelt summoned the power and moral authority of the majority—so-called ordinary folks—against the "economic royalists," Sparer tried to hem in the majority. Given the majority's wary attitude toward the poor, Sparer argued that the poverty lawyer's mission was "to utilize the legal process and to help change the ground rules of American society."

24. Sparer, "The Right to Welfare," p. 83 (emphasis in original). See also 3 *Law in Action* (May 5, 1968).

25. Edward Sparer, "The New Legal Aid as an Instrument of Social Change," address before the Midwestern Conference of the Law Students Civil Rights Research Council, The University of Illinois, April 24, 1965.

LSP lawyers were not to make the "welfare system conform to what the elected representatives . . . had decreed it should be."[26] Rather, welfare assistance was a matter of right, a principle of justice, and could not be bartered away in the pluralist political process.

As a direct result of this political philosophy, Sparer envisioned substantial changes in the American welfare system. He was quite open about the kinds of changes he hoped that LSP attorneys could bring about through litigation and social pressure:

> We must identify our primary concern. Is it to guarantee that people who cannot or should not work will have enough aid so as to live with minimum decency, or to assure that people who can work will do so regardless of work they are forced to accept? Suppose a welfare system offered an adequate grant to all those in need (with income below it), and a right to refuse work which paid less than the welfare grant. If as a result, private businesses and government were forced to reorganize the economy to ensure that it provided purposeful and well-paying work, would not that be desirable? Are we not producing the opposite result when we subsidize . . . the most pointless and exploitative jobs in the economy while denying decent welfare grants to those who cannot work?[27]

Sparer was especially critical of the two-tiered welfare system, which he traced to the Social Security Act of 1935; the Social Security Act, he believed, accorded respect and procedural protections to the so-called deserving poor, such as the disabled and the retired, but heaped scorn and bureaucratic restrictions on the "undeserving poor," such as ADC mothers. But though Sparer was attuned to the particular hardships borne by AFDC mothers, he hoped that the Supreme Court would extend substantive welfare rights and procedural safeguards to *all* poor people. After all, the very notion of citizenship rights, as encompassing subsistence needs, was predicated on the universal attributes of humanity that all people share. Furthermore, the idea of welfare as a right attached to citizenship would elevate the position of AFDC mothers who were stigmatized by government and the public as unfit parents and wards of the state.

Opponents of the "right to live" objected that it was a "positive" right requiring "affirmative government action," whereas the "nega-

---

26. Sparer, "The Right to Welfare," p. 84.
27. Ibid., p. 91.

tive" rights contained in the Bill of Rights simply demanded that government refrain from intrusive action. Blasting the distinction between "positive" and "negative" rights, Sparer responded by implicating government in the poor's miserable living conditions and holding it responsible for fulfilling an "affirmative duty under the Equal Protection Clause" to meet the poor's basic needs.[28] Whereas Roosevelt had tried to establish "positive" economic rights through legislative actions, Sparer proposed to graft such rights onto the Constitution itself through judicial interpretation.

In trying to establish a constitutional welfare right on the basis of the natural-law tradition Edward Sparer and other LSP attorneys consciously sought to raise the status of AFDC mothers, whose benefits government officials tended to consider a privilege, not a legal entitlement.[29] Those welfare-rights lawyers felt that AFDC recipients suffered from being disparaged as wayward mothers who failed to keep their families together. Hence, the lawyers advocated that AFDC mothers be presented in court as citizens possessed of a full spectrum of inalienable natural rights—citizens who were disadvantaged not because of personal moral deficiencies but because of the subordination of their economic class. Welfare rights, therefore, attached to universal citizenship and not to the particular identities, needs, and responsibilities of single mothers. In Sparer's judgment welfare rights could be legitimated only if detached from motherhood—only if, in other words, gender was effaced. However, some AFDC mothers were wary of Sparer's gender-neutral conception of universal rights. For in treating the rights of all indigent individuals the same, i.e., universal rights embedded in the ideal of the autonomous citizen, some NWRO members worried that welfare-rights leaders would deflect attention away from the *maternalist* concern for the unique circumstances, burdens, and responsibilities of AFDC mothers.[30]

28. Ibid.
29. Another legal thinker whose ideas helped to shape the welfare rights movement was Charles Reich, then a professor at Yale Law School. In an influential article Reich described the distinction between "rights" and mere "privileges," and how welfare and other government benefits were treated not as legal entitlements but as "gratuities" to be taken away at government's whim. He advocated that welfare benefits in particular be reconceptualized as "new property," eliciting the same constitutional and statutory protections accorded traditional property rights. Although Reich himself seemed to be uncomfortable, as a strategic matter, with the characterization of welfare benefits as a natural right, his attempt to unite subsistence needs with property rights was somewhat reminiscent of the Jacksonian-era Workingmen discussed in Chapter 2. See especially Reich, "The New Property," 73 *Yale Law Journal* 733 (April 1964).
30. We will see this gender dynamic more clearly in Chapter 6.

In the late 1960s, however, the AFDC mothers' reasons for optimism eclipsed any concerns voiced by NWRO members about the prominent role given to mostly white, male attorneys in the welfare rights movement. The Warren Court had shown itself to be hospitable to poor people's legal grievances. The fundamental-rights and wealth-discrimination doctrines struck AFDC mothers as especially promising avenues of legal reform. The principle articulated in *Harper*—that certain nonenumerated rights are "fundamental" by virtue of making "effective" the rights listed in the Bill of Rights—made good sense to AFDC mothers. They knew from personal experience that without the resources to feed their children, the First Amendment guarantee of participating in political rallies and engaging in lobbying, street protests, and other forms of expression was more of a privilege than a right. The only reason that AFDC mothers could afford to spend time and energy participating in the welfare rights movement was precisely because, at least for a time, they extracted material benefits from local and state governments. In that respect AFDC mothers never felt that their rights were regarded with the same degree of respect as those of middle-class citizens, in contravention of the wealth-discrimination doctrine. Thus, between the seemingly sympathetic Warren Court and savvy LSP lawyers willing to exploit every possible opening in the Constitution and federal law, in the late 1960s AFDC mothers were hopeful that the guarantee of subsistence needs ultimately would be theirs.

Chapter Six

The Failure of Constitutional Welfare Rights in the Warren Court

In the nitty-gritty world of litigation the Warren Court's Equal Protection doctrines offered two routes to constitutional welfare rights. One path, following the wealth-discrimination rulings in *Griffin v. Illinois* and *Harper v. Virginia Board of Election Commissioners*, led to the identification of the poor as an economic class entitled to added judicial protection.[1] The other path, following the fundamental-rights strand, led to the treatment of welfare as a constitutionally guaranteed right since it assures citizens the capacity to exercise the rights contained in the Bill of Rights. Here *Harper* and *Griswold v. Connecticut* were useful precedents.[2]

But notwithstanding Legal Services attorneys' short-lived success in goading the justices toward a constitutional welfare state, the

1. 351 U.S. 12 (1956); 383 U.S. 663 (1966).

2. *Griswold v. Connecticut*, 381 U.S. 479 (1965). As explained in Chapter 5, *Harper* reaffirmed the "fundamental right" to vote in a state election established in 1964 in *Reynolds v. Sims*, and *Griswold* identified privacy as a constitutionally protected right "emanating" from the rights enumerated in the Bill of Rights.

Warren Court declined in 1970 to incorporate subsistence needs into the Equal Protection Clause.

For a brief moment in the late 1960s it looked as though the arguments of the Legal Services attorneys might carry the day. In the 1968–69 term the Supreme Court overturned state durational residence laws governing welfare eligibility in a decision that might have prefigured the establishment of a *national* right to welfare. However, in conformity to the doctrinal distinction between negative and positive liberty (or between procedural and substantive economic rights), that decision was based on the *procedural* "right to interstate travel." When, in the following term, Legal Services lawyers argued directly for a *positive* right to welfare, the Supreme Court proved unwilling to violate the post-*Lochner* "double standard"—and flatly rejected the notion of a constitutional right to welfare. Ironically, it was the liberal Warren Court's fidelity to the post-*Lochner* "double standard"—originally intended to protect progressive legislation from the assaults of conservative judges—that doomed the efforts of the Legal Services attorneys to failure.

If the post-*Lochner* channeling of judicial natural-rights doctrine into strictly procedural channels was decisive in defeating constitutional welfare rights, the unwillingness of National Welfare Rights Organization leaders to offer a "maternalist" argument in support of welfare rights (and the probable unwillingness of liberal Supreme Court judges to have embraced such an argument even if it had been offered) certainly played a contributory role. In fact, that unwillingness seems to have contributed to conflicts *within* the NWRO.

The disagreements between the male strategists and the AFDC mothers went beyond tactical questions to disputes over the very language in which subsistence needs ought to be couched and legitimated. Although AFDC mothers and their children received tangible benefits from court victories, the language of welfare rights that the NWRO male leaders and LSP lawyers had used aroused ambivalence among some members of the NWRO, the nerve center of the welfare rights movement.

The understanding of the self and civic obligations underlying the CSWPL's legal briefs rankled the AFDC mothers. Although finding inspiration in a natural-law understanding of human rights, the NWRO women groped for a way to think about motherhood and subsistence needs that resonated more directly with their particular experiences raising children single-handedly under daunting circumstances. The disagreements between the men and women produced so much friction that the NWRO members ousted the male leaders in the early 1970s and rebuffed the men's entreaties to form a broader poor people's "movement for economic justice," one that would include the elderly poor, indigent workers, and the unemployed.

Section I of this chapter focuses on the doctrinal dilemmas the Warren Court faced when confronted with the claim of constitutionally based welfare rights. The case analysis is gleaned from the Earl Warren Papers and the William J. Brennan Papers, the latter first made public at the Library of Congress in 1985–86. Section II takes a glimpse at the splits within the National Welfare Rights Organization that surfaced in response to the litigation strategy the CSWPL pursued and to the ensuing Supreme Court opinions.[3] One irony was that judicial victories for welfare recipients helped to contribute to the fracturing of the welfare rights movement.

I.

As Executive Director of the CSWPL and counsel to the NWRO, Edward Sparer had envisioned center and other Legal Services attorneys filing welfare cases in a particular sequence, with individual principles favorable to welfare recipients building on one another and culminating in a constitutional guarantee of a minimum income. But as Susan Lawrence observes in her book on the Legal Services Program, the decentralized structure of the LSP thwarted the CSWPL's efforts to manage the flow of cases being brought to the Supreme Court.[4] In contrast to the discipline that the NAACP's Legal Defense Fund imposed on lawyers filing racial discrimination lawsuits, the CSWPL was unable to orchestrate the cases that LSP lawyers from all over the nation brought to the courts. At times, cases that Sparer felt were not ripe for a Supreme Court victory arrived in court prematurely because some LSP lawyers had filed them without regard to strategic concerns.

Shapiro v. Thompson was one such case that Sparer was dismayed

3. My archival research in the Earl Warren Papers and William J. Brennan Papers at the Library of Congress was supplemented by research at the Center on Social Welfare Policy and Law in New York City.

4. Susan E. Lawrence, *The Poor in Court: The Legal Services Program and Supreme Court Decision Making* (Princeton, N.J.: Princeton University Press, 1990), p. 50. See also Martha F. Davis, *Brutal Need: Lawyers and the Welfare Rights Movement, 1960–1973* (New Haven, Conn.: Yale University Press, 1993), chap. 6.

to see arrive at the Supreme Court in 1967.[5] He believed that the Court first would have to establish basic principles of welfare law favorable to the poor before agreeing to strike down durational residence requirements states used in the administration of welfare and other programs. *Shapiro* was a difficult case that was argued twice before the Warren Court in the 1967–68 and 1968–69 terms. The changes in the way the Court approached the constitutionality of the durational residence laws reflected the doctrinal and ideological complexities that the Court faced in welfare policy.

In the Court's original majority opinion Chief Justice Warren and five colleagues upheld the one-year durational residence requirements many states used in the administration of AFDC; as a budgetary measure, Connecticut and some other states barred AFDC mothers from receiving welfare assistance until they lived in the state for at least one year. Failing to resolve the case to its satisfaction, however, the Court agreed to rehear the case in 1968. In the second term the Court reversed itself, with six members voting to declare the durational residence laws a violation of the Equal Protection Clause. Noted for fostering consensus on the Court, Justice Brennan, who had initially voted to uphold the durational residence requirements, successfully built a coalition invalidating the laws on grounds that they created an "invidious discrimination" against newly arrived needy residents. The Court ruled that states' attempts to guard their budgets by inhibiting the migration of poor people into their jurisdictions were unconstitutional. According to the majority opinion, the durational residence requirements not only contained a discrimination between two groups of poor people but also penalized the "fundamental right to interstate travel."[6]

Far from perceiving the durational residence requirements as easy prey, the CSWPL was deeply worried about *Shapiro*. In fact, the center was not surprised when in the 1967–68 term the Court upheld the one-year residence laws. Henry Freedman, the current CSWPL director who worked closely with Sparer some thirty years earlier, offers three reasons for the center's doubts about winning *Shapiro*: (1) the durational residence requirements were a long-standing feature of American welfare policy; (2) the Social Security Act explicitly allowed states to use durational residence requirements of up to a year; and

5. Interview, February 25, 1987, with Henry Freedman, the current director of the Center on Social Welfare Policy and Law and the late Edward Sparer's assistant at the CSWPL in the 1960s.

6. *Shapiro v. Thompson*, 394 U.S. 618 (1969), at 634.

(3) Chief Justice Warren had been involved as a California attorney in *Edwards v. California*, in which he defended a state law making it a misdemeanor knowingly to bring or to assist in bringing an indigent person into the state who was not a California resident.[7]

So how was it that the Court changed its collective mind over the course of the two terms it heard oral arguments in *Shapiro*? In the 1967 term Legal Services lawyers pressed for a constitutional right to welfare under the Equal Protection Clause and contended that poverty (or "wealth") ought to be treated as constituting a "suspect classification," akin to race. But only Justices Fortas and Douglas accepted either of these claims. For example, in his original dissent Justice Douglas described the durational residence laws as inherently discriminatory: "The rich and prosperous no longer stop the migrants at the border . . . but make it difficult if not impossible for the indigent to reach the community where a new life is possible."[8] He cautioned his colleagues about the "sophisticated" means "the rich" use to subordinate the poor. Justice Fortas also found the durational residence requirements a manifestation of wealth discrimination.[9] A majority of the Court, including Justice Brennan, however, felt uneasy about the use of the wealth-discrimination doctrine in the area of social-welfare policy. After all, the application of the wealth-discrimination doctrine in the economic domain of welfare could render the capitalist motive itself constitutionally suspect in the face of unmet subsistence needs. Indeed, finding no such transgression of the Equal Protection Clause, Chief Justice Warren's opinion for the Court in the 1967 term upheld the durational residence laws as consistent with both the Constitution and the Social Security Act. Yet discomfort with this ruling led the Court to rehear *Shapiro* the next term.

Between the 1967 and 1968 terms Edward Sparer and his CSWPL colleagues decided to exploit the justices' unease about sustaining the durational residence laws. Sparer met with three attorneys who were litigating the durational residence requirements and proposed to submit one umbrella argument, consolidating the cases, in the next term. According to Freedman, Sparer proposed enlisting the legal assistance of Archibald Cox, a former solicitor general in the Johnson administration, or someone of his stature, who could present a convincing argument on behalf of the AFDC mothers in the 1968–69 term. Other

7. Interview with Henry Freedman, February 25, 1987.
8. Justice Douglas's original dissenting opinion, June 12, 1968, p. 5. Filed in the Earl Warren Papers, Library of Congress, container number 566.
9. Justice Fortas's original dissenting opinion, June 12, 1968, p. 30. Filed in the Earl Warren Papers, Library of Congress, container number 566.

lawyers' names appeared on the list of possibilities, but Sparer and the LSP attorneys all agreed that Cox's extensive experience before the Supreme Court made him the best choice. After meeting with Sparer, Cox signed on to reargue the newly consolidated cases before the Court.[10]

Cox agreed with Sparer that Legal Services lawyers had mistakenly advocated so abruptly for a constitutional welfare right that they left the Court little choice but to uphold the one-year residence laws. Cox made two significant changes in the original brief prepared for the AFDC mothers in the 1967 term. First, rather than characterizing the one-year residence requirement as creating a wealth discrimination against "the poor" by "the rich," Cox contended that the laws were really an example of in-staters discriminating against out-of-staters, of "neighbors" discriminating against "strangers."[11] Neutralizing the language of class peppered throughout Justices Douglas's and Fortas's draft dissents, Cox explained that the vulnerability of poor people lay not simply in their destitution but in their obvious lack of political representation in another state. Thus, whereas Justices Douglas and Fortas had highlighted the unequal effects of the durational residence laws on those with and without resources to move to another state, Cox stressed the Privileges and Immunities component of the right to travel: states are constitutionally forbidden from discriminating against citizen-strangers from out of state.

Cox's oral argument was so persuasive to Justice Brennan that he decided to switch sides and to join Justices Douglas and Fortas in striking down the durational residence laws.[12] In order to engineer a

10. Interview with Henry Freedman, February 25, 1987.

11. See the transcript of Archibald Cox's oral argument, reprinted in *Landmark Briefs and Arguments of the Supreme Court of the United States: Constitutional Law*, ed. Philip B. Kurland and Gerhard Casper (Arlington, Va., and Bethesda, Md.: University Publications of America, 1975), 68: 378–406. As Henry Freedman explained, Cox pounced on the argument made in the amicus curiae brief that the Iowa special assistant attorney general, Lorna L. Williams, submitted in support of the durational residence requirement. Attorney Williams defended the residence requirements as enabling states to first "take care of our own." Cox lambasted what he perceived as a "parochial" attitude fundamentally at odds with the national scope of the Bill of Rights. He drew the analogy between the durational residence laws and those sanctioning racial discrimination. See the transcript of the oral argument, p. 387. This point is examined more closely in Chapter 7.

12. The archival materials show that Brennan was particularly captivated by Justice Fortas's point, made in his original dissent in 1968, that the durational residence laws violated the "fundamental right" to interstate travel. One sees penciled on this draft the word "fundamental" in Justice Brennan's handwriting, in the margin adjacent to Fortas's argument about interstate travel. The significance for Brennan was that the

consensus Justice Brennan wrote his opinion along the lines Cox had presented, since Justices White and Stewart—two swing voters—had also been impressed by Cox's presentation. Likening the "hostile treatment of those who travel" to racial discrimination, Cox and later Justice Brennan railed against the state-sanctioned "local prejudice" against impecunious "strangers" or "outsiders."[13] This doctrinal revision, amplifying the distinction between in- and out-of-staters rather than between rich and poor, enabled Justice Brennan to make it "unnecessary to break new constitutional ground," as Justice Stewart pointed out in a concurring opinion.[14] In invalidating the durational residence requirements Justice Brennan made clear that the Court was merely barring states from denying formal equality to outsiders who settled in their jurisdictions. Thus, by affirming the value of formal equality rather than promoting economic equality, per se, Justice Brennan wooed Justices White and Stewart to his side; combined with Justices Douglas, Fortas, and Marshall, a six-member majority emerged to void the durational residence requirements.

The second doctrinal revision that Archibald Cox and, subsequently, Justice Brennan made in the LSP lawyers' original brief pertained to the issue of constitutional welfare rights. Cox himself was loath to rest his case against the durational residence laws solely on grounds that they denied "the bare essentials of life." Although Cox considered discrimination in relation to subsistence needs to be unconstitutional, he noted that a "much narrower ruling" was available.[15] The explosive legacy of the *Lochner*-era "liberty of contract" decisions led Cox and the CSWPL attorneys to define welfare assistance in *Shapiro* as a statutory entitlement rather than a fundamental constitutional right. Cox framed the constitutional question in terms of the even-handed distribution of a state-created good, AFDC, and of the fundamental right to interstate travel.

---

presence of such a right triggered the strict scrutiny, not reasonable basis, test. So it was this part of Justice Fortas's opinion and Archibald Cox's brief that was particularly instrumental to Justice Brennan in reworking the dissents to build a coalition invalidating the durational residence requirements. See Justice Fortas's draft and Justice Brennan's reaction, June 13, 1968. William J. Brennan Papers, Library of Congress, container number 184.

13. Transcript of the oral argument, reprinted in Kurland and Casper, eds., *Landmark Briefs and Arguments of the Supreme Court*, 68: 387.

14. The quote comes from Cox's oral argument, reprinted in ibid. In his concurring opinion Justice Stewart emphasized the long-standing recognition of the right to interstate travel. 394 U.S. 618 (1969), at 644, 646.

15. Archibald Cox, Supplemental Brief, reprinted in Kurland and Casper, eds., *Landmark Briefs and Arguments of the Supreme Court*, 68: 88.

Although not listed in the Constitution, the right to travel had deep roots in precedents.[16] Moreover, fastening on the right to travel enabled Cox, and later Justice Brennan, to give voice to the ideal of equal opportunity "to leave an old and personally unsatisfying environment for new opportunities . . . and different associations."[17] The constitutional hook supplied by the right to travel also allowed Cox and Justice Brennan to speak eloquently about the *negative* ideal of liberty—in Justice Brennan's words, the right of "all citizens to travel . . . uninhibited by statutes, rules, or regulations which unreasonably burden or restrict this movement."[18] In a concurring opinion Justice Stewart went so far as to call the right to travel "a virtually unconditional personal right."[19] Even Justice Harlan, who voted to uphold the durational residence requirements, considered the right to interstate travel "fundamental" under the Fifth Amendment's Due Process Clause.

Cox and the CSWPL lawyers with whom he collaborated ultimately won in *Shapiro* during the 1968 term. The Court's decision to strike down the durational residence laws enabled many poor mothers to claim AFDC benefits despite having recently moved to a new state. Yet Cox, Sparer, and CSWPL attorneys sensed that *Shapiro* portended problems for future welfare litigation. *Shapiro* became a victory only after Cox (1) convinced the Court that an "established constitutional right" was threatened by a welfare policy *and* (2) presented the case as involving an invidious discrimination "between two classes of needy residents" rather than between two economic classes, rich and poor. In embracing the distinction between in-staters and out-of-staters and in highlighting the right to interstate travel rather than the right to welfare, Justice Brennan shied away from an egalitarian ideology

16. Drawing on such precedents as *U.S. v. Guest*, 383 U.S. 745 (1966), and *Edwards v. California*, 314 U.S. 160 (1941), Justice Brennan located the right to interstate travel in the Fourteenth Amendment's Privileges and Immunities and Due Process Clauses, as well as the Commerce Clause of Article I, section 8. For example, Justice Brennan noted that the right was grounded in the Privileges and Immunities vision of the United States as a "national community" with open borders that bars states from discriminating against residents from other states. The Due Process source for the right to travel sprung from "our constitutional concepts of personal liberty," while the Commerce Clause underpins the view that labor must be unencumbered in its search for a market. 394 U.S. 618 (1969), at 629–30.

17. Archibald Cox, Supplemental Brief, reprinted in Kurland and Casper, eds., *Landmark Briefs and Arguments of the Supreme Court*, 68: 101. See also 394 U.S. 618 (1969), at 631–32.

18. *Shapiro v. Thompson*, 394 U.S. 618 (1969), at 629.

19. Ibid. at 643.

oriented to meeting basic human needs. He successfully galvanized a Court majority only by grounding *Shapiro* in the right to interstate travel and espousing the classical liberal values of equal opportunity (not "equal results") and negative freedom. In short, victory for AFDC mothers in *Shapiro* came only after Justice Brennan neutralized the language of class and of economic entitlement, thereby stripping the case of its downwardly redistributive policy potential.

The limits of the *Shapiro* opinion were starkly revealed in *Dandridge v. Williams*, a case the Court dealt with in the 1969–70 term involving Maryland's maximum family-grant regulation.[20] In this case Legal Services lawyers argued head on for a constitutionally protected right to welfare aid; however, in his majority opinion Justice Stewart rejected the claim that welfare policy necessarily implicates constitutional rights. Discerning no constitutional right at stake, he and five other colleagues upheld Maryland's regulation limiting AFDC monthly benefits to $250 per family regardless of family size.

Ironically, Sparer had singled out maximum family grants as ripe for early Supreme Court adjudication and as likely to establish a favorable precedent for AFDC mothers. As Henry Freedman recounts, Sparer thought that the Court would strike down the maximum family-grant regulation if the CSWPL sponsored a case from the deep South, where benefit levels were miserably low and welfare administration was often racially motivated.[21] For example, the flamboyant southerner Russell Long, chairman of the Senate Finance Committee, once lamented the number of births of black children born to the "broodish mares" having children out of wedlock. What happened instead was that Maryland's maximum family-grant regulation reached the Supreme Court *before* a case from the deep South could be adjudicated; Sparer was unable to stop the Maryland LSP attorneys from challenging their state law. Maryland's relatively generous AFDC benefit levels made *Dandridge* a "bad case" in Sparer's view, but once the litigation had been set in motion, there was nothing the CSWPL could do but submit an amicus curiae brief on behalf of the welfare recipients.

Lawyers representing the AFDC mothers had to confront the dichotomy that had arisen in Equal Protection decisions between a realm of fundamental rights eliciting judicial solicitude and a realm of eco-

20. 397 U.S. 471 (1970).

21. Interview with Henry Freedman, February 25, 1987. In addition see Jack Greenberg, "Litigation for Social Change: Methods, Limits, and Role in Democracy," 29 *Record of the Association of the Bar of the City of New York* 320 (1974).

nomic and social policy eliciting judicial deference toward legislators
and bureaucrats. While acknowledging that welfare policy involves
state legislatures in economic calculations that the Court has been
loath to question, the Maryland LSP attorneys cited two lower court
decisions distinguishing welfare policy from business regulation:

> Receipt of welfare benefits may not at the present time consti-
> tute the exercise of a constitutional right. But among our
> Constitution's expressed purposes was the desire to "insure
> domestic tranquillity" and "promote the general welfare." Im-
> plicit in these phrases are certain basic concepts of humanity
> and decency. One of these, voiced as a goal in recent years by
> most responsible governmental leaders, both federal and state,
> is the desire to insure that indigent, unemployable citizens
> will at least have the bare minimums required for existence,
> without which our expressed fundamental constitutional
> rights and liberties frequently cannot be exercised and there-
> fore become meaningless. Legislation with respect to welfare
> assistance, therefore . . . deals with a critical aspect of the
> personal lives of our citizens. . . . We believe that with the
> stakes so high in terms of human misery, the equal protection
> standard to be applied should be stricter than that used upon
> review of commercial legislation and more nearly approximate
> that applied to laws affecting constitutional rights.[22]
>
> *   *   *
>
> This natural movement toward assistance where assistance is
> needed, and the human terms of the problem permit the court
> somewhat greater latitude in deciding that this difference in
> the treatment of those in our midst who are in need amounts
> to unequal protection of laws than if the treatment were
> with respect to some matter less critical to their living condi-
> tions. . . .[23]

The LSP attorneys in *Dandridge* urged the Court to strike down the
maximum family-grant regulation as violations of the "fundamental
right" to procreation and to life guaranteed by the Equal Protection
Clause. To support a constitutional "right to live," the attorneys

22. Quoted from *Rothstein v. Wyman*, 303 F. Supp. 339 (S.D.N.Y., 1969), in Brief for
Appelles, reprinted in Kurland and Casper, eds., *Landmark Briefs and Arguments of
the Supreme Court*, 69: 152–53.
23. Quoted from *Harrell v. Tobriner*, 279 F. Supp. 22 (D.D.C., 1967), in Brief for
Appelles, ibid., p. 152.

invoked a nineteenth-century dissenting opinion that foreshadowed the natural-law style of reasoning used during the *Lochner* era. Ironically, perhaps fatally, they quoted from Justices Field's and Strong's dissenting opinion in *Munn v. Illinois*, written in 1877, singing the praises of a laissez-faire economy as against the encroachments of a regulatory state. The Maryland LSP lawyers included the following excerpt from Justices Field's and Strong's *Munn* dissent:

> By the term "life," as here used, something more is meant than mere animal existence. The inhibition against its deprivation extends to all those limbs and faculties by which life is enjoyed. . . . The deprivation not only of life, but of whatever God has given to everyone with life, for its growth and enjoyment, is prohibited by the provision in question, if its efficacy be not frittered away by judicial decision.[24]

Whereas Justices Field and Strong argued that this God-given right to life went hand in hand with "liberty of contract," the LSP attorneys in *Dandridge* contended that the right to life meant constitutionally guaranteed subsistence needs.

In its reply brief, the state of Maryland stressed the "irony inherent in the use of Justice Field's words" in *Munn*.[25] The LSP's attorneys' reliance on Justice Field's words was doubly ironic: not only was the *Munn* dissent a vigorous defense of a laissez-faire economy but it also was written in the natural-law style that became discredited during the Court-presidency battles of the 1930s.

Clearly uneasy about engaging in natural-law reasoning, the LSP attorneys tried to anchor the right to welfare in the Constitution, just as the Court had done in *Reynolds v. Sims*, concerning establishing the right to vote in a state election, and in *Griswold v. Connecticut*, concerning establishing the right to privacy.[26] The lawyers stated that "without the bare necessities of life the full and active exercise of guaranteed rights, such as freedom of speech and association, is curtailed. As a result of indigence, many have not participated in the political process."[27] That the Constitution does not mention a right to subsistence, the LSP lawyers claimed, does not deny its existence. Relying on the "nexus" argument that the Court had made in *Reynolds*, the lawyers representing the AFDC mothers wrote: "Certainly,

24. Ibid., p. 149.
25. Reply Brief for Appellants, reprinted in ibid., p. 199.
26. 377 U.S. 533 (1964); 391 U.S. 479 (1965).
27. *Dandridge v. Williams*, 397 U.S. 471, (1970), at 484.

in any hierarchy of rights the right to the bare necessities of life and minimal physical well-being ranks as high as the right to procreate, privacy, vote, marry or travel. Indeed, . . . these rights presuppose the existence of a basic right to life and are dependent upon such a right."[28] Just as the right to vote was considered fundamental because "preservative of other basic civil and political rights," so, too, the right to welfare gives the poor the capacity to exercise the rights enumerated in the Bill of Rights. The LSP lawyers cited *Shapiro* as requiring the application of the "strict scrutiny" test when laws impinge on the "basic necessities of life."

The LSP lawyers' identification of welfare assistance as a "fundamental right" safeguarded under the Equal Protection Clause did not wash with the Court. Justice Stewart placed social welfare policy into the category of economic policy, thereby triggering the lax "reasonable basis" test rather than strict scrutiny. The reasonable basis test gives wide latitude to the states in its policy judgments. *Lochner* cast a shadow over Justice Stewart's opinion, in which he warned: "For this Court to approve the invalidation of state economic or social regulation . . . would be far too reminiscent of an era when the Court through the Fourteenth Amendment gave it power to strike down laws because they may be unwise, improvident or out of harmony with a particular school of thought."[29] Although Justice Stewart conceded that "[t]he Constitution may impose certain procedural safeguards" in the dispensation of welfare benefits, the "intractable economic, social, and even philosophical problems presented by public welfare assistance programs are not the business of this Court."[30] As we can see, Justice Stewart held firmly to the procedure/substance distinction. This distinction is based on the assumption that consent is a precondition of political obligation, and since welfare is wrapped up in budgeting and taxation decisions, distributive decisions are properly made by elected officials who can check the pulse of public opinion.

In *Dandridge* the reinforcement of the boundary between the realm of individual rights and the realm of economic and social policy is apparent: "For here we deal with state regulation in the social and economic field, not affecting freedoms guaranteed by the Bill of Rights, and claimed to violate the Fourteenth Amendment only because

28. *Brief* for Appelles, reprinted in Kurland and Casper, eds., *Landmark Briefs and Arguments of the Supreme Court*, p. 151.
29. *Dandridge v. Williams*, 397 U.S. 471 (1970), at 484.
30. Ibid. at 487.

the regulation results in some disparity in grants of welfare pay-
ments. . . ."[31] In implying that inequalities spawned in the market
economy are constitutionally irrelevant outside the delineated sphere
of protected rights, the justices gave voice to one version of classical-
liberal theory that reconciled civic *equality* with economic *inequality*.
Interestingly, the Court showed its ambivalence while articulating
this classical-liberal tenet. For example, in his original *Shapiro* opinion in 1967 Chief Justice Warren stated: Poverty "has pricked the
nation's conscience in recent years. . . . To the extent that appellees
have attempted to show that durational residence requirements impose handicaps upon the poor of the nation, they appeal to the right
instincts of all men. *However, instinct cannot be our guide*."[32] Acting
on the basis of "right instincts," Chief Justice Warren admonished,
would be tantamount to acting subjectively.

In *Dandridge* Justice Stewart himself showed some ambivalence
about the majority's decision, admitting that sliding business regulation and social welfare policy under one doctrinal category subject to
the lax reasonable basis test glosses over the very real differences
between the two: "The administration of public welfare assistance, by
contrast [with state regulation of business or industry], involves the
most basic economic needs of impoverished human beings. We recognize the dramatically real factual difference between the cited cases
and this one, but we can find no basis for applying a different constitutional standard [to welfare and business regulation]."[33]

In sum, while the Warren Court was alarmed at the ways in
which poverty eroded the poor's constitutional rights, the decision in
Dandridge had the effect of divorcing the *content* of rights from the
capacity to exercise them. *Dandridge* thus exposed the frailty of the
Warren Court's Equal Protection doctrines in the economic domain of
distributive politics and the justices' difficulty in addressing the "para-
dox of poverty amidst plenty."[34]

31. Ibid. at 484.
32. Draft opinion, June 3, 1968, filed in the Earl Warren Papers, Library of Congress,
container number 566 (emphasis added).
33. *Dandridge v. Williams*, 397 U.S. 471 (1970), at 485.
34. The Supreme Court abandoned the wealth-discrimination doctrine in 1973, send-
ing the clear signal that class-based grievances could succeed only if first translated
into race- or gender-based claims under the Equal Protection Clause. See *San Antonio
Independent School District v. Rodriguez*, 411 U.S. 1 (1973). In this case the majority
criticized the wealth-discrimination doctrine and upheld the use of property taxes as a
basis for allocating state educational aid to local school districts.

II.

If natural law proved to be the deathblow to the LSP's claims of a constitutional welfare right, the lawyers never even considered maternalism as a source of subsistence rights. The CSWPL-NWRO's litigation strategy produced some judicial victories, but it also yielded damaging defeats for AFDC mothers.[35] Yet splits within the NWRO were not due simply to increased friction between the mostly white male lawyers and the predominantly black female membership over losses in Court. To the contrary, the very success of litigation spawned discontent among some AFDC mothers regarding the ideological premises of the LSP lawyers' briefs supporting welfare rights. Whereas LSP attorneys worked within an ethic of universal rights, some AFDC mothers protested their bleak conditions by blending a particularistic "maternalist" ethic of care and responsibility with the LSP's natural-rights language of citizenship rights.[36] The natural-law premise of individual "human dignity" and universal rights resonated with African-Americans' religious values, which, as Andrew Young once noted, informed their approach to politics.[37] But some of the AFDC mothers had reason to be wary of a concept of citizenship rights—even one incorporating subsistence needs—that treated the

35. Chapter 8, note 5 describes the victories for AFDC mothers in cases involving statutory interpretation.

36. See the archival materials on the NWRO located in the library of the Center on Social Welfare Policy and Law, New York City. See also the rich empirical study of the welfare rights movement found in Guida West's *The National Welfare Rights Movement: The Social Protest of Poor Women* (New York: Praeger Publishers, 1981). See also Susan Handley Hertz, *The Welfare Mothers Movement: A Decade of Change for Poor Women?* (Lanham, Md.: University Press of America, 1981). These books do not, however, say very much about the interaction between the welfare rights movement and the courts or Legal Services lawyers. Martha F. Davis's well-researched book, *Brutal Need*, helps to fill this gap in the literature. I do not suggest that the AFDC mothers were fifteen years ahead of Carol Gilligan's ground-breaking book, *In a Different Voice: Psychological Theory and Women's Development* (Cambridge, Mass.: Harvard University Press, 1982). Rather, beccause of their experiences the mothers did worry about the individualistic bias of rights talk and appreciated that all too often *individual* rights meant *men's* rights. "Motherhood" for them was a natural alternative model to "citizenship" for thinking about rights and governmental duties. For an insightful discussion of "the sameness and difference conundrum" that feminist lawyers face see Martha Minow, "Adjudicating Differences: Conflicts Among Feminist Lawyers," in *Conflicts in Feminism*, ed. Marianne Hirsch and Evelyn Fox Keller (New York: Routledge, Chapman and Hall, 1990), pp. 149–63.

37. See Nick Kotz and Mary Lynn Kotz, *A Passion for Equality: George A. Wiley and the Movement* (New York: W.W. Norton, 1977), p. 253.

needs of poor single mothers the same as those of poor men, fathers or not. Exclusive appeals to citizenship rights risked negating important gender differences and sidestepping the "special contingency of women in relation to male control and male power."[38]

AFDC mothers were understandably suspicious of efforts to extend welfare rights to working-class and other indigent men who did not share single mothers' burdens because all too often the inclusion of men's needs resulted in a diversion of resources to male recipients and in a redefinition of the NWRO's priorities. For example, when George Wiley, the first executive director of the NWRO, reached out to working-class men, he encountered among them a strong aversion to the NWRO's main goal: a guaranteed minimum income. The working-class men regarded that goal as degrading, a handout in lieu of hard work.[39] To bring those men into the fold, Wiley shifted the NWRO's objectives from a guaranteed income to tax reform, national health insurance, and improved housing. Although the redefinition of the NWRO's priorities was a strategic maneuver on Wiley's part to expand the base of the welfare rights movement, many AFDC mothers felt slighted. At the NWRO's 1971 convention AFDC mothers were angered when Wiley, stressing the need to steer clear of welfare reform because of the political controversy it aroused, brought with him representatives of tenant, consumer, working-class, white ethnic, and black nationalist organizations.[40]

The last straw for those AFDC mothers who wanted jobs and day care for their children came when they lost out to poor men in the Work Incentive Program.[41] Frustrated and feeling adrift, the AFDC mothers in 1972 decided to remove the male leadership and to install a black woman named Johnnie Tillmon to lead the NWRO. Tillmon understood that some AFDC mothers wanted their maternal obligations to be honored by retaining the option of staying at home to care for young children, while other mothers wanted to be placed in decent jobs, not tossed aside by men who felt they had a superior claim over

38. Valerie Polakow, *Lives on the Edge: Single Mothers and Their Children in the Other America* (Chicago: University of Chicago Press, 1993), p. 165.

39. For an excellent study of George Wiley's role in the National Welfare Rights Organization see Kotz and Kotz, *A Passion for Equality*.

40. Ibid., p. 289.

41. Johnnie Tillmon and other women leaders were angry that Wiley placed priority on obtaining decent jobs for unemployed men and downplayed the issue for poor women. The women leaders of NWRO pressed the issue of jobs for welfare mothers seeking employment. See, for example, "Focus," *Welfare Fighter*, February 1974, filed in the library of the Center on Social Welfare Policy and Law, New York City.

women to such employment. As Jackie Pope's study of a Brooklyn welfare-rights organization shows, AFDC mothers were principally concerned with having sufficient income "to provide new opportunities for their children, since many believed it was too late for themselves."[42]

Believing that guaranteed-income proposals were politically dead in 1972, Wiley then formed a Movement for Economic Justice aimed at attracting a wide spectrum of disadvantaged people. Wiley and his male colleagues were irked by the NWRO members' recalcitrance and opposition to joining a broad-based, poor people's political movement. In addition to sensing that welfare rights were no longer politically viable, Wiley and the CSWPL lawyers felt strongly that the NWRO members' emphasis on motherhood as a source of welfare entitlements was regressive. For one thing the NWRO members were calling attention to an aspect of their identities that the rest of society stigmatized—their status as single mothers who in the perception of many people lacked either the ability or the inclination to keep a husband. For another, as evident in the political battles over the Equal Rights Amendment, women's role as mothers was trumpeted by ERA *opponents* who wished to preserve the status quo on gender relations.[43] To Wiley and his lawyer friends, some NWRO members' emphasis on motherhood was tactically foolish and politically reactionary, enabling welfare mothers to be pawns in the struggle over gender stereotypes. In the lawyers' view it was prudent to downplay gender differences and present AFDC mothers as "citizens" with generalizeable attributes so that their *particular* identities as black single mothers would be invisible to the rest of society.

To the NWRO mothers, by contrast, an ideology linking subsistence needs to maternal nurturance was hardly regressive. It is true that some NWRO members, including Johnnie Tillmon, felt anxious about politicians exploiting an ideal of motherhood in order to domesticate AFDC mothers. Tillmon once lambasted politicians for thinking that welfare mothers had additional children solely for the sake of increased welfare benefits: "That's a lie that men tell women," she proclaimed. Men did not even understand women's desire to have children; yet male politicians were ever vigilant to mold AFDC mothers into their idealized image of motherhood. Some of those efforts to

42. Jackie Pope, "Women in the Welfare Rights Struggle: The Brooklyn Welfare Action Council," in *Women and Social Protest*, ed. Guida West and Rhoda Lois Blumberg (New York: Oxford University Press, 1990), p. 71.

43. Jane Mansbridge, *Why We Lost the ERA* (Chicago: University of Chicago Press, 1986).

promote "good mothering" were highly intrusive to the AFDC recipient. Some hard-fought court battles had been waged to overturn laws authorizing government officials to double-check that AFDC mothers' homes provided a "suitable" environment for their children.[44] There was always the risk of politicians imposing an antiquated and austere Victorian morality on welfare recipients in exchange for government aid. But for AFDC mothers the notion of citizenship rights at times spoke inaudibly to their real-life experiences, relationships, and living conditions. Furthermore, in the real world of politics, citizenship rights too often became translated into men's rights. As the Kotz's observe in their biography of George Wiley, "the welfare women were suspicious of many black male leaders, who, they felt, ignored [and] then exploited them and sometimes degraded them."[45]

NWRO members did not view motherhood and legal equality as mutually exclusive. Yet, in calling attention to their special obligations as mothers, neither did NWRO members insist that all AFDC recipients should stay at home to care for their children. Those with very young children naturally wanted to be free of job duties, but a good number of NWRO members wished to combine motherhood with employment. The union of motherhood and work came naturally to NWRO members, whose history never included a division between the public sphere of work and the private sphere of home. As Eileen Boris observes, the ideological use of motherhood had a long history in the annals of African-American women's resistance to oppression: whereas white women's understanding of motherhood "fed into the hegemonic culture's equation of motherhood with biology and female dependence on men, . . . black women's reliance on motherhood, a status and experience disrupted and denied to their mothers and grandmothers, challenged the subordination of African-Americans."[46] Patricia Hill Collins notes that far from being viewed as caring, responsible mothers, black women have repeatedly been stereotyped in the most derogatory of images.[47] To the extent that it challenged

---

44. *King v. Smith*, 392 U.S. 309 (1968). In that decision the Supreme Court declared the "substitute-father" rule a violation of the Social Security Act.

45. Kotz and Kotz, *A Passion for Equality,* p. 208.

46. Eileen Boris, "The Power of Motherhood: Black and White Activist Women Redefine the 'Political,' " in *Mothers of a New World: Maternalist Politics and the Origins of Welfare States*, ed. Seth Koven and Sonya Michel (New York: Routledge, Inc., 1993), pp. 235–36.

47. Patricia Hill Collins describes the stereotypes as "mammies, matriarchs, welfare recipients, and hot mommas." Patricia Hill Collins, *Black Feminist Thought: Knowledge, Consciousness, and the Politics of Empowerment* (New York: Routledge, Chapman and Hall, 1991), p. 67.

those stereotypes, the NWRO members' use of motherhood had a politically subversive edge. Their conception of motherhood, moreover, went to the very heart of AFDC mothers' lived experience of being not only biological mothers to their own kids but also "community othermothers" to the children of relatives and friends.[48] Their experience as "othermothers" continues to underpin the political activism of African-American women.

Thwarted by conflicts over how best to conceptualize and to organize politically for welfare rights, the NWRO lost financial resources and political support after 1972. By 1975, ten years after it was formed, the NWRO closed down, although some local affiliates continued to agitate for welfare reform.

And so the obstacles that the welfare rights movement faced were not completely external, for the AFDC mothers were themselves distrustful of a vocabulary of economic class and entitlement that negated their identities as impoverished single mothers responsible for the care of their children. However tactically unwise it may have been for AFDC mothers to refuse to press for redistributive policies by linking up with a broader poor people's movement, they correctly perceived that the history of American welfare policy has been one in which women's claims have generally taken a back seat to men's claims, although the Progressive era was certainly an exception. Overall, the unemployed, veterans, and retired men have fared far better than AFDC mothers in political conflict over welfare policy.[49] In that respect the gender obstacles to coalition building in the welfare rights movement were deeply rooted.

While the Warren Court's Equal Protection doctrines *did* result in many incremental gains in the legal status of poor people, the peculiar cast of the Court's "judicial liberalism" ultimately doomed the effort to establish a constitutionally guaranteed right to welfare. Because of its fidelity to the post-*Lochner* "double standard," the Court's collective liberal instincts were almost all channeled into aggressive innovations in the sphere of "procedural" rights. In many cases, such as *Shapiro*, the expansion of "procedural" safeguards resulted in substantive economic gains for the poor. However, the judges ultimately proved unwilling to jump the doctrinal fence erected by the double standard

48. Ibid., p. 129.
49. Barbara J. Nelson, "The Origins of the Two-Channel Welfare State: Workmen's Compensation and Mothers' Aid," in *Women, the State, and Welfare*, ed. Linda Gordon (Madison: University of Wisconsin Press, 1990), pp. 123–51.

and to assert a positive "fundamental right" to subsistence. Unlike Franklin Roosevelt, whose "Economic Bill of Rights" carried a *positive* strand in the Anglo-American natural-rights tradition (one articulated a hundred years earlier by the Jacksonian workingmen), the Warren Court was doctrinally constrained by a much narrower "proceduralist" conception of natural rights—one grounded in the post-*Lochner* double standard.

If the Supreme Court's peculiar fidelity to the double standard doomed the case for constitutional welfare rights on the basis of a universalistic conception of natural law, the Court's commitment to Equal Protection also created what would have been a hostile environment for any sort of "maternalist" argument for welfare rights based on the particular vulnerabilities of poor women and their children. As it happened, such arguments were never even made, in part because male NWRO leaders and attorneys shared the Court's commitment to universal (as opposed to particularistic) standards of Equal Protection—and in part because such arguments would have cut so strongly against the grain of 1960s feminism. Perhaps the only people who might have wanted to offer such a "maternalist" argument in court and elsewhere were the welfare mothers themselves—who registered their disapproval of the tactics of the NWRO lawyers by ousting their black male director and the white male leadership of their organization in 1972, just a few years before the movement's collapse. Ironically, the very strength of judicial liberalism's commitment to *universal* standards of Equal Protection helped to preclude the establishment of a constitutional welfare right—an outcome that tended to set different groups of poor people against each other in the pluralist political arena, thus pitting one particularistic claim against another in a fierce competition for diminishing public resources.

Chapter Seven

Constitutional Obligation and the Liberal "Persuasion" of the Warren Court

The tensions embedded in the Warren Court's Equal Protection decisions were reflected not only at the level of jurisprudence but also at the level of political theory or ideology. Canvassing some of its landmark Equal Protection and First Amendment rulings, this chapter pieces together the Warren Court's conception of constitutional obligation and especially public obligation toward the poor. As made manifest in the Jacksonian and New Deal periods, natural law offered a vocabulary with which to assimilate subsistence needs into the Equal Protection concept of "fundamental rights." Nevertheless, the Warren Court ultimately rejected a natural-law philosophy that enshrined communal responsibilities to the poor as a basic principle of justice. The Court did not perceive natural-law principles of economic justice as a viable constitutional framework, for reasons that were fraught with irony. First, as shown in the previous chapter, the Court was constrained by the constitutional doctrines created by their *liberal* predecessors who, at the behest of President Franklin Roosevelt, had completely discredited natural law as a source of "extraconstitutional" values.[1] The "Roosevelt Court" did not simply repudiate its predecessor's *conservative* interpretation of natural law, defined as "liberty of contract"; it repudiated natural law *altogether* as a basis for *judicial* decision making in economic cases. Second, as I argue in this chapter, an individualistic and pluralist understanding of constitutional obligations prevailed over a class- or community-based understanding in the Warren Court. Although the wealth-discrimination doctrine reflected the Warren Court's sensitivity to economic disparities, the justices did not regard poverty as a structural problem demanding affirmative constitutional obligations toward the poor as an economic class. In construing welfare primarily as a matter of economic policy rather than a "fundamental right," the Court ultimately relegated the poor's subsistence needs to the rough-and-tumble of interest-group politics. In the pluralist political arena the poor were left to compete against more powerful and more popular groups in thrashing out the terms of the American social contract.

Yet the Supreme Court's refusal to "constitutionalize" a right to welfare was by no means inevitable. It would be a mistake to think of the Warren Court as mimicking the "possessive individualism" of bourgeois liberal ideology on behalf of the dominant class in society. That Marxist portrait strips the Court of human agency, rendering it passive and either completely unaware or falsely conscious of the ideological implications of its decisions. The fact is that the Warren Court's Equal Protection innovations were creative and deliberate acts. The case of *Shapiro v. Thompson*, involving the durational residence laws, is particularly striking in that regard. The changes in constitutional doctrine that Justice Brennan penned to the draft opinions of Justices Douglas and Fortas were quite ingenious. They enabled him to cobble together a majority declaring the durational residence requirements used in welfare policy an unconstitutional

---

1. The term "extraconstitutional" values refers to values that are said to lie beyond the words or structure of the document. Legal scholars sometimes refer to the use of "extraconstitutional" values as "noninterpretive review." See John Hart Ely, *Democracy and Distrust: A Theory of Judicial Review* (Cambridge, Mass.: Harvard University Press, 1980), chap. 3.

I want to make clear at the outset that my argument is not in any way intended as a political attack on contemporary liberals. Rather, I suggest that it was the set of political exigencies in 1937 that helped to influence the behavior of liberals who were genuinely committed to providing Americans with a modicum of economic security. That same set of political exigencies created the parameters within which the welfare rights movement subsequently sought unsuccessfully to obtain a constitutional right to subsistence.

violation of the right to interstate travel.[2] The *Shapiro* cases made clear that while *Lochner*'s shadow still darkened the road to economic justice, the Warren Court had an alternative doctrinal route through the protection of civil liberties in welfare cases.

But another reason for the appeal of Justice Brennan's arguments in *Shapiro* appears to have been the resonance of his arguments with powerful and enduring American ideals. In his majority opinion Justice Brennan wrote evocatively of the connection between equal opportunity and geographic mobility in American society. The durational residence laws used in the administration of welfare policy, he explained, unconstitutionally "deterred" the poor single mother from "seeking to make a better life for herself and her children."[3] The themes of equal opportunity, geographic mobility, and individual liberty were intricately sewn together in Justice Brennan's *Shapiro* opinion. He knew that his centrist colleagues, including Justices Harlan, Stewart, and White, could embrace those values as readily as the liberal bloc if tethered to existing Equal Protection doctrines. The support of the centrists, moreover, would help to quell criticism that the Court was seriously considering the "kooky" idea of a constitutional "right to live."[4] Indeed, Justice Brennan's *Shapiro* opinion was so convincing that he—or, more exactly, Archibald Cox, whose arguments the justice and his centrist brethren found so compelling— wrested a victory for AFDC mothers from the states, which had won the case in the Supreme Court the previous year. Given that the states had the liberal chief justice on their side throughout the argument *and* reargument of the case, the final decision in *Shapiro* was all the more impressive.

It would be an oversimplification, however, to conclude with the legal realists that justices are free willy-nilly to inject their own values into the Constitution. As Michael McCann observes, "judges are constrained routinely by their dependence upon the inherited ideas, symbols, and other conventions of legal narrative as well as by institutional factors which shape the particular political contexts of judicial action."[5] It is true that the justices sometimes offer "novel" interpreta-

2. 394 U.S. 618 (1969).

3. Ibid. at 631–32.

4. Martha F. Davis notes that even Lee Albert of the Center on Social Welfare Policy and Law regarded Sparer's "right-to-live" idea as "kooky" and doubted that the Supreme Court would ever take it seriously. See Davis, *Brutal Need: Lawyers and the Welfare Rights Movement, 1960–1973*, (New Haven, Conn.: Yale University Press, 1993), p. 103.

5. Michael W. McCann, "Equal Protection for Social Inequality: Race and Class in Constitutional Ideology," in *Judging the Constitution: Critical Essays on Judicial Lawmaking*, ed. Michael W. McCann and Gerald L. Houseman (Boston: Scott, Foresman and Co., 1989), p. 236.

tions of the Constitution; certainly, some members of the Warren Court introduced new doctrines to Equal Protection review that provoked skepticism from other members.[6] But Supreme Court justices are just as often constrained by the unforeseen doctrinal consequences of earlier ventures in jurisprudential innovation or creativity. And what appears to be one Court's decisive resolution of a constitutional issue in one era might contain ambiguities and paradoxes that are not revealed until a later Court confronts them in new cases and in a different institutional and political environment. For example, the Stone Court's repudiation of the "liberty of contract" doctrine and simultaneous creation of the double standard in constitutional law—the separation of "economic justice" from "individual rights"—unleashed new and unforeseen problems for its successor, the Warren Court.

In this chapter I turn from constitutional doctrines to the political theory or what might be called the "liberal persuasion" of the Warren Court. I borrow the concept of "persuasion" from historian Marvin Meyers, who introduced it in his classic *The Jacksonian Persuasion*.[7] As Meyers explained the concept, a "persuasion" is a shared "set of attitudes, beliefs, projected actions: a half-formulated moral perspective."[8] A "persuasion" is at once less formal, less self-conscious, and less concerted than an ideology as used in the behaviorist sense, and yet it can ultimately be more powerful in that its premises are rarely challenged (if only because they tend to be taken for granted within the discourse of believers). I use the concept of "persuasion" more as a heuristic device than as a causal variable in this chapter in order to capture the cluster of ideas embedded in many of the Warren Court's seminal Equal Protection and First Amendment decisions.[9] Rather

6. R. Shep Melnick, *Reading Between the Lines: Interpreting Welfare Rights* (Washington, D.C.: The Brookings Institution, 1994). Melnick demonstrates that the Court has greater maneuvering room in statutory than in constitutional interpretation. See especially pp. 83–111, 249–51.

7. Marvin Meyers, *The Jacksonian Persuasion: Politics and Belief* (Stanford, Calif.: Stanford University Press, 1960), pp. 9–10. My thanks to historian Daniel A. Cohen for suggesting Meyers's concept to me.

8. Ibid., p. 10.

9. Perhaps "heuristic" is not the exact word I'm looking for, insofar as heuristic implies an artificial device that is merely the product of the scholar's imagination. To the extent that "persuasion" incorporates a readable set of background presumptions, attitudes, understandings, and values that are shared by those who sign onto a judicial opinion representing the position of "the Court," it is hardly a pure abstraction. I am hedging here only because I am reluctant to identify these political ideas, suppositions, and so forth as *the* engine of causal forces and factors behind the Warren Court's decision making. Persuaded by Michael McCann that ideological factors are far more

than try to assign a causal weight to "ideological" factors, I adopt a more modest goal here: to describe the ideas and values underlying the Court's decisions and to sketch their implications for a politics of welfare rights.

The approach to the case material taken here is intended to supplement rather than supplant alternative lines of inquiry into the role of ideas in judicial decision making. The amorphous quality of "persuasion" may actually prove to be a virtue insofar as it lacks the baggage attached to the more polarizing concept of ideology. For years the concept of ideology has sent behaviorists and critical-legal scholars in opposite directions—or at each others' throats.[10] But the notion of a "persuasion" is sufficiently open-ended to incorporate both the personal attitudinal factors emphasized by behaviorists and the interactions between ideology and class structure highlighted by critical-legal scholars.

Whatever the concept one employs, there is a danger in ascribing *one* "persuasion," or *one* theory, or *one* ideology to an institutional body consisting of nine justices.[11] Behaviorists, who analyze legal ideas at the level of the individual justice, will likely balk at the concept of persuasion.[12] To avoid the pitfalls in placing the Warren Court's decisions in the collectivist mold of a "persuasion," I use the concept to refer to ideas embedded in the *aggregate* of the justices' majority opinions. No doubt each justice's own value choices emanate from a welter of background influences, including socioeconomic status, party affiliation, and prior professional experience. But surely it is worthwhile to delineate certain broad ideas that appear and reappear throughout the Warren Court's majority opinions.

---

complex than I had originally understood, I am qualifying the argument I made in my article "The Failure of Constitutional Welfare Rights in the Warren Court," *Political Science Quarterly* 109 (Spring 1994): 105–31.

10. This is one element of the broader division in the field that Rogers M. Smith discussed in his seminal article "Political Jurisprudence, the 'New Institutionalism,' and the Future of Public Law," *American Political Science Review* 82 (March 1988): 89–108. My effort here is inspired by Smith's important article. I hope that the concept of "persuasion" is sufficiently accessible and ideologically neutral to help foster intellectual exchange between behaviorist social scientists, at one end, and traditional public law and critical-legal theorists, at the other end.

11. My thanks to Michael McCann for alerting me to this problem. He provides a clear and accessible explication of the problems of "reification" in his book *Rights at Work: Pay Equity and the Politics of Legal Mobilization* (Chicago: University of Chicago Press, 1994), pp. 300–303.

12. See, for example, David W. Rohde and Harold J. Spaeth, *Supreme Court Decision Making* (San Francisco: W.H. Freeman, 1976).

After all, Supreme Court opinions are not purely idiosyncratic but are themselves filtered through the stock of values and ideas in the political culture at large. The justices not only craft their opinions so that they make sense as *legal* argument, but they also speak a shared language that has meaning in the dominant political culture.[13] As Rogers Smith has explained, the justices' values are a part of the broader intellectual currents that are "carried . . . via particular traditions" embedded in the political culture.[14] Those "traditions" form an intellectual "comfort zone" of sorts, and set the general parameters within which the justices resolve cases and justify their opinions.[15] The Warren Court sometimes reworked and stretched the bounds of the traditions and conventions bequeathed to it. In general, however, the Court ventured only so far beyond the comfort zone of the liberal persuasion that the justices themselves had helped to define.[16]

This chapter describes the "liberal persuasion" of the Warren Court. That persuasion had three distinct, but interrelated, components. First and most prominently, the Court adopted a "proceduralist" approach

13. John Brigham, *Constitutional Language: An Interpretation of Judicial Decision Making* (Westport, Conn.: Greenwood Press, 1978), pp. 127–28.

14. Smith, "Political Jurisprudence," p. 105.

15. The resurgence of interest in the "justificatory" dimensions of judicial decision making has led some scholars to think about law as a kind of cultural artifact, a symbolic system with multiple layers of meaning that sometimes exhibits "striking parallels [to] other spheres such as history, politics, economics. . . ." David Sugarman, "Law, Economy, and the State in England, 1750–1914: Some Major Issues," in *Legality, Ideology, and the State*, ed. David Sugarman (New York: Academic Press, 1983), p. 249. This article contains an illuminating discussion of the debate over law's "autonomy" and "legal consciousness." See also McCann, *Rights at Work*, pp. 303–9. In addition to Sugarman's and McCann's work there are other works that focus on the ways in which law "constitutes" social, economic, and political relations. See, for example, Susan S. Silbey, "Ideals and Practices in the Study of Law," 9 *Legal Studies Forum* 7 (1985); Sally Engle Merry, *Getting Justice and Getting Even: Legal Consciousness Among Working-Class Americans* (Chicago: University of Chicago Press, 1990); Austin Sarat and Thomas R. Kearns, eds., *The Fate of Law* (Ann Arbor: University of Michigan Press, 1993).

16. Critical-legal scholars may suggest I use the term "hegemony" rather than comfort zone. Insofar as "ideological hegemony" connotes structures of power that induce passivity by generating "false consciousness," the concept is too rigid for my purposes. Supreme Court justices are among the most intellectually self-conscious and deliberative of government officials in the United States. The liberal bloc on the Court was all too aware of the problems posed by the idea of constitutional welfare rights. Rather than throw up their arms in resignation, Justices Brennan and others tried to work creatively within the bounds of doctrinal structures and political values in order to derive constitutional support for welfare rights and to elicit judicial solicitude for poor people. They were not lacking in *imagination*, as the concept of ideological hegemony implies.

to many constitutional issues involving claims of discrimination or denial of individual rights. Specifically, proceduralism encompassed the Court's commitment to several principles: (1) that governmental procedures—electoral, judicial, and administrative—be fair; (2) that individual rights be protected when violations occurred; and (3) that government refrain from imposing its political, religious, and moral values on the citizenry. Outside of the economic domain proceduralism gave priority to individual liberty over collective obligations—based, at least partly, on natural-law assumptions regarding human dignity. A second component of the Court's "liberal persuasion" was its particular conception of liberty as essentially at odds with government intervention. As such, its understanding of individual rights fit the "negative libertarian" one, according to which rights buttressed the individual *against* the encroachments of the majority or community that government claimed to represent. A third element of the Warren Court's "liberal persuasion" was its hostility to notions of local community coupled with a faint sense of national community.

Section I takes another look at two of the wealth-discrimination cases examined in Chapter 5 in order to underscore the Warren Court's proceduralist orientation. Surveying some landmark First Amendment cases, section II highlights the conflict between individual liberty and government restrictions, as the Warren Court perceived it, and the justices' wariness of community prerogatives that in any serious way impinged on individual rights. The third section pursues the individual versus community theme more vigorously by concentrating on the normative tensions in Archibald Cox's brief and in Justice Brennan's majority opinion in *Shapiro v. Thompson*. Those documents also reflected the Warren Court's discomfort with the use of natural-law arguments in economic cases. Exploring the difficulty posed by natural-law arguments in the economic domain, section IV examines the Legal Services lawyers' brief in *Dandridge v. Williams* and the Supreme Court's rejection of a constitutional right to welfare and of the wealth-discrimination doctrine. The chapter concludes by drawing out the implications of the Court's "liberal persuasion" for the welfare rights movement.

I.

The Warren Court's commitment to procedural fairness was clearly exhibited in its creation of the wealth-discrimination doctrine. The wealth-discrimination doctrine stood as a constitutional ban on laws that discriminated against individuals on the basis of their poverty. In such wealth-discrimination rulings as *Griffin v. Illinois* and *Harper v. Virginia Board of Election Commissioners* the Court made clear that henceforth it would consider the unequal *effects* on rich and poor of laws that were otherwise neutral in their intent and statutory language.[17] In so doing, Justice Black's opinion for the Court in *Griffin* echoed philosopher Jean-Jacques Rousseau's famous argument in "A Discourse on the Origin of Inequality": economic inequality makes a sham of the equal rights ostensibly guaranteed to all citizens by the social contract.[18] When the poor's rights are reduced to a "worthless thing," to use Justice Black's words, then the Court has a constitutional obligation to intervene.[19] For "law," Justice Frankfurter stressed in his concurring opinion, "addresses itself to actualities," not surface logic.[20]

In his dissenting opinion Justice Harlan characterized the opinions of Justices Black and Frankfurter as embracing a "philosophy of leveling" that imposed on the states "an affirmative duty to lift the handicaps flowing from differences in economic circumstances."[21] Justice Frankfurter's insistence that "a State need not equalize economic conditions" failed to assuage Justice Harlan's concerns about the downwardly redistributive policy implications of the Court's new reading of the Equal Protection Clause in *Griffin*.[22]

In *Harper v. Virginia Board of Election Commissioners* the Court struck down a poll tax as constituting an "invidious distinction between rich and poor" and as violating the "fundamental political right" to vote in a state election. In his majority opinion Justice Douglas wrote that "[w]ealth . . . is not germane to one's ability to participate intelligently in the electoral process" and is therefore a "capricious or irrelevant factor."[23] Although Justice Douglas invoked *Griffin v. Illinois* as precedent to bolster the majority's conclusion in *Harper*, Justice Black found no parallel between the two cases and joined the dissenting side.

17. 351 U.S. 12 (1956); 383 U.S. 663 (1966). The third of the major wealth-discrimination rulings, also discussed in Chapter 5, was *Douglas v. California*, 372 U.S. 353 (1963).

18. Jean-Jacques Rousseau, "A Discourse on the Origin of Inequality," in *The Social Contact and Discourses*, trans. G.D.H. Cole (London: J.M. Dent and Sons, Ltd., 1973), pt. 2, pp. 76–105.

19. *Griffin v. Illinois*, 351 U.S. 12 (1956), at 17.

20. Ibid. at 23.

21. Ibid. at 34.

22. Ibid. at 23.

23. 383 U.S. 663 (1966), at 668.

Justice Black distinguished between the two cases on the basis of a comparative assessment of the relevance of wealth to the procedures at stake—criminal procedures versus electoral procedures—and of the substantive importance of criminal appeals and voting to the individual. According to Justice Black's calculus, appellate review is an indispensable procedural protection because a person pays so dearly for a miscarriage of justice: ". . . while man has strived throughout history to provide equal justice for rich and poor, history is on the side of the 'rationality' of the State's poll tax policy."[24] Justice Black elaborated:

> State poll tax legislation can "reasonably," "rationally," and without "invidious" or evil purpose be found to rest on a number of state policies including (1) the State's desire to collect its revenue, and (2) its belief that voters who pay a poll tax will be interested in furthering the State's welfare when they vote. . . . Property qualifications existed in the Colonies and were continued by many States after the Constitution was adopted.[25]

The historical record supported Justice Black's position; the founding fathers hardly shared the conception of equal representation found in the majority opinion. The elitist strand of civic republicanism that influenced early American politics sanctioned the restriction of voting to property holders. The premise was that only property holders possessed the necessary independence to understand—and the material stake to want to pursue—the community's well-being.[26] Although Justice Black and the other dissenting justices did not disguise their dislike of poll taxes, they emphasized that their "personal" judgment was constitutionally immaterial. For constitutional purposes all that mattered was the *rationality* and not the *desirability* of the poll tax.

Harper thus elicited two competing views of political equality. The majority argued that the meaning of "equal protection of the laws" changed over time and that in modern America political equality required equal access to the ballot box. The majority found the poll tax to be especially noxious because it signaled the unequal worth of the

24. Ibid. at 19.
25. Ibid. at 674–75.
26. Rowland Berthoff, "Independence and Attachment, Virtue and Interest: From Republican Citizen to Free Enterpriser, 1787–1837," in *Uprooted Americans: Essays to Honor Oscar Handlin*, ed. Richard L. Bushman et al. (Boston: Little, Brown & Co., 1979), pp. 99–124.

poor. In stirring language used in an earlier speech before the Civil Liberties Education Foundation Justice Douglas declared that voting restrictions violated the "equality, liberty, and *dignity of man*."[27] His use of resounding natural-law phrases outside the courtroom may have unwittingly encouraged critics to pin the *Lochner* label on the *Harper* majority opinion. Justice Black himself referred disparagingly to what he called Justice Douglas's "natural law-due process" reasoning.[28] In the eyes of the dissenting justices the majority's definition of Equal Protection merely reflected their colleagues' subjective aversion to "the political theory" of an earlier era and their misplaced desire to "keep [the nation] abreast of this Court's enlightened theories of what is best for our society."[29]

More broadly one sees a "proceduralist" emphasis underlying the Warren Court's wealth-discrimination rulings.[30] Proceduralism, which is concerned principally with protecting the integrity of the criminal justice and political processes, had its origins in the Supreme Court decision that gave rise to the post-*Lochner* "double standard" in constitutional law. In *United States v. Carolene Products Company* (1938), an otherwise innocuous case involving a business regulation, then-Associate Justice Harlan Fiske Stone explained that judicial restraint was appropriate in economic cases, since the Constitution endorsed no one particular economic theory. In other words, without natural law as a source from which to divine economic liberties, as the *Lochner*-era Court had done, Justice Stone stated that the "political" branches, not the judiciary, were responsible for making economic policy.

But while heeding the lesson of *Lochner* and binding the Court to value-neutrality and judicial restraint on economic matters, Justice Stone signaled the Court's willingness to become "activist" in certain other kinds of cases.[31] Specifically, he suggested that in the future the

27. Speech before the Civil Liberties Education Foundation, November 17, 1962; emphasis added.

28. Justice Black's attack on "natural-law reasoning" was even more pointed in *Griswold v. Connecticut*, 381 U.S. 479 (1965). Justice Douglas's majority opinion declared that, although not explicitly enumerated in the Bill of Rights, the right to privacy was "fundamental" because embedded in the "penumbras" or "emanations" of the First, Third, Fourth, Fifth, and Ninth Amendments. In voting to uphold a Connecticut birth control law Justice Black stated in a dissenting opinion that "I cannot rely on the Due Process Clause or the Ninth Amendment or any mysterious and uncertain natural law concept as a reason for striking down this state law."

29. *Harper v. Virginia Board of Election Commissioners*, 383 U.S. 663 (1966), at 677.

30. See Ely, *Democracy and Distrust*.

31. *U.S. v. Carolene Products Co.*, 304 U.S. 144 (1938), at 152–53, n. 4. The "double

Court would apply a strict standard of review to laws involving individual rights, political processes, or "discrete and insular minorities":

> It is unnecessary to consider now whether legislation which restricts those political processes which can ordinarily be expected to bring about repeal of undesirable legislation, is to be subjected to more exacting judicial scrutiny under the general prohibitions of the Fourteenth Amendment than are other types of legislation . . . Nor need we enquire whether similar considerations enter into the review of statutes directed at particular religious, . . . or national, . . . or racial minorities . . . whether prejudice against discrete and insular minorities may be a special condition, which tends seriously to curtail the operation of those political processes ordinarily to be relied upon to protect minorities, and which may call for a correspondingly more searching judicial inquiry.[32]

The Court justified the "double standard" as a vindication of democratic principles. Judicial restraint in the economic domain fostered democracy by allowing "the people" a voice in economic arrangements. But, according to the Court, the democratic argument for judicial

---

standard" articulated by Justice Stone to some degree echoed the philosophy of Justice Oliver Wendell Holmes, who had urged his colleagues to eschew "liberty of contract" and to follow judicial restraint in economic cases but who also had carved out an activist role for the Court in freedom of speech cases. My thanks to Jeffrey B. Abramson for elucidating the conceptual components of proceduralism and the nuances of First Amendment law.

32. Ibid. As indicated in Chapter 4, some scholars, such as Michael W. McCann, suggest that most academics and legal commentators have mistakenly cast the double standard as emblematic of a contrast between the *Lochner*-era and Warren Court decisions. McCann argues that the *Lochner*-era conception of "liberty of contract" fit much more comfortably with Anglo-American law (supported by the inegalitarian and individualistic strains of liberalism) than most scholars are willing to concede. See McCann, "Equal Protection for Social Inequality," p. 232. By contrast, Edward Keynes argues that the denigration of the *Lochner*-era decisions obscures the historical importance and acceptance of substantive due process as a source of liberty and property interests. He also contends that the contemporary substantive due process decisions involving reproductive rights have proven too subjective, and proposes instead an alternative model called "police-power jurisprudence," which he believes provides a more objective, less arbitrary way of deciding when government oversteps its authority and encroaches on individuals' liberty and property interests as guaranteed by the Fourteenth Amendment. See Keynes, *Liberty, Property, and Privacy: Toward a Jurisprudence of Substantive Due Process* (University Park: Pennsylvania State University Press, 1996).

restraint lost credibility when legislative majorities restricted the access of minorities or otherwise corrupted the political process. The exclusion of certain individuals from the political arena not only demeaned those excluded but also weakened the whole democratic system by depriving the citizenry of a "free marketplace of ideas"—a concept that Justices Oliver Wendell Holmes and Louis Brandeis, following British philosopher John Stuart Mill, had introduced into First Amendment review during the 1920s.[33] In short, proceduralism established the Court as a gatekeeper of the democratic process, ensuring the equal access of all individuals and groups. The assumption was that so long as the democratic process operated fairly, the substantive outcomes were not to be second-guessed by the judiciary. In other words, the Court had no authority to judge the substantive content of legislation (particularly economic legislation), only its procedural integrity.

II.

Between 1943 and 1949 the Stone Court began to expose legislation impinging on individual rights to "more searching judicial inquiry."[34] It was not until the Warren Court era, however, that a majority of justices followed through on the proceduralist logic of Justice Stone's famous footnote in *Carolene Products* and regularly began to apply the strict scrutiny test. In addition to the wealth-discrimination rulings, proceduralism provided the normative basis for the landmark legislative-apportionment decisions in such cases as *Baker v. Carr* and *Reynolds v. Sims*, and the criminal-procedure decisions in *Mapp v. Ohio, Gideon v. Wainwright, Escopedo v. Illinois*, and *Miranda v. Arizona*.[35] Warren Court rulings in the areas of school desegregation and voting rights revealed the Court's deep suspicion of race-based laws and its endorsement of statutory efforts to redress racial inequal-

33. See, for example, Justice Holmes's dissenting opinion in *Abrams v. U.S.*, 250 U.S. 616 (1919).

34. Craig R. Ducat and Harold W. Chase, *Constitutional Interpretation*, 4th ed. (St. Paul: West Publishing Co., 1988), p. 69.

35. *Baker v. Carr*, 369 U.S. 186 (1962); *Reynolds v. Sims*, 377 U.S. 533 (1964); *Gideon v. Wainwright*, 372 U.S. 335 (1963); *Mapp v. Ohio*, 367 U.S. 643 (1961); *Escopedo v. Illinois*, 378 U.S. 478 (1964); *Miranda v. Arizona*, 384 U.S. 436 (1966).

ity.[36] In all of those decisions the Court showed its belief in what Chief Justice Warren called the "procedural slant" of the Bill of Rights.[37]

Yet the Warren Court's procedural emphasis went beyond a narrow, instrumental understanding of individual rights as protective of the integrity of the criminal-justice or democratic processes. Its decisions reflected the Court's belief in the primacy of the individual in a democracy.[38] For example, while the poll tax and legislative-reapportionment decisions fit the "process model" very well, one is hard pressed to describe the Court's free-speech decisions in exclusively procedural terms. To be sure, the justices believed that freedom of speech was a prerequisite to democratic debate and majority rule. But many on the Court regarded freedom of speech as essential to preserving the very "dignity" and "worth" of the individual. For example, Justice Brennan employed natural-law phraseology to the Court's Fourteenth Amendment rulings, which he believed accelerated "mankind's pursuit of the age-old dream for recognizing the inherent dignity and the equal and inalienable rights of all members of the human family."[39] Referring to the Court's Equal Protection decisions in particular, Justice Brennan asserted that mankind's "inherent dignity" could not be preserved unless the Court "protects freedom and equality in a realistic and not merely a formal sense."

Another Warren Court liberal, the chief justice himself, also used natural-law rhetoric in a speech outside the courtroom. Judicial review, he explained, "came into being in our nation because our people

36. See, for example, *Brown v. Board of Education of Topeka*, 347 U.S. 483 (1954); *Brown v. Board of Education, II*, 349 U.S. 294 (1955); *Cooper v. Aaron*, 358 U.S. 1 (1958); *Green v. School Board of New Kent County*, 391 U.S. 430 (1968); *Heart of Atlanta Motel, Inc., v. U.S.*, 379 U.S. 241 (1964); *South Carolina v. Katzenbach*, 383 U.S. 301 (1966), and *Katzenbach v. Morgan*, 384 U.S. 641 (1966).

37. Speech delivered at New York University Law School, October 1968.

38. In contrast, some proceduralist theories define free-speech rights mainly as utilitarian instruments designed to aggregate individual preferences and to crystallize "the greatest good for the greatest number" in legislation. John Hart Ely's *Democracy and Distrust* treats rights to freedom of speech in this way because, arguing against those who contend that the Court is essentially a countermajoritarian anomaly, he contends that the Court's decisions striking down laws on First Amendment grounds actually enhance majority rule by making sure that all voices, all "preferences," are registered in the political process.

39. Compare text accompanying footnote 27 with the quote of Justice Brennan here. Justice William Brennan, "Landmarks of Legal Liberty," address to New York University Law School, October 1, 1968. In a 1996 article expressing opposition to the death penalty, the former justice wrote: "Our Constitution is a charter of human rights, dignity, and self-determination." William J. Brennan, Jr., "What the Constitution Requires," *New York Times*, April 28, 1996, sec. 4, p. 13.

recognized that it provided a useful weapon in the struggle for the preservation of fundamental human rights—for the protection of the individual human beings from the tyranny of the majority. . . . Human dignity and freedom gain from the stability of government to which a judicial umpire contributes. . . ."[40] Such transcendent natural-law language showed a greater affinity with the aspirational assertions of the Declaration of Independence than with the more legalistic articles of the United States Constitution.

The natural-law language that permeated some of the justices' off-the-Court speeches was less frequently found in their actual rulings. While natural-law rhetoric worked well as oratory, the Warren Court justices generally avoided it in their opinions—perhaps for fear of being compared with the discredited *Lochner* Court. After all, the *Lochner* Court's natural-law reasoning was savagely attacked for thirty years and brought the Supreme Court into disrepute. Yet, in some cases involving an enumerated right in the Bill of Rights, the Warren Court justices exhibited much less hesitation in using natural-law language, presumably because specific wording in the document supported (even if it was not dispositive of) their decisions.[41] Whatever the language used, the Warren Court's rulings exhibited both a proceduralist commitment to preserving the integrity of the democratic and criminal-justice systems and a humanist commitment to the primacy of "individual human beings."

While proceduralist and humanist values ultimately parted company in welfare cases, they converged in the Warren Court's First Amendment decisions. More than any other area of law, the latter revealed the individualistic thrust of the Warren Court's jurisprudence. Although in earlier decisions the Supreme Court's main interest was in effecting more robust democratic communication, gradually the Warren Court came to define freedom of speech in terms of the intrinsic value of personal self-expression.[42] This individualistic

40. Address to New York Law School, December 2, 1960.

41. See, for example, *Rochin v. California*, 342 U.S. 165 (1952), decided the year before Earl Warren became chief justice; *Mapp v. Ohio*, 367 U.S. 643 (1961), and *Stanley v. Georgia*, 394 U.S. 557 (1969).

42. Compare, for example, the First Amendment theories of Alexander Meiklejohn and Thomas Emerson. Meiklejohn took a functionalist approach to the First Amendment and argued that the Court should provide *absolute* protection to "public speech" but only conditional protection to "private speech." Meiklejohn defined public speech as essential to the proper workings of a robust democracy, namely political speech. According to this definition, commercial and artistic speech ought to receive less protection than political speech. Thomas Emerson, by contrast, believed that personal speech was entitled to the same strong protection as political speech since the former was an important part of

conception of speech was perhaps most evident in the Warren Court's development of the "neutrality principle," which was first articulated by Justices Holmes and Brandeis and was later embraced by the Stone Court in the 1940s.[43] The principle of content-neutrality requires government to remain neutral regarding the content of individuals' values and life choices. To put the point more colloquially, the Warren Court became impatient with government attempts to "legislate morality," which, they believed, stifled the full flowering of individuality. Since the principle of content-neutrality in First Amendment law appears to have reinforced the Warren Court's value-neutrality over questions of *economic* justice, a closer look at a few landmark rulings is in order.

Our own familiarity with the content-neutrality principle should not obscure the shift in First Amendment review that has taken place over the course of the twentieth century. The shift may be described as one from a "self-government" model to a "self-expression" model of free speech and free press.[44] In the 1940s Alexander Meiklejohn, a leading constitutional scholar and proponent of the self-government model, claimed that "the primary purpose of the First Amendment is . . . that all the citizens shall, so far as possible, understand the issues which bear upon our common life."[45] From this premise, he argued that the First Amendment gave priority to "political" speech over "private" speech. The hierarchy of values in the First Amendment, according to Meiklejohn, meant that government was constitutionally obligated to provide absolute protection to political speech; however, government could, within reason, regulate the "private freedom of this or that individual" to assert his or her views on nonpolitical issues.[46]

---

individual identity and "self-fulfillment." The Warren Court was influenced by both of these First Amendment theories, although it put greater emphasis on the latter than previous Courts had. Alexander Meiklejohn, *Free Speech and Its Relation to Self-Government* (New York: Harper and Row, 1948); Meiklejohn, *Political Freedom* (New York: Harper Brothers, 1960); Thomas Emerson, *The System of Freedom of Expression* (New York: Random House, 1970). For a fuller discussion see Jeffrey Abramson and Elizabeth Bussiere, "Free Speech and Free Press: A Communitarian Perspective," in *New Communitarian Thinking: Persons, Virtues, Institutions, and Communities*, ed. Amitai Etzioni (Charlottesville: University Press of Virginia, 1995), pp. 218–32; and Rogers M. Smith, *Liberalism and American Constitutional Law* (Cambridge, Mass.: Harvard University Press, 1985), pp. 106–8.

43. The Stone Court's clearest statement of the neutrality principle actually came in a religion case, *West Virginia Board of Education v. Barnette*, 319 U.S. 624 (1943).

44. Abramson and Bussiere, "Free Speech and Free Press," pp. 218–32. The Warren Court did not abandon the self-government model; rather, the self-expression model became more heavily accented in the 1960s.

45. Meiklejohn, *Free Speech and Its Relation to Self-Government*, p. 89.

46. Ibid., p. 88.

The blurred line in real life between political and private speech made Meiklejohn's argument controversial; nevertheless, it captured an earlier conception of the First Amendment as intended to promote vigorous debate and democratic community. For example, during the 1940s and 1950s the Supreme Court upheld group-libel and obscenity laws and thereby gave communities the democratic space to make substantive judgments about the worth of speech. The Court considered "hate speech" beyond the First Amendment's protection because it rested on base emotions and undermined the very conditions for rational discussion among citizens by intimidating its targets.[47] Thus, for example, in *Beauharnais v. Illinois* the Court upheld the conviction of the president of a white supremacist organization under an Illinois group-libel (or hate-speech) law.[48] The Court argued that the vile residue of racial hostility gave the state a "reasonable basis" for assuming that hate speech "promote[s] strife and tend[s] powerfully to obstruct the manifold adjustments required for free, ordered life in a metropolitan, polyglot community."[49]

The self-government model at the heart of *Beauharnais* stood in tension with the self-expression model that began its ascendancy in the late Warren Court years and that now predominates in the Supreme Court's rulings.[50] While the former model was predicated on the community's power to render moral judgments and to regulate the expression of hate groups, the latter has rested on an individualistic conception of the First Amendment as assuring the individual a personal haven from government regulation—in Justice Douglas's words, a "sanctuary of belief and conscience."[51] That view of the First Amendment found expression in *Brandenburg v. Ohio* (1969), in which the Warren Court invalidated an Ohio law that was used to prosecute the Ku Klux Klan for making incendiary speeches about Jews and blacks while burning a wooden cross.[52]

47. See *Roth v. U.S.*, 354 U.S. 476 (1957), and *Beauharnais v. Illinois*, 343 U.S. 250 (1952), respectively. Regarding the exclusion of "fighting words" and commercial speech see *Chaplinsky v. New Hampshire*, 315 U.S. 568 (1942), and *Valentine v. Christensen*, 316 U.S. 52 (1942).

48. 343 U.S. 250 (1952).

49. Ibid. at 259.

50. The line between the two models, of course, should not be overdrawn, for in real life they sometimes overlap and are mutually reinforcing. But the normative underpinnings of the self-government and self-expression models *are* different.

51. *Brandenburg v. Ohio*, 395 U.S. 444 (1969), Justice Douglas concurring.

52. Ibid. Even more dramatic was a Burger Court case challenging the constitutionality of three ordinances passed by Skokie, Illinois, in response to the announcement of an American Nazi march through the town. The Nazis, or National Socialist Party, had

Paralleling its shifting treatment of hate speech, the Supreme Court has gone from accepting obscenity regulations, on the premise that obscenity appeals not to reason but to "prurient interest," to limiting the reach of such restrictions in order to protect individual self-expression. The unanimous decision in *Stanley v. Georgia* in 1969 was emblematic of the Warren Court's movement toward the self-expression model of the First Amendment. Departing from precedents, the Court in *Stanley* struck down a Georgia law that punished the possession of obscene materials in the home.[53] Challenging Georgia's purported interest in "social order and public morality," Justice Marshall's opinion proclaimed: "[The] right to receive information and ideas, *regardless of their social worth* . . . is fundamental to our free society."[54] Two years later, in a political and not a pornography case, the Burger Court reinforced the self-expression model by asserting that "one man's vulgarity may be another man's lyric."[55] If government were granted the power to make moral judgments about the form and content of speech, Justice Harlan stated in *Cohen v. California*, "the premise of individual dignity and choice upon which our political system rests" would be eroded.[56]

In each of the cases just scanned the Supreme Court elevated the individual's right of self-expression over the community's interests in

---

deliberately designated Skokie as the site of the march because of the town's large Jewish population, which included Holocaust survivors. The Burger Court let stand two lower federal court rulings that had voided the ordinances as violations of the Nazis' First Amendment right to parade through Skokie and even to display swastikas. Most recently the Supreme Court declared unconstitutional St. Paul, Minnesota's Bias-Motivated Crime Ordinance, under which a young white man was given an additional punishment for burning a cross on the lawn of an African-American family. In a complicated opinion that reflected shifting coalitions of justices on several key points a majority ruled that the ordinance violated the content-neutrality principle. *R.A.V. v. St. Paul*, 120 L. Ed. 2d 305 (1992).

53. 394 U.S. 557 (1969).

54. Ibid. at 564, emphasis added.

55. *Cohen v. California*, 402 U.S. 15 (1971), at 25. In this case the Court overturned the conviction of a man for wearing a jacket with "Fuck the Draft" emblazoned on the back. While really a *mix* of the self-government and self-expression models, the case is famous for Justice Harlan's emphasis on the inherent subjectivity and individuality of values.

56. Ibid. at 24. As *Cohen* demonstrated, the principle of content-neutrality is capable of supporting both the self-government and the self-expression models. Indeed, sometimes, as in *Cohen*, the models commingled in the same ruling. But when a case arose in which the two models led to opposing conclusions, the Warren, Burger and Rehnquist Courts have all tended to favor the self-expression model. Since the 1960s, the Supreme Court has given very little leeway to community efforts to restrict speech, even when the regulations were aimed at buttressing democratic dispositions and institutions.

preventing vulnerable groups from being frightened into silence by hate speech, in minimizing the degradation wrought by pornography, and in maintaining a certain level of civility in public discourse in a courthouse. Although the Court thought otherwise, the communities that enacted the regulations saw themselves as strengthening rather than undermining democracy. For instance, the intent of the Illinois hate-speech law adjudicated in *Beauharnais* was to foster an environment in which all groups felt safe, none degraded. Moreover, by refusing to tolerate hate speech, citizens were affirming the union of individual and collective well-being. The ordinances expressed the conviction that the pain suffered by an African-American in the shadow of a burning cross was the community's pain as well.

But as in other areas of law the Warren Court was particularly suspicious of communitarian assertions because they posed a risk to individual rights. Perhaps that is why the Court sometimes found refuge in natural law when having to defend unpopular decisions, such as overturning a criminal conviction because of a procedural error or because of the right of the Ku Klux Klan to spew racial hatred. While its critics viewed group-libel laws as essential to preserving the equal respect of all citizens, including the decendants of former slaves, the Warren Court suggested that it was group-libel laws themselves that failed to accord equal respect to each individual, especially to members of unpopular fringe groups. By protecting the purveyors of hate, the Court implied, government actually recognized the "dignity and choice"—the equal respect—of every individual. Unbending First Amendment rights implicitly acknowledged that even members of the Ku Klux Klan were not beyond the pale of human discourse.[57]

At least for some of the justices the Equal Protection and First Amendment decisions emanated alike from a natural-law premise of universal human rights and dignity. Although reluctant to make explicit use of natural-law language in Fourteenth Amendment cases, the Warren Court sometimes hinted at it in First Amendment cases. Meanwhile, in some of their off-the-court speeches a few of the justices did make explicit use of natural-law phraseology regarding the "dignity of the individual human being." According to those justices, the Court's Equal Protection and First Amendment decisions not only maximized freedom by lifting government constraints on individual choice but also preserved human dignity by compelling government to accord equal respect to all individuals and groups.

57. David A. J. Richards, *Toleration and the Constitution* (New York: Oxford University Press, 1986), p. 192.

Since the liberal repudiation of *Lochner*-era decisions tended to block the application of natural law in the economic domain, however, the Warren Court's ideas of human dignity and liberty did not take them very far in social-welfare cases. The Court's strong attachment to the "double standard" posed an insurmountable barrier for welfare-rights advocates, who pressed for affirmative government obligations to meet the poor's subsistence needs. As Michael Sandel has argued, the citizen of the "procedural republic" is an "unencumbered self" for whom public obligations, nearly always burdensome, must be freely chosen.[58] In the proceduralist framework (established in the economic sphere), therefore, the "liberty" of the nonpoor is counterpoised against the "needs" of the poor. That normative conflict was not strictly philosophical; it was politically acted out in the form of tax revolts during the late 1960s and early 1970s, and once again during the Reagan and Bush presidencies. Furthermore, *states'* references to human "dignity" and "respect" increasingly justified government *curtailment* rather than expansion of the safety net. As sketched in the remainder of this chapter, the idea of a constitutional obligation to meet the poor's subsistence needs faced formidable obstacles at the level of political theory and not just jurisprudence—obstacles, that is, to providing a normative basis for a collective obligation to meet the poor's subsistence needs. But before arriving at that denouement there was the climactic case of *Shapiro v. Thompson*, which aroused hope among AFDC mothers that the Court might declare welfare a constitutional entitlement for all.

III.

When *Shapiro v. Thompson* was first argued in the 1967 term, Chief Justice Warren's majority opinion characterized welfare benefits as a "privilege," which states could distribute largely at their own discretion so long as their regulations were "reasonable" and complied with federal law. But when *Shapiro* was reargued the next term, the majority declared the one-year residency requirements unconstitutional. Justice Brennan's majority opinion closely followed the supplemental brief and oral argument of Archibald Cox, a Harvard professor

---

58. Michael J. Sandel, "The Procedural Republic and the Unencumbered Self," *Political Theory* 12 (February 1984): 81–96.

and former U.S. solicitor general, whom the Center on Social Welfare Policy and Law had enlisted once the Court decided to rehear the case.

Henry Freedman, Edward Sparer's colleague at the CSWPL, recalled why Cox's oral argument was so enticing as to persuade three justices to change their minds to strike down the durational residence laws. To assuage the Court's discomfort in the uncharted waters of welfare policy "Cox presented the case as if it were in the grand tradition of case law."[59] Having served as solicitor general, he knew the justices' language, and his demeanor was confident and reassuring. According to Freedman, the knockout punch came when Cox "pounced on the argument made in the Iowa amicus curiae brief," as well as during the appellants' oral presentation. The Iowa amicus curiae brief asserted the principle that a state is primarily obligated to take care of its *own* poor but not the poor of another state; Lorna Lawhead Williams, the special assistant attorney general of Iowa, repeated that claim during the oral argument in which she participated along with Francis J. MacGregor, Connecticut's assistant attorney general. Cox lambasted Iowa's argument for its "insular localism" and said that the durational residence laws were an affront to the Commerce Clause as well as the Fourteenth Amendment's Equal Protection and Privileges and Immunities Clauses.

At the same time that LSP attorneys and AFDC recipients were buoyed by the victory that Cox had helped wrest from the states, the CSWPL was anxious because the Court suggested that only if a welfare regulation impinged on an *established* constitutional right would the Court seriously consider invalidating the law.[60] Yet the dichotomy between economics and rights that the Warren Court had amplified was not the center's only problem. *Shapiro* also contained normative tensions that foreshadowed stormy waters for welfare-rights activists trying to chart new constitutional obligations to the poor.

Cox's argument succeeded mainly because he based *Shapiro* on the right to interstate migration and the value of equal opportunity. The right to interstate travel was both doctrinally and ideologically alluring because it was well established in precedents and was the essence of "negative liberty," freedom from restrictive government regulations. Furthermore, by reconceptualizing the laws as involving government "discrimination against 'outsiders,' " Cox avoided the more incendiary assertions of Justices Douglas and Fortas, who had

59. Interview with Henry Freedman, February 25, 1987.
60. Ibid.

attributed the laws to the desire of "the rich" to keep out "the poor."
In short, Cox offered Justice Brennan a way to adhere to the ideals of
formal and procedural equality. The Constitution, he emphasized,
requires the *formal* equality of in-staters and out-of-staters vis-à-vis
the right to interstate travel and the *procedural* equality of in-state
and out-of-state indigent families vis-à-vis access to welfare assistance. By casting *Shapiro* in procedural terms, Justice Brennan es-
chewed the controversial substantive ideal of equality defined as the
right to government satisfaction of subsistence needs.

But Archibald Cox and Justice Brennan paid a price for their
doctrinal and ideological repackaging of *Shapiro*. Ironically, that price
was attached to the very part of Cox's argument that the CSWPL
believed was responsible for the Court's change of mind—namely, his
bitter and sarcastic attack on Iowa's defense of the durational residence law contained in its amicus curiae brief. The problem was that
his argument encapsulated rather than transcended the travails of
American politics and the fraying of civic bonds. While Iowa's brief
may have been unpersuasive to the Court as *legal* argument, it was
politically prescient.

The power of Cox's *Shapiro* brief as legal argument lay in its
alignment with both American national politics and the Warren
Court's jurisprudence. Ever since the New Deal, a staple in American
politics has been the appeal to national citizenship in order to justify
federal curtailments of the states' traditional police powers.[61] That
development was hardly confined to the federal courts. President
Franklin Roosevelt envisioned an Economic Bill of Rights that would
have ultimately taken economic-security programs out of the states'
hands and placed them in a federal bureaucracy under presidential
control. Twenty years later President Lyndon Johnson obtained passage of federal antipoverty programs that were deliberately designed
to circumvent traditional power structures at the state and local levels
by mandating the direct participation of local community groups in
the formulation of policies. At the same time Congress enacted civil
rights legislation to fortify the position of vulnerable minority groups
with the protections of the federal government.

But it was the Warren Court's almost complete incorporation of the
Bill of Rights into the Fourteenth Amendment that accelerated the
nationalization of American politics during the 1950s and 1960s. Here
it is important to remember that for most of American history the Bill

---

61. Samuel Beer, "Liberalism and the National Idea," *The Public Interest* (Fall
1976): 70–82.

of Rights applied only against federal, and not state, action. Citizens were especially mistrustful of the federal government because of its distance from the citizenry. State governments, by contrast, were closer and presumably more attuned to their residents' values and needs than the federal government. To a certain degree communities were *expected* to be insular. The assumption was that people of similar backgrounds and values would settle in the same community, and their views of justice would reflect their community identity. Federalism was an institutional expression of different standards of justice that mirrored the diversity of communities within and among the states as distinct geographic, religious, and political collectivities. As J. Anthony Lukas has observed, "the notion that communities ought to control their own destinies—even at the expense of outsiders—was a deeply held American value."[62] Until the nationalization of the Bill of Rights during the twentieth century, justice in America often had a local hue, imbued by community values.

The Warren Court decisively changed the federal-state balance through its constitutional decisions. It imposed national standards of justice on the states and locales through its interpretations of the Fourteenth Amendment's Due Process and Equal Protection Clauses. The Court came to regard local notions of justice as perversions of national (or universal) standards rather than merely different forms of justice unique to different communities. In case after case the justices incorporated a right contained in the Bill of Rights into the Fourteenth Amendment and extended that particular federal constitutional protection to the individual at the state level. Uniform rights of national citizenship came to take priority over "states' rights" and "local control," which by the 1960s the Court increasingly believed were euphemisms for bigotry and intolerance. The Warren Court used the universalizing logic of rights in explaining why it extended federal constitutional safeguards to citizens at the state level. A constitutional right is a *right*; how can a citizen have one set of federal constitutional protections in Massachusetts and quite a different set in Mississippi? With its arsenal of rights, the Warren Court became *the* symbol of the nationalization of politics. It also became the lightning rod for political attacks on the federal government and eventually on "liberalism" itself.

In *Shapiro v. Thompson* Archibald Cox and CSWPL attorneys exploited the Warren Court's hypersensitivity to the erosion of individual

---

62. J. Anthony Lukas, "Community and Equality in Conflict," *New York Times*, September 8, 1985, sec. 4, p. 25.

rights at the hands of prejudiced and "moralistic" communities. With flair and savvy Cox presented the durational residence laws as raising a classic conflict between the individual's rights of national citizenship and the prerogatives of community. As indicated, during the oral argument he illustrated that conflict by fastening on the position staked out in the Iowa amicus curiae brief. Iowa's special assistant attorney general defended her state's durational residence law on communitarian grounds: "[AFDC] is an overall program, where the children are tied to a community where the people care about them, where we are more or less tied, because of our occupations, in rearing children. . . . [People] are more or less tied, because that's what they want to give to the children—some security."[63]

Special Assistant Attorney General Williams's emphasis in her oral argument on the rootedness of civic ties stood in stark contrast to Cox's portrait of ceaseless individual mobility. He attacked the Iowa brief and oral presentation for displaying thinly veiled "discrimination against strangers" at odds with the individual rights that attach to national citizenship.[64] In the eyes of the Court, Cox successfully discredited Iowa's communitarian line of argument as harking back to the Elizabethan Poor Laws, which he described as entailing: "[the] notion that each vicinage should take care of what Mrs. Williams calls 'our people,' those who are settled, and that it had no obligation to those strangers, those out-siders, who come from somewhere else and whom we don't quite know, we don't quite trust, and don't owe any obligation to."[65]

In their own amicus curiae brief CSWPL attorneys also used harsh language to repudiate Iowa's assertions. The durational residence laws were no more than "the vestigial remnants of a localism which changed conditions and attitudes, and a *national society* have rendered insidious."[66] While conceding that in the past "community member-ship was more important than national citizenship," the CSWPL proclaimed that "today the rights of national citizenship have priority over community standards."[67]

Within the terms of their liberal "persuasion" Archibald Cox and

63. Reprinted in Philip B. Kurland and Gerhard Casper, eds., *Landmark Briefs and Arguments of the Supreme Court of the United States: Constitutional Law* 68 (Arlington, Va., and Bethesda, Md.: University Publications of America, 1975): 336.

64. Archibald Cox, Supplemental Brief, reprinted in ibid., p. 387.

65. Ibid., p. 379.

66. Amicus curiae brief filed at Center on Social Welfare Policy and Law, New York City, p. 9. See also the center's amicus curiae reprinted in ibid., pp. 215–60.

67. Filed at Center on Social Welfare Policy and Law, p. 13.

Justice Brennan naturally perceived Iowa's communitarian stance as anachronistic and disingenuous. And, indeed, the image of "neighbors helping neighbors" struck them and many other people as empty rhetoric since most Americans, even well before the late 1960s, lived in large and anonymous metropolitan areas. Furthermore, an industrial state like Connecticut, whose brief underlined the necessity of saving money, could not convincingly invoke communitarian principles.

The scorn that Cox heaped upon the Iowa brief, however, has obscured two important points. First, in reducing Iowa's communitarian argument to a mere pretext—a cover for discrimination against "outsiders"—Cox was blind to a political truth contained in the state's brief that was as old as Western political philosophy itself. That truth pertained to the inextricable connection between the social and political bonds of community. Although unrepresentative of the states as a whole, Iowa's relatively small and homogeneous population, its largely rural character, and its political decentralization provided the foundation for Attorney General William's position. At the local level, at least, Iowans perceived themselves as "neighbors" whose civic relations were characterized by a sense of mutuality and affective ties. Williams lamented that "if this Court were to strike [the durational residence law] down, . . . every one of our women who are [sic] planning to keep their children on a certain standard of living, they'd have to drop proportionately, because it [would] now be equal for everyone—whether they come on the rolls new, whether they've been there ten years. . . ."[68]

In that context the durational residence laws expressed a feeling of membership among Iowans by stipulating that the first obligation was to meet the needs of their own residents.[69] Even the poor among them

68. Transcript of the oral argument, reprinted in Kurland and Casper, eds., *Landmark Briefs and Arguments of the Supreme Court* 68: 338.

69. No doubt, some readers will chafe at such communitarian insularity, deeming it reactionary and inconsistent with any notion of "progressive politics." I have two responses. First, I am using communitarianism in this context as an explanatory rather than a strictly normative model. In other words, I am suggesting that the general lack of a sense of community in most states (Iowa being an exception in the late 1960s) made it difficult for government officials to summon the political will to help the poor. Second, on normative terms alone, from Jean-Jacques Rousseau in the seventeenth century to Michael Walzer in our own day, there is a longstanding communitarian tradition associated with a deep and abiding concern for the poor and the problem of economic inequality; conservatives do not have a monopoly on communitarian critiques. In fact, I would argue that the "new Democratic" politics associated with President Clinton is partly a reaction against the individualism (some would say atomism) of contemporary liberalism. But liberals like Senator Edward Kennedy of Massachusetts understandably become frustrated when the "new Democrats" use their communitarian perspective to attack rather than strengthen existing programs for the poor.

were presumed to have contributed in some way to the state. During the course of the oral argument the state attorneys general or assistant attorneys general justified the durational residence laws as directing resources toward those indigent persons who have made an "investment in the community." Cox ridiculed that phrase as a "euphemistic way of expressing . . . discrimination against strangers, or outsiders."[70] Probing Cox on his skeptical attitude toward the states' position, one of the justices asked him if he believed the notion of community investment *did* properly apply to voting. The question, the justice posed, was whether "knowledge of local parties and politics . . . would be relevant" in distributing the franchise, thus justifying the use of durational residence requirements. Cox responded to the Court:

> I was using investment more in the sense of what one had contributed to the community and was not focusing, as you suggest, on concern for the community, interest in the character of the community. . . . I would certainly agree [in the voting case] this might well be a justifying consideration.
>
> But I suggest it is not relevant here because . . . I don't think one can use this kind of "benefit" any more than one may use schools, or fire or police protection, as a reward for what people have been supposed to contribute.[71]

In Cox's view the durational residence laws amounted to a requirement that the poor first "pay" for their state benefits through taxes for one year prior to actually receiving welfare assistance. But as the question about voting revealed, more was at stake than just money. The durational residence law was aimed at affecting the dispositions of poor people and thereby shaping the very character of the state, its cities, and local communities. More specifically, it was aimed at encouraging the poor to seek employment upon arriving in a new state. To be sure, there were legitimate criticisms of the laws; some states were overly optimistic about the ready availability of jobs, and the waiting-period requirement certainly made the pursuit of employment quite onerous for AFDC mothers, who had to have independent means of supporting their families while looking for a job. The point here, though, is that the states' interest went beyond the purely economic. "Community investment" in a state like Iowa

70. Archibald Cox, oral argument, reprinted in Kurland and Casper, eds., *Landmark Briefs and Arguments of the Supreme Court* 68: 396.
71. Ibid., pp. 396–97.

encompassed the variegated contributions that citizens make to the state in which they put down roots. In the words of Iowa's Lorna Lawhead Williams, states "participate in ADC because they can help their local citizens to a greater extent," and the durational residence requirement enabled them to help out their own community members to a greater degree than if the rule were "as long as they need the money, they share equally."[72]

In short, in a small and rural state like Iowa the durational residence law was predicated on the feeling that "we are all more or less tied [to a community] in rearing our children." Quoting further from the Iowa brief, the law was designed to assist those "who want to have a sort of permanency in [the] community" and to let the poor know that "[t]hey have a friend in the community, besides just bread and butter." In essence, the law was "tied to helping people."[73]

Since, however, Iowa's small-scale democratic communities were not typical of most other states, Archibald Cox convinced the Warren Court that the communitarian defense of the durational residence laws was disingenuous. But a second point has been obscured because of Cox's public discrediting of the Iowa brief and the fact that he won the case for the welfare recipients in the Supreme Court. Cox's derisive treatment of Iowa's brief belied his *own* communitarian assumptions. Assailing Iowa's small-town "insular localism," he characterized the United States as a *"national* community" within which individuals have a constitutional right to move freely across state borders. Justice Brennan followed suit in his majority opinion, quoting from a Supreme Court decision rendered in 1849: " 'We are all citizens of the United States; and, *as members of the same community*, must have the right to pass and repass through every part of it without interruption, as freely as in our own States.' "[74]

So while the express basis of *Shapiro* was the right to interstate migration—what Hannah Arendt called "the most elementary of negative liberties"—Cox and Justice Brennan also pointed toward a positive conception of freedom.[75] Underlying that positive notion of freedom was a national community obligation to meet the poor's needs.

72. Oral argument of Lorna Lawhead Williams, on behalf of appellant, reprinted in ibid, p. 337.

73. Ibid., p. 339.

74. 394 U.S. 618 (1969), at 630, quoting from Chief Justice Taney's opinion for the Court in *The Passenger Cases*, 7 How. 283, 492 (1849); emphasis added.

75. Hannah Arendt, "The Evolutionary Tradition and Its Lost Treasure," in *Liberalism and Its Critics*, ed. Michael J. Sandel (New York: New York University Press, 1984), p. 255.

For, as a matter of policy if not ideology, *Shapiro* required the states to open up their coffers to *all* needy persons who otherwise qualified for public assistance. By dismantling the geographic barriers posted by the durational residence laws, the Court implicitly granted the poor a claim on the common resources of all the states—of the nation.

In fact, during the oral argument Attorney General William C. Sennett of Pennsylvania expressed concern that granting a right to interstate travel was tantamount to recognizing a constitutional right to welfare assistance. He asked the justices: "Is this Court now prepared to say that the welfare right can be extended to everyone without any discrimination whatsoever?"[76] Cox suggested that human need was the only relevant factor in the distribution of welfare assistance and so, by that measure, any non-need-eligibility condition was "arbitrary and capricious" and a violation of the Equal Protection Clause. The logical implication of the need norm, as Attorney General Sennett observed, was to dismantle the categorical structure of the welfare system established in the Social Security Act of 1935. Since means-tested categorical programs, such as AFDC, were the bane of welfare-rights activists, they wanted to believe that the Court's nullification of the durational residence laws was a precursor to a uniform national welfare system in which human need would be the basic principle of justice. Edward Sparer and other activists thought that, as a matter of logic, it was not such a large step from *Shapiro* to a welfare system in which the poor were assured a constitutional claim on the common resources of the nation at large.[77]

But as Michael Ignatieff has explained, "a claim of right to common resources" is difficult to sustain in the absence of "fraternity" among citizens.[78] Perhaps that is why the Warren Court ascribed the poor's "claim of right to common resources" to the individual's *negative* right to interstate migration—emphasizing the *liberty* of the poor rather than the *obligations* of the public to meet the needs of indigent people. The Court may have thought that it was one thing to invoke a national community as the basis for a right to interstate migration—or freedom

76. Oral argument, reprinted in Kurland and Casper, eds., *Landmark Briefs and Arguments of the Supreme Court* 68: 413.

77. Edward V. Sparer, "The Right to Welfare," in *The Rights of Americans: What They Are—What They Should Be*, ed. Norman Dorsen (New York: Random House, 1971), p. 76.

78. Michael Ignatieff, *The Needs of Strangers: An Essay on Privacy, Solidarity, and the Politics of Being Human* (New York: Viking Penguin, 1984), p. 137. As Ignatieff elaborates, without civic solidarity the nonpoor feel resentful that their right to liberty is being sacrificed to the poor's claim of right to equality.

of religion, speech, assembly, and so forth. But the sheer size and social diversity of the United States alone would have impeded the cultivation of a strong sense of national community that extended to helping impoverished strangers. As Aristotle appreciated, when human bonds are diffuse, people have only a weak and "watery" feeling of public obligation rather than a genuine stake in one another's well-being.[79] Yet even more relevant is that a history of virulent hostility among various regional, racial, religious and ethnic groups has impaired the development in the United States of a sense of national community in which individuals feel they have a stake in one another's well-being. In the final analysis Archibald Cox's brief, highlighting the constitutional ban on discrimination against "intruders" and "strangers," not only resonated very powerfully with the Warren Court's "liberal persuasion" but also foreshadowed the problems raised by a constitutional right to welfare.

IV.

Mistrustful of communal solidarity at the local level and recognizing its absence at the national level, Edward Sparer of the Center on Social Welfare Policy and Law pursued an alternative path to constitutional welfare rights than that etched by Archibald Cox in *Shapiro v. Thompson*. Instead of trying to awaken national goodwill towards the poor, Sparer embraced a class-based notion of justice that linked the "fundamental-rights" and "wealth-discrimination" doctrines. Sparer believed that:

79. Aristotle made this argument in response to Socrates' proposal in Plato's *Republic*. In the *Politics* Aristotle considered three kinds of states in which members hold, alternatively, (1) all things in common; (2) nothing in common; or (3) some things in common and some things in private. He criticized the first, contending that when children are raised in common "everybody is more inclined to neglect the duty which he expects another to fulfill. . . . Each citizen will have a thousand sons who will not be his sons individually, but anybody will be equally the son of anybody, and will therefore be neglected by all alike." In such a state where particular blood ties are not allowed to be felt between parents and children "love will be watery" because "there is no reason why the so-called father should care about the son, or the son about the father, or brothers about one another. Of the two qualities which chiefly inspire regard and affection—that a thing is your own and that it is your only one—neither can exist in such a state as this." See *Politics*, in *Aristotle's Politics and Poetics*, trans. Benjamin Jowett and Thomas Twining (New York: Viking Press, 1957), pp. 27 and 29.

Even assuming traditional concepts, does not an affirmative duty under the Equal Protection Clause arise when, as a result of government action designed to enrich one group of citizens, other citizens are stripped of the means of survival? Cannot a substantial case be made that there is a direct, causal relation between affirmative government policy on behalf of the middle class and rich and the substandard condition of the poor?[80]

As we saw in Chapter 5, Sparer devised a litigation strategy that he hoped would result in a constitutional "right to live." Believing that individuals have a natural, inalienable right to subsistence, Sparer argued that no citizen could ever consent to a social contract in which their very survival was in doubt. Yet, in Sparer's view the poor *as a class* were systematically denied their right to subsistence, in violation of the Fourteenth Amendment's Equal Protection Clause. He perceived the Warren Court's fundamental-rights and wealth-discrimination doctrines as the conduits to constitutional welfare rights.

The Center on Social Welfare Policy and Law was unable to execute Sparer's litigation strategy, however, because local Legal Services agencies were not about to be told whether and when to file lawsuits challenging particular welfare laws. The local LSPs had their own indigent clients, and so their first loyalty was to them rather than to the CSWPL's master plan. Moreover, as Mark Kessler's work shows so vividly, since there were vast differences among the local political environments in which LSPs operated, a uniform national strategy might not even have been viable or effective had one been implemented.[81] Consequently, much to Sparer's frustration and disappointment, the first maximum family-grant law to reach the Supreme Court came from Maryland and not a state in the deep South. From Sparer's perspective the Maryland law made for a "bad case" because of its relatively high AFDC benefit levels.[82] A case from the deep South, which was rife with racial discrimination against black AFDC mothers, would have been far preferable as a strategic matter. But once the Maryland case—*Dandridge v. Williams*—reached the Supreme Court, all the CSWPL could do was to submit an amicus curiae brief and hope for the best.[83]

80. Sparer, "The Right to Welfare," p. 91.

81. Mark Kessler, *Legal Services for the Poor: A Comparative and Contemporary Analysis of Interorganizational Politics* (Westport, Conn.: Greenwood Press, 1987).

82. Jack Greenberg, "Litigation for Social Change: Methods, Limits, and Role in Democracy," 29 *Record of the Association of the Bar of the City of New York* 320 (1974).

83. 397 U.S. 471 (1970).

In *Dandridge v. Williams* the Supreme Court squarely confronted the question of whether welfare was a constitutionally protected right under the Fourteenth Amendment's Equal Protection Clause.[84] Finding no such right in the Constitution, Justice Stewart's majority opinion revealed just how much of an obstacle *Lochner*'s legacy was to natural-law arguments supporting the welfare rights of the indigent:

> For this Court to approve the invalidation of state economic or social regulation . . . would be far too reminiscent of an era when the Court thought the Fourteenth Amendment gave it power to strike down laws "because they may be unwise, improvident or out of harmony with a particular school of thought." That era long ago passed into history.[85]

While acknowledging the importance of welfare benefits to the poor who received them, Justice Stewart argued that the Court was compelled to apply the reasonable basis test rather than the strict scrutiny test in order to remain faithful to the post-*Lochner* double standard: "[I]t is a standard that is true to the principle that the Fourteenth Amendment gives the federal courts no power to impose upon the states their views of what constitute wise economic or social policy."[86] Doctrinally, the majority found no relevant difference between the asserted "right to live" and the discredited "liberty of contract."

Ironically, the Legal Services lawyers challenging the Maryland regulation were the ones who made it especially easy for the Court to pin the *Lochner* label on the right-to-live doctrine.[87] In support of a constitutional right to live the LSP attorneys cited a controversial dissenting opinion in a case that was a preview of the *Lochner* era. As shown in the previous chapter, the LSP attorneys cited a nineteenth-century dissenting opinion in *Munn v. Illinois* that lay the foundation for the natural-law reasoning used during the infamous *Lochner* period.[88] That opinion was an odd choice because in it Justice Field

84. Ibid. at 484.
85. Ibid.
86. Ibid. at 485.
87. As I noted earlier, it also didn't help welfare-rights advocates that *Dandridge* involved the Maryland law rather than one from the deep South, where welfare policy was entangled in racial politics, thus raising serious Equal Protection issues. Edward Sparer and CSWPL attorneys were frustrated by their inability to stop the Maryland LSP attorneys from initiating the litigation, and once *Dandridge* reached the Supreme Court the CSWPL could do nothing else but submit an amicus curiae brief.
88. *Munn v. Illinois*, 94 U.S. 113 (1877), at 142.

had sung the praises of a laissez-faire economy and defined natural law in terms of the primacy of freedom of contract and near-absolute property rights over government regulation. In their brief the Maryland Legal Services attorneys quoted approvingly from that opinion, which stated: "The deprivation not only of life but of whatever God has given to everyone with life, for its growth and enjoyment, is prohibited by the provision in question, if its efficacy be not frittered away by judicial decision . . . "[89] In essence, both Justice Field and the Maryland LSP attorneys believed that a natural right to life set limits on government action; in *Dandridge* the limit on government action was the denial of welfare assistance to those in need. For those who found the use of the *Munn* dissenting opinion implausible, the Maryland LSP attorneys also quoted from two recent lower federal court opinions hinting that welfare ought to be constitutionally protected.[90]

The principle of the *Munn* dissenting opinion—that there is a God-given right to life—*was* therefore similar to the LSP attorneys' notion of universal "human rights" setting ethical constraints on government action. Embracing the idea of universal human rights, Justices Marshall and Brennan included a reference to the United Nations Declaration of Human Rights in their *Dandridge v. Williams* dissenting opinion.[91] Underlying the UN Declaration is the philosophical tenet that all individuals possess certain inalienable rights by virtue of being human. Or, in Justice Brennan's words, there are basic human rights because all individuals are "members of the human family."[92]

Yet anticipating the criticism that the United States Constitution protects *constitutional* rights and not *human* rights per se, the Maryland LSP attorneys included a second line of argument in their brief. They tried to show the affinity between a constitutional right to welfare and other nonenumerated rights that the Supreme Court had already deemed "fundamental": "Certainly, in any hierarchy of rights the right to bare necessities of life and minimal physical well-being

89. Brief for Appellees, reprinted in Kurland and Casper, eds., *Landmark Briefs and Arguments of the Supreme Court* 69: 149.

90. See ibid., pp. 152–53, which quotes from *Rothstein v. Wyman*, 303 F. Supp. 339 (S.D.N.Y., 1969), and *Harrell v. Tobriner*, 279 F. Supp. 22 (D.D.C., 1967).

91. 397 U.S. 471 (1970), at 521, n. 25. The United Nations Declaration is a charter of civil, political, and economic rights that forms a part of international law. A right to subsistence is among the economic rights included in the charter, but the United States has never signed that particular provision.

92. Justice William Brennan, "Landmarks of Legal Liberty," Address, New York University Law School, October 1, 1968.

ranks as high as the right to procreate, privacy, vote, marry or travel. Indeed, . . . these rights presuppose the existence of a basic right to life and are dependent upon such a right."[93]

Blending the fundamental-rights and wealth-discrimination doctrines, the lawyers declared that "without the bare necessities of life, the full and active exercise of guaranteed rights, such as freedom of speech and association, is curtailed. As a result of indigence, many have not participated in the political process."[94] The LSP lawyers cited *Shapiro v. Thompson* as precedent for the use of the rigorous strict scrutiny test when a law obstructed access to the "basic necessities of life."

In sum, the LSP attorneys maintained that without a guaranteed constitutional right to subsistence, the poor's personal privacy, ability to participate politically, and very physical survival would continue to be jeopardized. Their brief derided the state's defense of the maximum family-grant law as a means of *protecting* AFDC by placating an increasingly embittered and restive electorate: "[The Court] has, in the past, refused to allow the constitutional rights of a few to be sacrificed because of general public disapproval."[95] Justice Marshall's dissenting opinion likewise held that constitutional rights do not depend on the goodwill of the public. Rights, he emphasized, *insulate* the individual from the hostile actions of a community or of society at large.

Thus, in the end the LSP attorneys failed to persuade the Supreme Court of either a natural "human right" or a constitutionally based right to subsistence. In contrast to Thomas Paine and the Jacksonian artisans, the justices had come to regard natural law as anathema in constitutional interpretation involving economic cases. Hence the natural-law assumption of an original common to which the poor have an inviolable right of access was a weak reed for constitutional welfare rights for two reasons. First, the Roosevelt Court's thoroughgoing repudiation of natural-law reasoning rendered a "natural" right to subsistence very flimsy as a matter of constitutional interpretation. Second, as a philosophical and ideological proposition the idea of an original community of goods to which the poor can lay claim presupposed a degree of civic solidarity that has long been lacking in modern America. And so, repairing to its familiar proceduralist vocabulary,

93. Brief for Appellees, reprinted in Kurland and Casper, eds., *Landmark Briefs and Arguments of the Supreme Court* 69: 151.
94. Ibid., p. 150.
95. Ibid., p. 142.

Justice Stewart's majority opinion in *Dandridge* noted that although the "Constitution may impose certain procedural safeguards upon systems of welfare administration," the "intractable economic, social, and even philosophical problems presented by public welfare assistance programs are not the business of this Court."[96] After *Dandridge*, LSP lawyers had to find new ways to protect the poor's needs in court.

V.

Though the principal explanation for the Warren Court's refusal to identify subsistence as a constitutional right was doctrinal, its legal doctrines were grounded in much broader philosophical and ideological assumptions that seemed to shape its understanding of constitutional obligations toward the poor. For heuristic purposes I have labeled those broad assumptions (embedded in the aggregate of the Warren Court's majority opinions) a "liberal persuasion." One component of that persuasion, inherited from its predecessor, was the Warren Court's deliberate commitment to proceduralism, which encompassed a judicial duty to intervene when laws: (1) undermined the fairness of democratic and criminal justice procedures; (2) violated a right protected by the Bill of Rights; and (3) failed to remain neutral toward citizens' own value choices. Two related components of the Warren Court's "liberal persuasion" were its "negative libertarian" definition of freedom and its enduring suspicion of local communities, sometimes asserted in contradistinction to its support for a somewhat abstract and amorphous conception of a single *national community*. In case after case involving the First and Fourteenth Amendments the Court characterized its role as the nation's guardian of individual "fundamental rights" against (local) community prerogatives or majority will.

The Court's doctrinal constructs—its evaluation of the rights strand of the "double standard," its creation of the "fundamental-rights" doctrine under the Equal Protection Clause, and its development in First Amendment jurisprudence of the principle of value-neutrality— all evinced the primacy of the individual over the community. In the Warren Court's "proceduralist republic," to use Michael Sandel's term, liberty essentially meant the individual's negative right to be free of government restraints and obligations. So when the time came to

---

96. *Dandridge v. Williams*, 397 U.S. 471 (1970), at 487.

decide whether the Constitution contained positive economic rights, an individualist and proceduralist approach placing individual liberty *over* community obligations was, in some respects, the natural outcome.

Yet, as this book has shown, concepts of individual rights and freedom are not *inherently* hostile to community obligations and prerogatives. After all, the Jacksonian artisans and Progressive-era maternalists embraced a communitarian understanding of rights. And as we will see in the final chapter, many AFDC mothers defined individual rights by reference to their particular obligations as mothers, and many contemporary feminist theorists have followed suit. Individual rights and communal obligations collide with one another, however, when the individual is abstracted from concrete social relations and liberty is defined as freedom *from* government intervention.

The tension between individual rights and communal responsibilities was particularly vivid in Archibald Cox's brief in *Shapiro v. Thompson*, which so influenced the Warren Court that it changed its mind about the constitutionality of the durational residence laws. Although his brief did not hinge on it, Archibald Cox intimated that the "national community" had a constitutional obligation to meet the poor's subsistence needs. Yet that argument, presupposing a web of communal obligations, stood in tension with the heart of Cox's brief: the assertion of an individualist and libertarian definition of freedom—the right to interstate migration. Given the weight of its own doctrines, it is not surprising that the Warren Court proclaimed a constitutional right to interstate migration rather than a right to welfare.

The irony is that, although the Warren Court spoke eloquently about the need for "equal justice between rich and poor," the "liberal persuasion" that flowed from and reinforced its doctrines ultimately left little space for a constitutional obligation to fulfill the poor's most basic needs. Thus the welfare rights movement pinned its hopes on creative statutory interpretations of the Social Security Act in an effort to widen the safety net. However, when that strategy failed, LSP lawyers were left with no overarching constitutional principle to fall back on, and the welfare rights movement became increasingly dependent on the "natural sympathies" of judges and legislatures alike. Such sympathies were on the wane with the replacement of the Supreme Court's liberal justices and lower court judges by conservative appointments during the twelve years of the Reagan and Bush administrations.

Chapter Eight

Whither Welfare Entitlements?

The decisive defeat that the Supreme Court had dealt welfare recipients in 1970 in *Dandridge v. Williams* did not end the poor's quest for "welfare rights." In fact, just two weeks before *Dandridge* was announced, the Court had rendered its decision in *Goldberg v. Kelly*, establishing a welfare recipient's constitutional right to a fair hearing prior to having her benefits terminated.[1] Influenced by the innovative ideas of Yale Law School Professor Charles Reich, who had likened welfare benefits to "property" protected by the Fifth and Fourteenth Amendments, the Court stated unequivocally in *Goldberg* that welfare assistance is a "legal entitlement" to be administered in accordance with "due process of law."[2] *Goldberg*'s significance went beyond the

---

1. 394 U.S. 254 (1970).

2. Reich's two seminal articles that reached well beyond an academic audience were: "The New Property," 73 *Yale Law Journal* 733 (April 1964), and "Individual Rights and Social Welfare: The Emerging Legal Issues," 74 *Yale Law Journal* 1245 (June 1965). Justice Brennan cited Reich's work in *Goldberg v. Kelly* in order to justify the characterization of welfare assistance as a legal entitlement for those who qualify for it rather

Court's *constitutional* guarantee of procedural protections against capricious bureaucratic actions. The decision also turned out to be a
political boon to Legal Services Program lawyers and welfare-rights
activists who recruited new members into the movement and organized recipients at the actual sites of the fair hearings. *Goldberg's*
stimulus to welfare-rights organizing led Henry Freedman, executive
director of the Center on Social Welfare Policy and Law, to identify it
as the "most significant" welfare decision of the Supreme Court.[3]

Coming so quickly on the heels of *Goldberg*, which had buoyed the
spirits of LSP lawyers, *Dandridge* was a big disappointment for
CSWPL legal strategists and their colleagues throughout the country.
But rather than paralyze LSP lawyers, *Dandridge* was a catalyst for
CSWPL attorneys and others to pursue more promising avenues of
welfare reform through statutory interpretation. Although scholars
tend to place a premium on constitutional decisions, which are generally more dramatic than statutory rulings, in AFDC policy it was the
latter that arguably had the most significant policy consequences.
An exclusive focus on constitutional decisions, as R. Shep Melnick
illuminates, obscures the federal courts' prominent role in welfare
reform during the late 1960s and early 1970s.[4]

---

than as a "privilege" or "gratuity" to be given at government whim. For an interesting
discussion of how Reich came into contact with welfare-rights advocates see Martha
Davis, *Brutal Need: Lawyers and the Welfare Rights Movement, 1960–1973* (New Haven,
Conn.: Yale University Press, 1993), pp. 82-86.

3. Interview with Henry Freedman, February 1987. In a 1996 article former Associate
Justice William Brennan singled out *Goldberg* as one of the great rulings with which
the Supreme Court has "been able to erect some of liberty's most enduring monuments."
William J. Brennan, Jr., "What the Constitution Requires," *New York Times*, April 28,
1996, sec. 4, p. 13. *Goldberg* should caution critical-legal scholars against dismissing
the case as a mere procedural victory. See, for example, Rand Rosenblatt, "Legal
Entitlement and Welfare Benefits," in *The Politics of Law*, ed. David Kairys (New York:
Pantheon Books, 1982), pp. 262–78. For, as Michael McCann amplifies in his book on a
pay equity movement, social-movement activists can be quite ingenious in gaining
political mileage even out of those court decisions that on their surface appear quite
insignificant as a matter of legal doctrine. See especially his concluding chapter in
Rights at Work: Pay Equity and the Politics of Legal Mobilization (Chicago: University
of Chicago Press, 1994) for an insightful discussion of the dynamic between the legal
and political dimensions of judicial decisions within a social movement. See also Joel F.
Handler, *Social Movements and the Legal System: A Theory of Law Reform and Social
Change* (New York: Academic Press, 1978).

4. R. Shep Melnick, *Reading Between the Lines: Interpreting Welfare Rights* (Washington, D.C.: The Brookings Institution, 1994), chap. 4. Melnick's book is an engaging
study of judicial decision making in AFDC, Food Stamps, and Education for the
Handicapped and the practice of the Supreme Court and lower federal courts of drawing
inferences from statutory language and legislative history that actually *contradicted*

Through statutory litigation Legal Services lawyers racked up numerous victories, along with constitutional and statutory defeats, in welfare cases that expanded eligibility criteria and increased the number of program recipients.[5] Strikingly, some of the Court's inter-

---

Congress's understanding of the objectives of particular government programs. For example, Melnick argues that the Warren Court distorted the language and history of AFDC by privileging the objective of meeting the needs of dependent children over other goals, such as discouraging out-of-wedlock births, that Congress considered to be equally if not more important. Once set in judicial ruling, Melnick emphasizes, the courts' statutory interpretations were difficult to overturn because of the built-in institutional obstacles to change in the United States political process. Not until the presidency of Ronald Reagan did Congress reverse some of the federal courts' earlier "liberal" rulings.

5. The most important decisions affected the scope of "eligible individuals." Almost from the beginning of LSP statutory-based litigation, the Supreme Court set down two principles: (1) since meeting the needs of dependent children was the "paramount purpose" of AFDC, only those state eligibility restrictions explicitly authorized by federal statute were valid; and (2) only income that was "actually available" for a child's care could be calculated as part of the AFDC grant. The latter meant that states could not factor into the calculation of the grant level the income of any caretaker relative that was not acknowledged to be "available" for the care of a dependent child. In *King v. Smith* the Court ruled that states could not calculate into a family's grant the income of a man who did not adopt his stepchild(ren), since such a man was not "legally obligated" to support his wife's offspring. The result, in some cases, was to increase the overall income of an eligible welfare family who did receive financial assistance from a man or caretaker relative. The trilogy, which substantially restricted state discretion in the administration of AFDC, consists of: *King v. Smith*, 292 U.S. 309 (1968); *Townsend v. Swank*, 404 U.S. 282 (1971), in which the Court, against Congress's express policy, ruled that states that opted to participate in the AFDC-U program (intact families with an unemployed caretaker) must include in its coverage all students up until age twenty-two rather than mark the cut-off point at age eighteen; and *Carleson v. Remillard*, 406 U.S. 598 (1972), in which the Court ruled that a father's absence from the family on account of military service constituted deprivation of parental support in violation of federal law, despite evidence that Congress had not intended AFDC coverage for families with an absent father in the military and despite the practice of the administering agency—the Department of Health, Education, and Welfare—of approving state plans with such an exemption. At least as stated in the trilogy the Court's presumption was in favor of AFDC coverage: even if the states provided documentary evidence of federal statutory intent (e.g., legislative reports) indicating congressional support for, or at least not opposition to, a particular eligibility restriction, the Supreme Court held that eligibility limits were only valid if explicitly stated in Title IV itself.

In a few other cases involving the Equal Protection Clause the Court for a brief time declared unconstitutional those state laws and regulations that contained an "irrebuttable presumption" against a particular category of prospective recipients. See, for example, *U.S. Department of Agriculture v. Murry*, 413 U.S. 508 (1973), invalidating a state presumption of Food Stamp ineligibility for unrelated boarders; *Vlandis v. Kline*, 412 U.S. 441 (1973), regarding residence requirements involving tuition preferences for in-state students at state universities; and *Stanley v. Illinois*, 405 U.S. 645 (1972),

pretations of AFDC were at odds with congressional intent; such was the case in *King v. Smith* (1968), in which the Court struck down Alabama's "man-in-the-house" rule as a violation of the federal mandate that AFDC be given to all "eligible individuals."[6] The Court asserted that the primary and "enlightened" purpose of AFDC, at least as the program had evolved since 1935, is to meet the subsistence needs of dependent children who are deprived of a father's support.

---

regarding a child-custody rule. Perhaps because of the criticism that the Court's "irrebuttable presumption" doctrine was substantive Due Process reasoning in disguise, the Court substantially backtracked in *Weinberger v. Salfi*, 422 U.S. 749 (1975).

Confusingly, at the same time that the Court handed down the trilogy of decisions in favor of recipients, it also announced some rulings that enhanced state discretion in AFDC and other policy areas associated with the welfare state, thus narrowing the scope of poor people's legal "rights." There were several victories for states on constitutional grounds that followed in the footsteps of *Dandridge v. Williams*. For example, in *Wyman v. James*, 400 U.S. 309 (1971), the Court rejected a Fourth Amendment challenge to New York's home visits to AFDC recipients. The Court declined to side with LSP lawyers, who had described the mandated home visits as a "search" in violation of the Fourth Amendment's guarantee against "unreasonable searches and seizures" and of HEW regulations, which stipulated that caseworker visits be *voluntary* only. (The Court responded that the searches were voluntary, for all a recipient had to do was to turn the caseworker away. That s/he lost benefits for her family, in the Court's view, did not make the consent coercive.) In *James v. Valtierra*, 402 U.S. 137 (1971), the Court upheld a California constitutional requirement that low-rent housing projects first be approved by state referendum. Rejecting an Equal Protection challenge based on the claim of a wealth discrimination, the Court stated that the referendum requirement reflected the state's commitment to democracy and not prejudice against low-income people. That same year, in *Jefferson v. Hackney*, 406 U.S. 535 (1972), the Court upheld a state law against an Equal Protection challenge that paid a lower percentage of "need" to AFDC recipients than to recipients of Old-Age Assistance and other categorical assistance programs contained in the Social Security Act. The Court also refused to identify housing as a "fundamental interest" subject to heightened judicial protection under the Equal Protection Clause; see *Lindsay v. Normet*, 405 U.S. 56 (1972). And in *San Antonio Independent School District v. Rodriguez* the Court dealt a severe blow to social reformers seeking equity in school financing. The Court ruled that education is not a "fundamental right" under the Equal Protection Clause, nor is wealth (poverty) a "suspect classification." It was in *Rodriguez* that the Court explicitly and unequivocally abandoned the wealth-discrimination doctrine, although criticism of that doctrine was implied in *Valtierra*. An important statutory ruling that favored the states over the claims of LSP lawyers came in *N.Y. State Department of Social Services v. Dublino*, 413 U.S. 405 (1973). There, following the traditional stance in federal preemption cases, the Court upheld New York's work program against a challenge that it was preempted by the federal Work Incentive Program. Although Congress had not explicitly authorized state work and training programs, the court did not think such silence indicated a congressional intent to "occupy the field" in this area of law. In requiring AFDC recipients to prove an express congressional intent to preempt, the Court went against its line of decisions in *King-Townsend-Remillard*. Finally, a crucial victory for the states and a blow to the welfare rights movement came in *Rosado v. Wyman*, 397 U.S.

But imputing such an "enlightened" purpose to Congress was ironic in light of the 1967 amendments to the Social Security Act, which threatened to withhold federal matching funds to any state that failed to rein in out-of-wedlock births. In addition, the Court's general pronouncement that only those state eligibility restrictions explicitly *authorized* (rather than *prohibited*) by federal law would survive judicial scrutiny ruling went against the grain of federal-preemption rules. Yet the fact that the Burger Court for a time ignored and even defied congressional intent attests to the capacity of the Court to act independently of political forces. The hold of legal doctrines on the justices' imaginations provides the Court with some insulation from changing political winds.

In the long run, however, the statutory victories handed to AFDC recipients were incapable of buffering them from political assaults on welfare between 1980 and 1996. An even fiercer political attack on the poor than in 1981–82 has been the zealous movement since the 1994 congressional elections, under the banner of the Contract with America, to scale way back the obligations of the welfare state in the United States. The principle established by the Warren Court that welfare is a statutory and not constitutional entitlement produced some important benefits for the poor, but it has also meant that AFDC mothers' legal claims to subsistence have ultimately been dependent on the sustained sympathy of the electorate and elected officials. Not surprisingly, when the political winds began to change in the early

---

397 (1970), in which the Court ruled that, although the states must adjust their *standards of need* to reflect inflation, they are not obligated to adjust their *benefit levels.* In a reverse situation to that in *Goldberg v. Kelly* the Court's upholding New York's maintenance of AFDC benefit levels despite elimination of its special-needs grant hurt AFDC recipients in their pocketbooks as well as deprived the movement of an effective recruitment and organizing tool.

The intricacies of legal doctrine are lucidly exhibited in: Fred C. Doolittle, "State-Imposed Nonfinancial Eligibility Conditions in AFDC: Confusions in Supreme Court Decisions and a Need for Congressional Clarification," 19 *Harvard Journal on Legislation* 1 (1982); and Kenneth M. Davidson, "Welfare Cases and the 'New Majority': Constitutional Theory and Practice," 10 *Harvard Civil Rights-Civil Liberties Law Review* 513 (Summer 1975).

For good discussions of the doctrines in a broader political context, in addition to Melnick, see Davis, *Brutal Need*; Susan E. Lawrence, *The Poor in Court: The Legal Services Program and Supreme Court Decision Making* (Princeton, N.J.: Princeton University Press, 1990); and Samuel Krislov, "The OEO Lawyers Try to Constitutionalize a Right to Welfare: A Study in the Limits and Uses of the Judicial Process," 58 *Minnesota Law Review* 211 (1973).

6. 392 U.S. 309 (1968). For a lucid discussion of Court-Congress conflict on this point see Melnick, *Reading Between the Lines*, pp. 85–88.

1970s, the welfare rights movement became increasingly disabled in its efforts to fend off political retrenchment in welfare policy notwithstanding all the incremental changes in AFDC brought about by statutory victories.[7]

Part intellectual history, part legal analysis, this book has offered an interpretation of the Supreme Court's refusal to identify subsistence as a constitutional right and has considered the consequences for the politics of welfare in the United States. While recognizing the contribution of the AFDC-mother activists to the welfare rights movement, the book's central actor has been the Warren Court. Amidst a national debate over a guaranteed minimum income, the Court rendered decisions that seemed to point down the road toward a constitutional "right to live." But when it reached that juncture, the Court decided it could not take that road without veering off the proper path of constitutional law and institutional duty.

The reason for the Warren Court's rejection of a constitutional right to welfare was not strictly ideological—at least not in the behaviorist or critical-legal sense. More specifically, the Court's refusal to accept a constitutional right to welfare was not a mere reflection of the justices' personal values, for those values were mediated by intra-Court deliberation and negotiation. Nor was it an inevitable by-product of an inegalitarian market society.[8] This book, after all, has highlighted two long-standing traditions in American politics— natural law and maternalism—that provided strong ideological support for the idea that subsistence needs supersede the market's needs.

The central argument of this book is that the Warren Court declined

---

7. The constitutional rulings from the Warren Court era did have some sticking power, however. For example, the Burger Court reaffirmed the Warren Court's ruling in *Shapiro v. Thompson* and struck down durational residence requirements attached to emergency medical care. See *Memorial Hospital v. Maricopa County*, 415 U.S. 250 (1974). Interestingly, although the Rehnquist Court had an opportunity to overturn the right-to-travel ruling in a California welfare case during the 1994–95 term, it used a procedural mechanism in order to avoid revisiting the Warren Court's ruling in *Shapiro v. Thompson*. As of this writing, the constitutional implications of the 1996 welfare law are unclear, but even some Clinton administration officials concede that parts of it may violate the U.S. Constitution. Despite the fact that Wisconsin's waiting-period requirement for new residents conflicts with *Shapiro v. Thompson*, the Clinton administration approved the state plan anyway. See Robert Pear, "State Officials Conclude Some Provisions of the Welfare Law May be Unconstitutional," *New York Times*, October 6, 1996, sec. 1, p. 30.

8. In an insightful critique of the literature, Michael McCann warns critical-legal scholars of the dangers of "reifying" ideology. While he notes that legal ideas can exert some degree of autonomy, scholars should not go to the other extreme and divorce those ideas from a material or institutional referent. See McCann, *Rights at Work*.

to "constitutionalize" a right to welfare primarily because of the impact of legal doctrines. My understanding of the relationship between legal doctrines and political ideology is informed by the insights of the "new institutionalism." As outlined by Rogers Smith, this theoretical perspective takes seriously the independent influence of legal doctrines, which are the conceptual lenses through which judges resolve cases.[9] Yet it is also attuned to the ideological dimensions of legal doctrines. Embedded in legal doctrines is a pattern of interpreting the political world—an intellectual structure—that gives them ideological content. I contend that the Warren Court's Equal Protection doctrines embodied a particular political ideology—or what I preferred to call a political "persuasion" in Chapter 7—that made constitutional welfare rights harder to support.

The predominant influence of legal doctrines observed in this book supports the argument of Lee Epstein and Joseph Kobylka in *The Supreme Court and Legal Change*. In their study of abortion and death-penalty decisions Epstein and Kobylka concluded that "the language of the law seems to have a reality and motive force that shapes . . . the paths that the law enunciated by the Court takes."[10] Qualifying Justice Oliver Wendell Holmes's observation that "the life of the law is experience," not formalistic reasoning, Epstein and Kobylka appropriately emphasized that "it is experience filtered through a peculiarly legalistic logic."[11]

My argument diverges from recent scholarly literature and is apt to provoke criticism in some quarters. Some scholars may believe I have given insufficient weight either to the resourcefulness of Legal Services attorneys or to the Warren Court's solicitude of poor people. For example, in her sophisticated quantitative study, *The Poor in Court*, Susan Lawrence concluded that the LSP victories in the Supreme Court have been mistakenly undervalued in the academic literature.[12] I agree with Lawrence's emphasis on the LSP's victories, for they improved the poor's lives in the course of shaping the Supreme Court's policy agenda. Similarly, as artfully demonstrated in R. Shep Melnick's *Reading Between the Lines*, through its interpretations of

9. Rogers M. Smith "Political Jurisprudence, the 'New Institutionalism,' and the Future of Public Law," *American Political Science Review* 82 (March 1988): 89–108.

10. Lee Epstein and Joseph F. Kobylka, *The Supreme Court and Legal Change: Abortion and the Death Penalty* (Chapel Hill: University of North Carolina Press, 1992), p. 309.

11. Ibid., p. 2.

12. Lawrence, *The Poor in Court*, pp. 127, 147.

federal statutes the Supreme Court expanded the safety net.[13] Anyone who has studied or has had personal contact with the welfare rights movement must acknowledge the palpable, often poignant, effects that the Court's decisions had on poor mothers and children.

Having conceded as much, I disagree with Lawrence that critical evaluations of the Legal Services Program are inappropriate because it never had a strategy that was "orchestrated to achieve" the goal of constitutional welfare rights.[14] To be sure, the Legal Services Program as a whole had no such overarching plan beyond "law reform." But the most successful LSP backup center—the Center on Social Welfare Policy and Law—was explicit about its mission: to persuade the Supreme Court of a constitutional "right to live." The CSWPL tried very hard to be the nerve center of LSP welfare litigation. Although unable consistently to control the pace and location of welfare litigation, the center largely carried out its litigation plan. As Martha Davis has since revealed in her meticulously researched and eloquently written book *Brutal Need*, sometimes the center's litigation went perfectly. Its challenge of Alabama's "substitute-parent" rule in *King v. Smith* was a case in point.[15] In other cases, such as the litigation over the durational residence laws in *Shapiro v. Thompson*, the CSWPL dramatically wrested control from less experienced local LSPs. In fact, the CSWPL's propensity to pursue its own agenda led many LSP attorneys and welfare-rights activists to accuse the center of being too much of a litigation-interest group![16]

Current developments in welfare politics, I believe, compel scholars to consider the consequences of the Warren Court's decision to exclude subsistence from the panoply of constitutional rights. With the Congress's and President Clinton's decision in 1996 to end AFDC's "entitlement" status, federal law might soon cease to cushion poor people from antiwelfare crusades in the fiscally pinched states if Clinton continues to accommodate Republicans on the direction of welfare. Whatever else they might be, the welfare "reforms" that were widely touted during the 1996 election campaigns are not a "new deal" for America's poor single mothers. Republicans' explicit attack on (and Democrats' ambivalence about) 1960s liberalism—especially that of the activist federal courts—thus makes frank evaluations of earlier reform efforts all the more important.

13. Melnick, *Reading Between the Lines.*
14. Lawrence, *The Poor in Court*, p. 127.
15. Davis, *Brutal Need*, chap. 5; Martin Garbus, *Ready for the Defense* (New York: Farrer, Straus, and Giroux, 1971), chap. 3.
16. See Davis, *Brutal Need*, pp. 73–75.

One purpose of this book has been to track the fate of natural-law and maternalist ideas, since they offered ideologically rich sources for subsistence rights. The Jacksonian Workingmen's movement revealed the strength of a natural-law ethic that conditioned property rights on the satisfaction of subsistence needs.[17] The Progressive-era movement for mothers' pensions showed the maternalist ethic that privileged the needs of indigent single mothers and their dependent children in the social contract. In fact, maternalism was so powerful that even the conservative *Lochner*-era Supreme Court, which was hostile to government intervention in the economy, upheld maternalist justifications for social-welfare legislation.[18]

But ultimately neither natural law nor maternalism was a viable vocabulary for constitutional welfare rights in the late 1960s and early 1970s.[19] The problem was not that conservative justices blocked the way of constitutional subsistence rights. To the contrary, it was *liberal* justices and reformers who inadvertently impeded the later effort to obtain constitutional welfare rights by discrediting both natural-law and maternalist ideas during the Progressive and New Deal periods.[20]

How these paradoxical developments came to pass was complicated. But essentially there were two parallel developments. The recalcitrance of the Supreme Court in protecting business interests through the "liberty of contract" decisions during the *Lochner*-era precipitated

17. I do not mean to suggest that natural law was *necessarily* aligned with egalitarian policies. After all, as we have seen during the *Lochner* era the Supreme Court utilized a conservative version of natural law to try to nip in the bud progressive social legislation to help the vulnerable. And in the mid-1990s we witness a resurgence of thinking that links natural-law ideas to arguments in support of judicial fortification of property rights under the Constitution's Fifth Amendment. See, for example, recent legislative initiatives and court challenges chronicled in "Land Grab: Property Rights Challenges Are Raising the Ante in Environmental Protection," *The Boston Globe*, December 11, 1995, p. 29. For an excellent overview of the concept of property see John Brigham, *Property and the Politics of Entitlement* (Philadelphia: Temple University Press, 1990).

18. *Muller v. Oregon*, 208 U.S. 412 (1908). In this case the Court upheld Oregon's ten-hour work day for women laborers.

19. My treatment of natural law and maternalism as two distinct political traditions should not obscure the fact that, in the protest language of the AFDC mothers, the two traditions converged. That should come as no surprise given the deeply rooted universalizing language of religion in the African-American community. See the quotes of welfare recipients provided in Jackie Pope, "Women in the Welfare Rights Struggle: The Brooklyn Welfare Action Council," in *Women and Social Protest*, ed. Guida West and Rhoda Lois Blumberg (New York: Oxford University Press, 1990), pp. 57–74.

20. As noted in chapter 7, my point here is an analytic one and is not intended in any way as "liberal-bashing."

President Franklin Roosevelt's attack on the Court in 1937. Having had so many of his New Deal programs declared unconstitutional, Roosevelt felt he had little choice but to rein in the "nine old men." Roosevelt scoffed at the *Court's* natural law-"liberty of contract" decisions, echoing British philosopher Jeremy Bentham's derisive remark about natural-law philosophies as essentially "nonsense on stilts." Roosevelt's landslide re-election in 1937 fortified his confidence that Congress and the public would support his Court-Packing Plan.

What was most significant about the Court-Packing Plan, for my purposes, was that even though it failed to be enacted, it was the catalyst for the Court's abandonment of its "liberty of contract" interpretation and, along with it, natural-law reasoning. Renouncing "liberty of contract," the Court declared in 1938 that henceforth it would refrain from using natural law to overturn economic legislation. At the same time, however, the Court indicated that it would carefully scrutinize laws that violated individual rights, that discriminated against minority groups, and that compromised the integrity of the political process. The Stone Court bequeathed the "double standard" to the Warren Court.

The Warren Court introduced innovations in Equal Protection review—thus showing the creative capacity of judges. Those innovations led legal scholars to dub them the "new Equal Protection" because the Court was willing to examine whether poverty eroded the constitutional rights of indigent persons in any specific case. In several landmark cases the Court ruled that it was not enough for the law to accord formal equality to all citizens by treating them exactly the same. If, because of economic inequality or poverty, a law "operated unequally on rich and poor," the Warren Court questioned its constitutionality. For such distinctions in the law, the Court held, created a wealth-based discrimination.

In addition to the wealth-discrimination rulings, the Warren Court's "fundamental-rights" doctrine opened an avenue of reform litigation to Legal Services lawyers. In several key decisions the Court declared that certain fundamental rights were constitutionally protected, *despite* not being enumerated in the document. These rights, including the right to privacy, the right to vote in a state election, and the right to interstate travel, were fundamental because they made possible the exercise of the rights listed in the Bill of Rights. The apparent malleability of the concept of fundamental rights gave Legal Services attorneys the hope that subsistence needs could be incorporated into it.

But the Stone Court passed on to the Warren Court a powerful doctrinal filter—the double standard—that shaped the justices' views

of what constituted a "wealth discrimination" or a "fundamental
right." The legacy of the *Lochner* debacle hovered over the Warren
Court, and its most important lesson was that natural law was but a
repository of the justices' own political preferences rather than an
objective source of constitutional rights. The Court was to steer clear
of natural-law reasoning on the assumption that it tempted the justices to substitute their own idiosyncratic, "subjective" values for the
"objective" principles in the Constitution.

The fear of judicial subjectivity that lay at the heart of the double
standard was so strong that the liberal chief justice, Earl Warren,
exhorted his colleagues in *Shapiro v. Thompson* to reject a constitutional right to welfare.[21] "Efforts to fight poverty," the chief justice
asserted, "appeal to the right instincts of all men, but . . . instinct
cannot be our [the Court's] guide. . . ."[22] Yet Chief Justice Warren was
not averse to treating privacy and voting in a state election as
"fundamental rights," despite their lack of explicit textual support in
the Constitution. Thus, the double standard led the Warren Court to
create a dichotomy between the realm of "fundamental rights" under
the Fourteenth Amendment—the Court's domain—and a realm of
economics—a "political" responsibility of the legislative and executive
branches. In contrast to Franklin Roosevelt's Economic Bill of Rights,
the Warren Court's Equal Protection doctrines generally failed to
recognize in a sustained way that constitutional rights cannot be
effectively exercised in the absence of basic economic security.

Building on the distinction between individual rights and economic
policy contained in the double standard, the Warren Court articulated
a proceduralist political theory, or political "persuasion," that held
little space for constitutional welfare rights. The Court defined justice
primarily in procedural terms, as encompassing fairness in the electoral and criminal-justice systems, the protection of individual rights,
and government neutrality toward citizens' value choices. Not surpris-

21. For illuminating feminist critiques of "liberal" notions of impartiality and subjectivity see Iris Marion Young, *Justice and the Politics of Difference* (Princeton, N.J.:
Princeton University Press, 1990); and Seyla Benhabib, "The Generalized Other and
the Concrete Other: The Kohlberg-Gilligan Controversy," in *Feminism as Critique*, ed.
Seyla Benhabib and Drucilla Cornell (Minneapolis: University of Minnesota Press,
1987), pp. 77–95.

22. As a constitutional matter, individual rights were seen as objective and definable,
whereas needs were seen as flimsy and ever-changing. For a philosophical critique of
the treatment of rights as possessions see Judith E. Grbich, "The Body in Legal Theory,"
in *At the Boundaries of Law: Feminism and Legal Theory*, ed. Martha Albertson
Fineman and Nancy Sweet Thomadsen (New York: Routledge, Chapman and Hall, Inc.,
1991), pp. 61–75.

ingly the Court ruled in *Goldberg v. Kelly* and subsequent welfare decisions that the Fourteenth Amendment provided procedural safeguards in the administration of welfare policy but did not itself contain substantive subsistence rights.[23] So just as the Constitution did not stand in the way of legislators who wished to establish entitlement programs for the needy, neither did it prevent them from abrogating those statutory obligations when they felt so inclined. Therein lay the difference between judicial and political liberalism: while judicial liberals believed that constitutional rulings should be value-neutral on questions of economic justice, political liberals of the New Deal coalition supported government programs that provided economic security, especially for the disadvantaged.

The Court's commitment to procedural justice ought not to be dismissed as purely symbolic. In big ways and small, the Court appreciably expanded the breadth of individual liberty for rich and poor alike. Yet the Court's conception of constitutional justice rested on a rather pale view of civic obligations that made constitutional subsistence rights more difficult to support. This was vividly illustrated in *Shapiro v. Thompson*, involving the one-year residence laws used in AFDC policy. During the oral argument in the Supreme Court Archibald Cox contemptuously dismissed the argument made by Iowa's assistant attorney general, Lorna Williams, in her brief. In defending the one-year requirement Williams appealed to communitarian principles, explaining that the policy enabled the communities to provide care first and foremost for their "neighbors," their own residents. Cox dismissed that argument as a cover for discrimination against impoverished "strangers." His argument won in the Supreme Court, which regarded Iowa's communitarian claims as dangerously insular and as defiling the idea of a *national* community. Iowa might have wished to provide better care for its own neighbors, Justice Brennan reasoned in his majority opinion, but it could not do so at the expense of allowing others the right to interstate travel. In short, although the LSP ultimately won the *Shapiro* case, it did so not on the basis of the poor's *positive* right to welfare assistance but on the *negative* right of all individuals—of all "strangers"—to travel freely throughout the nation without regard to state boundaries.

Without a constitutional right to welfare the poor's subsistence needs were reduced to the level of interest-group desires. In other words, since the Court relegated welfare to the category of "economics" and not "rights," subsistence needs were conceptualized as the subjec-

23. 397 U.S. 254 (1970).

tive preferences of just another interest group, the National Welfare Rights Organization. To its credit, in the course of statutory interpretation the Warren Court did underline the fact that AFDC deals with the needs of helpless, dependent children and not, say, with the commercial interests behind tobacco subsidies. But, as we saw in the majority's ambivalent decision in *Dandridge v. Williams*, the Court found no constitutional language with which to distinguish between welfare policy and business regulations. Although scholars such as Theodore Lowi like to think of the Supreme Court as providing an island away from the rough-and-tumble of interest-group struggles, it may be more accurate, at least in some policy areas, to see the Court as an institutional actor in what Ira Katznelson has described as a decisive shift of post-World War II American politics away from a "social-democratic" to an interest-group pluralist model.[24]

The language of maternalism might have served welfare recipients well here. For surely, the AFDC mothers were right to insist that their children's needs were not on the same moral plane as commercial interests.[25] Maternal obligations to dependent children were qualitatively different from the question of corporate freedom to pursue private profits—sometimes, as with the tobacco industry, at the public's expense.[26] But maternalism was no longer a viable constitutional ethic by the 1970s. The male leaders of the welfare rights movement

24. Theodore Lowi, *The End of Liberalism* 2d ed. (New York: W.W. Norton, 1979); Ira Katznelson, "Was the Great Society a Lost Opportunity?" in *The Rise and Fall of the New Deal Order, 1930–1980*, ed. Steve Fraser and Gary Gerstle (Princeton, N.J.: Princeton University Press, 1989), pp. 185–211.

25. Susan Handley Hertz, *The Welfare Rights Movement: A Decade of Change for Poor Women?* (Lanham, Md.: University Press of America, 1981), p. 107. AFDC recipients' unique status as mothers made them opposed to the idea of uniting with indigent men, including the unemployed, in order to create a broader social movement. See Guida West, *The National Welfare Rights Movement: The Social Protest of Poor Women* (New York: Praeger Publishers, 1981), p. 95; and Pope, "Women and the Welfare Rights Struggle," pp. 57–74.

26. In a thought-provoking and carefully argued book Nancy J. Hirschmann shows how past and contemporary liberal theory privileges individual freedom over social and political obligations. She argues that the superior position that liberal theory gives to individual freedom rests implicitly on a male model of the self, i.e., as unencumbered by social relations that are not of his "choosing." See Nancy J. Hirschmann, *Rethinking Obligation: A Feminist Method for Political Theory* (Ithaca, N.Y.: Cornell University Press, 1992). See also Robin L. West, "The Difference in Women's Hedonic Lives: A Phenomenological Critique of Feminist Theory," in *At the Boundaries of Law: Feminism and Legal Theory*, ed. Martha Albertson Fineman and Nancy Sweet Thomasden (New York: Routledge, Chapman, and Hall, 1991), pp. 115–34.

were uneasy about the AFDC mothers' maternalist claims and their unwillingness to join with indigent men in organizing for welfare rights.[27] For one thing, the Supreme Court's gender-based decisions in the early 1970s, in which the justices, reacting against traditional gender stereotypes, often interpreted the Equal Protection Clause as requiring government to treat women the *same* as men, did not make maternalism a winnable legal vocabulary. Maternalism, after all, elevated the needs of AFDC mothers as single caretakers over the needs of other citizens.[28] But even if maternalism had been a viable legal discourse, it was *politically* suspect because the women's movement was battling Phyllis Schafley and those on the Republican Right

27. The divisions were further complicated by the fact that the predominantly male and middle-class memberships of the National Urban League, the National Association for the Advancement of Colored People, and the Southern Christian Leadership Conference were averse to becoming associated with AFDC mothers, whom the public held in such low regard. See Jacqueline Jones, *Labor of Love, Labor of Sorrow: Black Women, Work, and the Family from Slavery to the Present* (New York: Vintage Books, 1986), p. 307. Andrew Young, the former Mayor of Atlanta, has explained the opposition by noting that, at least in the South, the Southern Christian Leadership Conference was constantly being branded as Communist. "Everything we did," Young has stated, "was considered Communist, and I think almost to survive we tended to phrase everything in religious terms and to avoid issues that smacked of economic change." Quoted in Nick Kotz and Mary Lynn Kotz, *A Passion for Equality: George A. Wiley and the Movement* (New York: W.W. Norton, 1977), p. 253.

28. In the early 1970s the Supreme Court began to consider whether the Equal Protection category of "suspect classifications" ought to include gender, along with race, alienage, and national origin. The women's movement was moving into high gear, galvanized in part by the proposed Equal Rights Amendment. And because the concept of "suspect classification" seemed so applicable to sex discrimination, women's organizations began to bring lawsuits based on the Fourteenth Amendment's Equal Protection Clause. For a time the Court proved fairly receptive to gender-based Equal Protection arguments, challenging laws that were predicated on gender stereotypes. See, for example, *Reed v. Reed*, 404 U.S. 71 (1971), in which the Supreme Court struck down an Idaho law that favored men over women in the appointment of administrators of estates (as if women were less capable than men of managing financial details); *Frontiero v. Richardson*, 441 U.S. 677 (1973), in which the Court invalidated a law that allowed male members of the armed forces to claim their wives as their dependents for purposes of obtaining increased quarters allowances and medical/dental benefits—*regardless* of whether the wives were actually dependent on their spouses—yet which disallowed female members of the services to claim their husbands as dependents (thus embodying traditional notions of female dependence and male independence); and *Weinberger v. Weisenfield*, 420 U.S. 636 (1975), in which the Court struck down on Equal Protection grounds a law that gave social security benefits to a deceased husband's surviving children and wife but gave benefits only to the surviving children if the wife died (on the assumption that women were primarily homemakers, not wage earners).

who sought to maintain traditional gender roles, such as women's primary identity as mothers.[29] In short, to feminists and the liberal and moderate justices committed to "equal rights" under the Fourteenth Amendment, maternalism was a questionable source of constitutional subsistence rights.[30]

But many AFDC mothers had a very different perspective on issues of gender equity, one based on their own experiences of economic hardship and, in many cases, male abandonment. In good feminist spirit they stressed that unless their particular burdens and needs were privileged, they would lose in the contest for public jobs and other benefits. To these women, *citizenship* rights would in practice become *men's* rights.[31] Besides, for African-American women who had

29. The traditional gender roles espoused by Phyllis Schafley and the Republican Right were particularly ominous for African-American women, given the racial politics of welfare. Especially in the southern states, restrictive welfare eligibility requirements were often based on a romantic (and white) ideal of motherhood to which black women were held in direct opposition. For example, in *King v. Smith*, involving Alabama's "substitute-father" rule, the state's brief defended the law as follows: "Nature places a great privilege and a great responsibility on women. Neither Appellees nor *amici* have shown exactly why saying a judicial 'yes' to cohabitation out of wedlock is going to help a deserted mother, widow, or unwed poor mother or affluent mother, get a husband. . . . Continence and chastity make better mothers and fathers." Quoted in Garbus, *Ready for the Defense*, pp. 187–88. Alabama's attorney, Mary Lee Stapp, insisted that the substitute-father regulation was not racially motivated but simply "antifornification," although her remark at a dinner, held prior to the oral argument before the High Court, with LSP attorney Martin Garbus belied her assertion: "Good Alabama citizens," she told Mr. Garbus, "don't think there should be sex outside of its 'proper' domicile—the wedded couple. You know that they aren't like us." Mr. Garbus responded: "Mrs. Stapp, they can't afford to see a lawyer to get a divorce. There are no black lawyers in Alabama they can turn to to get legal advice or help—and white lawyers don't want any part of them." Mrs. Stapp, in turn, asserted: "It's just wrong. They can do like other folks. What about the Seventh Commandment? . . . Why don't they get married? We don't have the money to support all those children." Ibid., pp. 189–90.

For an examination of the intersection of race and gender conflicts in the War on Poverty see Jill Quadagno, *The Color of Welfare: How Racism Undermined the War on Poverty* (New York: Oxford University Press, 1994), chap. 6.

30. I do not mean to imply that maternalism was a panacea. Precisely because sex differences were too often used to discriminate against women, women's organizations like the National Organization for Women Legal Defense Fund were loath to broach arguments regarding gender differences in the early 1970s, when feminist litigation under the Equal Protection Clause was launched.

31. The charismatic female leader of the National Welfare Rights Organization (i.e., the successor to George Wiley), Johnnie Tillmon, took a feminist perspective on welfare issues and used her acerbic wit to criticize the particularly shabby treatment of poor black women. Although the racial cleavages in welfare politics were deep in the late 1960s and early 1970s, the heightened consciousness among African-American women led to conflict within the black community along gender lines.

been defiled in countless ways, the attachment of entitlements to motherhood was not as politically retrograde as it appeared to white women supporters of the Equal Rights Amendment.[32]

The unavailability of natural law and maternalism as constitutional discourses left the welfare rights movement with nothing to fall back on in the judicial arena. Therefore, their only recourse was to try to press their claims of legal entitlement to welfare in the political arena.

32. For an analysis of the subversive possibilities of AFDC mothers' employing maternal images see Eileen Boris, "The Power of Motherhood: Black and White Activist Women Redefine the 'Political,'" in *Mothers of a New World: Maternalist Politics and the Origins of Welfare States*, ed. Seth Koven and Sonya Michel (New York: Routledge, Inc., 1993), p. 217; and Patricia Hill Collins, *Black Feminist Thought: Knowledge, Consciousness, and the Politics of Empowerment* (New York: Routledge, Chapman and Hall, Inc., 1991), chap. 4. Katha Pollitt observes that men are not the only ones to embrace negative stereotypes of AFDC mothers. For example, in a congressional debate two Republican representatives, Representative Barbara Cubin of Wyoming and Representative John L. Mica of Florida, referred to women on welfare as "wolves" and "alligators." Katha Pollitt, "Devil Women," *The New Yorker Magazine*, February 26 and March 4, 1996, p. 58. Such villification of AFDC mothers as conniving predators of the welfare system usually occurs to justify laws terminating their statutory entitlements.

But such rhetoric often disguises another legislative trend (including one in Florida!) that reflects a different view of many teenage mothers. Recent studies show that in two-thirds of the cases of out-of-wedlock teenage births, the father is twenty years of age or older and that in many instances the age disparity between the teenage girl and the father of her children is significant. Researchers are discovering that, particularly in cases where the age gap between the teenage mother and the father is significant, there is a greater chance that the young girl experienced sexual abuse as a chid and is simply repeating the exploitative pattern that is so familiar to her (although she herself may not perceive her relationship with the man as coercive). Concerned that some older men view teenage girls as easy prey, quickly impregnating and just as quickly abandoning them, several states have passed laws strengthening statutory rape laws. Such efforts are partly the result of resource-hungry states using such laws to deter the behavior as well as to collect child support from the fathers. But they also reflect concern about the vulnerability of teenage girls, who may mistakenly regard an older man as a ticket to greater opportunity. In short, such legislative efforts reveal an abandonment in some jurisdictions of the negative images of welfare mothers as impulsive and hopelessly promiscuous and the replacement with a more sympathetic image of them as vulnerable victims. (Feminists will likely note, however, the familiar dichotomy between "whore" and "virginal victim.")

Yet there is concern raised in some quarters that efforts to criminalize the behavior of indigent men who accidentally or deliberately impregnate a teenage girl will ultimately prove ineffective. Critics contend that many of the boyfriends or male acquaintances of the teenage mothers are also impoverished and may simply be modeling the abusive behavior that was the norm in their own childhoods. In that scenario, counseling and job training rather than imprisonment of the men might be more fruitful remedies to a complex problem. For a discussion of these issues, see Mireya Navarro, "Teenage Mothers Viewed as Abused Prey of Older Men," *New York Times*, May 19, 1996, p. A1.

But given the realities of the political process, the fate of America's poor has been left largely to the "natural sympathy" of elected officials and the people they claim to represent. The state of that sympathy has recently been tested in political conflicts over the Republican Party's Contract with America and the welfare law enacted in 1996.

I began this book with a description of the *DeShaney* case because Chief Justice Rehnquist's opinion for the Supreme Court illustrated a particular pattern of judicial thinking about government's obligations under the Fourteenth Amendment. But the case is also a powerful metaphor for recent developments in welfare politics in the United States. When I present the *DeShaney* case at the start of my civil liberties course, most of my students are shocked by the Court's refusal to hold the state liable under the Fourteenth Amendment for violating Joshua's "right to life." Often, a student will boldly (if erroneously) invoke the Declaration of Independence and declare that United States citizens have a constitutional right to "life, liberty, and the pursuit of happiness." By the end of the course, however, far fewer students would still challenge Chief Justice Rehnquist's majority opinion. Echoing the learned discourse of Supreme Court justices, students rather lament their inability "under the law" to give a battered little boy a substantive right to life and a grieving mother the power under the Constitution to hold the state accountable for her son's abuse at the hands of a violent father. To grant Mrs. DeShaney's claim on behalf of her permanently brain-damaged son, they argue, would amount to a repetition of the *Lochner* Court's errors and would compromise the Court's institutional integrity. When pressed to consider Justice Blackmun's suggestion that "natural sympathy" be accorded a place in judicial reasoning, students coolly respond that "subjective" feelings like sympathy should have no place in impartial constitutional judgments.

And so the *DeShaney* case embodies, in microcosm, the social and ideological plight of welfare recipients during the waning years of the twentieth century. In 1985, deprived of the protection of his natural mother and abandoned by the agents of a well-meaning but ineffectual welfare bureaucracy, Joshua DeShaney was pummeled into permanent disability by his brutal and enraged father. A decade later the dismantling of sixty-two years of national welfare policy has threatened to put America's most deprived citizens in a situation disturbingly analogous to that of young DeShaney. On the one hand, welfare recipients have been largely stripped of the particularistic protections of a maternalist ideology that has historically acknowledged the special needs and vulnerabilities of women and children. On the other hand, they have been denied the universalistic principle of a constitutionally sanctioned "natural right" to subsistence. And so America's AFDC children and their beleaguered advocates have been left to fend for themselves in the pluralist political arena, intermittently exposed to the chill winds of hostile (or indifferent) public opinion and to the punitive discipline (or "tough love") of angry and powerful men. In the aftermath of the decision to transform AFDC from a statutory entitlement into block grants to be administered by the states in accordance with work rules and time limits on assistance, the nation's impoverished children would seem to be at the mercy of an uncertain coalition of liberal Democrats and moderate Republicans drawn together not by any fixed ideological or constitutional principle but by various contingent political considerations.[33] Perhaps some are also motivated by those same intuitive sentiments of "natural sympathy" so glibly dismissed by Chief Justice Rehnquist in *DeShaney*—the Supreme Court's belated epitaph to the welfare rights movement. Whether those sentiments will prove more effective in the political realm than they have in the judicial sphere remains to be seen.

33. As of this writing, welfare reform is likely to continue to be a prominent policy issue as the federal and state governments work out their respective roles in implementing the 1996 welfare law. Interestingly, on two earlier Republican welfare bills President Clinton was moved to reject them after Marian Wright Edelman, president of the Children's Defense Fund, criticized the bills. Using the evocative language of natural law, Ms. Edelman attacked one bill as an affront to "God's mandate to protect the poor and the weak and the young." Quoted in Robert Pear, "Clinton Endorses the Most Radical of Welfare Trials," *New York Times*, May 20, 1996, p. A1. And in protest against Clinton's signing the 1996 welfare law, Peter Edelman, Ms. Edelman's husband, who had served as Clinton's assistant secretary for planning and development, resigned, contending that the law took the fight against poverty in the wrong direction. Notwithstanding the passage of the controversial welfare law, there is likely to be a flood of litigation challenging it on assorted constitutional grounds. See Robert Pear, "State Officials Conclude Some Provisions of the Welfare Law May Be Unconstitutional," p. 30. The litigation will come despite the recent prohibition on Legal Services lawyers to file class-action suits challenging welfare programs. It is too early to know whether President Clinton will have the political will or the clout to soften the harsher parts of the 1996 welfare law in his second presidential term—and in what remains of the twentieth century.

Bibliography

Books

Aaron, Henry J. *Why is Welfare so Hard to Reform?* Washington, D.C.: The Brookings Institution, 1973.

Abbott, Philip, and Levy, Michael, eds. *The Liberal Future in America: Essays in Retrieval.* Westport, Conn: Greenwood Press, 1985.

Abramovitz, Mimi. *Regulating the Lives of Women: Social Welfare Policy from Colonial Times to the Present.* Boston: South End Press, 1988.

Appleby, Joyce. *Capitalism and a New Social Order: The Republican Vision of the 1790s.* New York: New York University Press, 1984.

———. *Liberalism and Republicanism in the Historical Imagination.* Cambridge, Mass.: Harvard University Press, 1992.

Arendt, Hannah. *On Revolution.* New York: Penguin Books, 1965.

Aristotle. *Politics.* In *Aristotles's Politics and Poetics*, translated by Benjamin Jowett and Thomas Twining. New York: Viking Press, 1957.

Ashcraft, Richard. *Revolutionary Politics and Locke's Two Treatises of Government.* Princeton, N.J.: Princeton University Press, 1983.

Ashford, Douglas E. *The Emergence of the Welfare States.* London: Basil Blackwell, 1986.

Auerbach, Jerold. *Unequal Justice: Lawyers and Social Change in Modern America.* New York: Oxford University Press, 1976.

Badger, Anthony J. *The New Deal: The Depression Years, 1933–1940.* New York: Farrar, Straus, and Giroux, 1989.

Baer, Judith A. *Equality Under the Constitution: Reclaiming the Fourteenth Amendment.* Ithaca, N.Y.: Cornell University Press, 1983.

Bailyn, Bernard. *The Ideological Origins of the American Revolution.* Cambridge, Mass: Harvard University Press, 1967.

Bailis, Neil. *Bread or Justice: Grassroots Organizing in the Welfare Rights Movement.* Lexington, Mass.: Lexington Books, 1974.

Bartlett, Katharine T., and Kennedy, Rosanne. *Feminist Legal Theory: Readings in Law and Gender.* Boulder, Colo.: Westview Press, 1991.

Bassin, Donna; Honey, Margaret; and Mahrer Kaplan, Meryle, eds. *Representations of Motherhood.* New Haven, Conn.: Yale University Press, 1994.

Bawden, Lee, ed. *The Social Contract Revisited.* Washington, D.C.: The Urban Institute Press, 1984.

Beiner, Ronald, *Political Judgment.* Chicago: University of Chicago Press, 1983.

Bender, Thomas. *Community and Social Change in America.* New Brunswick, N.J.: Rutgers University Press, 1978.

Benson, Lee. *The Concept of Jacksonian Democracy*. Princeton, N.J.: Princeton University Press, 1961.

Berlin, Isaiah. *Four Essays on Liberty*. New York: Oxford University Press, 1969.

Bestor, Arthur. *Backwoods Utopias: The Sectarian Origins and the Owenite Phases of Communitarian Socialism in America, 1663–1829*, 2d ed. Philadelphia: University of Pennsylvania Press, 1970.

Bikel, Alexander. *The Morality of Consent*. New Haven, Conn: Yale University Press, 1975.

Blasi, Vincent, ed. *The Burger Court: The Counter-Revolution That Wasn't*. New Haven, Conn.: Yale University Press, 1983.

Bowler, Kenneth M. *The Nixon Guaranteed Income Proposal: Substance and Process in Policy Change*. Cambridge, Mass.: Ballinger Publishing Co., 1974.

Bridges, Amy. *A City in the Republic: Antebellum New York and the Origins of Machine Politics*. Ithaca, N.Y.: Cornell University Press, 1984.

Brigham, John. *Constitutional Language: An Interpretation of Judicial Decision Making*. Westport, Conn.: Greenwood Press, 1978.

——— *Property and the Politics of Entitlement*. Philadelphia: Temple University Press, 1990.

Brinkley, Alan. *The End of Reform: New Deal Liberalism in Recession and War*. New York: Alfred A. Knopf, 1995.

Brown, Peter G.; Johnson, Conrad; and Vernier, Paul. *Income Support: Conceptual and Policy Issues*. Totowa, N.J.: Rowman and Littlefield, 1981.

Burke, Vincent J., and Burke, Vee. *Nixon's Good Deed: Welfare Reform*. New York: Columbia University Press, 1974.

Bushman, Richard L., et al., eds. *Uprooted Americans: Essays to Honor Oscar Handlin*. Boston: Little, Brown & Co., 1979.

Byllesby, Langston. *Observations on the Sources and Effects of Unequal Wealth*. New York: Russell and Russell, 1961. First published in 1826.

Byrdsall, Fitzwilliam. *The History of the Loco-Foco or Equal Rights Party: Its Movements, Conventions, and Proceedings*. New York: Burt Franklin, 1967. First published in 1842.

Casper, Jonathan D. *Lawyers Before the Warren Court: Civil Liberties and Civil Rights, 1957–1966*. Urbana: University of Illinois Press, 1972.

Champagne, Anthony, and Harpham, Edward J., eds. *The Attack on the Welfare State*. Prospect Heights, Ill.: Waveland Press, 1984.

Cobb, James C., and Namorato, Michael V., eds. *The New Deal and the South*. Jackson: University Press of Mississippi, 1984.

———. *The Terms of Political Discourse*. 2d ed. Princeton, N.J.: Princeton University Press, 1983.

Cohen, Wilbur; Ball, Robert; Pifer, Alan; and Chisman, Forrest, contributors. *Fiftieth Anniversary Edition: The Report of the Committee on Economic Security of 1935 and Other Basic Documents Relating to the Development of the Social Security Act*. Washington, D.C.: National Conference on Social Welfare, 1985.

Collins, Patricia Hill. *Black Feminist Thought: Knowledge, Consciousness, and the Politics of Empowerment*. New York: Routledge, Chapman and Hall, Inc., 1991.

Commons, John R., et al., eds. *A Documentary History of American Industrial Society*, Vols. 4–7. New York: Russell and Russell, 1958.

Conkin, Paul. *Prophets of Prosperity: America's First Political Economists*. Bloomington: Indiana University Press, 1980.

Danziger, Sheldon H., and Weinberg, Daniel, eds. *Confronting Poverty: Prescriptions for Change*. Cambridge, Mass.: Harvard University Press, 1994.

———. *Fighting Poverty: What Works and What Doesn't*. Cambridge, Mass.: Harvard University Press, 1986.

Davis, Kenneth S. *FDR: Into the the Storm, 1937–1940, A History*. New York: Random House, 1993.

Davis, Martha F. *Brutal Need: Lawyers and the Welfare Rights Movement, 1960–1973*. New Haven, Conn.: Yale University Press, 1993.

Dawley, Alan. *Class and Community: The Industrial Revolution in Lynn*. Cambridge, Mass.: Harvard University Press, 1976.

Derthick, Martha. *The Influence of Federal Grants: Public Assistance in Massachusetts*. Cambridge, Mass.: Harvard University Press, 1970.

———. *Uncontrollable Spending for Social Services Grants*. Washington, D.C.: The Brookings Institution, 1975.

Diggins, John P. *The Lost Soul of American Politics: Virtue, Self-Interest, and the Foundations of Liberalism*. New York: Basic Books, 1984.

Donzelot, J. *The Policing of Families*. London: Hutchinson, 1979.

Dorsen, Norman, ed. *The Rights of Americans: What They Are—What They Should Be*. New York: Random House, 1971.

Ducat, Craig R., and Chase, Harold W. *Constitutional Interpretation*, 4th ed. St. Paul: West Publishing Co., 1988.

Dworkin, Ronald. *Laws Empire*. Cambridge, Mass.: Harvard University Press, 1986.

———. *A Matter of Principle*. Cambridge, Mass.: Harvard University Press, 1985.

———. *Taking Rights Seriously*. Cambridge, Mass.: Harvard University Press, 1980.

Ellwood, David T. *Poor Support: Poverty in the American Family*. New York: Basic Books, 1988.

Elshtain, Jean Bethke. *Democracy on Trial*. New York: Basic Books, 1995.

———. *Public Man, Private Woman: Women in Social and Political Thought*. Princeton, N.J.: Princeton University Press, 1981.

Ely, John Hart. *Democracy and Distrust: A Theory of Judicial Review*. Cambridge, Mass.: Harvard University Press, 1980.

Emerson, Thomas. *The System of Freedom of Expression*. New York: Random House, 1970.

Epstein, Lee, and Kobylka, Joseph F. *The Supreme Court and Legal Change:*

Abortion and the Death Penalty. Chapel Hill: University of North Carolina Press, 1992.

Evans, Peter R.; Reuschemeyer, Dietrich; and Skocpol, Theda, eds. *Bringing the State Back In.* New York: Cambridge University Press, 1985.

Evans, Sara M., and Boyte, Harry C. *Free Spaces: The Sources of Democratic Change in America.* New York: Harper & Row, 1986.

Faler, Paul G. *Mechanics and Manufacturers in the Early Industrial Revolution: Lynn Massachusetts, 1780–1800.* Albany: State University of New York Press, 1981.

Feinberg, Joel. *Rights, Justice, and the Bounds of Liberty: Essays in Social Philosophy.* Princeton, N.J.: Princeton University Press, 1980.

Ferguson Clement, Priscilla. *Welfare and the Poor in the Nineteenth-Century City: Philadelphia, 1800–1854.* Rutherford, N.J.: Fairleigh Dickinson University Press, 1985.

Fineman, Martha Albertson, and Thomadsen, Nancy Sweet, eds. *At the Boundaries of Law: Feminism and Legal Theory.* New York: Routledge, Chapman and Hall, Inc., 1991.

Fischer, David Hackett. *Albion's Seed: Four British Folkways in America.* New York: Oxford University Press, 1989.

Fishkin, James S. *Justice, Equal Opportunity, and the Family.* New Haven, Conn.: Yale University Press, 1983.

Foner, Eric. *Tom Paine and Revolutionary America.* New York: Oxford University Press, 1976.

Foster, James C., and Segers, Mary C., eds. *Elusive Equality: Liberalism, Affirmative Action, and Social Change In America.* Port Washington, N.Y.: National University Publications, 1983.

Fraser, Derek. *The New Poor Law in the Nineteenth Century.* New York: St. Martin's Press, 1976.

Fraser, Steve, and Gerstle, Gary, eds. *The Rise and Fall of the New Deal Order, 1930–1980.* Princeton, N.J.: Princeton University Press, 1989.

Freeman, Michael, and Robertson, David, eds. *The Frontiers of Political Theory: Essays in a Revitalized Discipline.* New York: St. Martin's Press, 1980.

Friedman, Kathi V. *Legitimization of Social Rights and the Western Welfare State: A Weberian Perspective.* Chapel Hill: University of North Carolina Press, 1981.

Frisch, Michael H., and Walkowitz, Daniel J., eds. *Working Class America: Essays on Labor, Commmunity, and American Society.* Urbana: University of Illinois Press, 1983.

Furniss, Norman, and Tilton, Timothy. *The Case for the Welfare State: From Social Security to Social Equality.* Bloomington: Indiana University Press, 1977.

Galloway, Russell. *The Rich and Poor in Supreme Court History.* Greenbrae, Calif.: Paradigm Press, 1982.

Garbus, Martin. *Ready for the Defense.* New York: Farrar, Strauss, and Giroux, 1971.

Garland, David. *Punishment and Welfare: A History of Penal Strategies.* Brookfield, Vt.: Gower Publishing Co., 1985.

Gilbert, Neil. *Capitalism and the Welfare State: Dilemmas of Social Benevolence.* New Haven, Conn.: Yale University Press, 1983.

Gillespie, Ed, and Schellhas, Bob, eds. *Contract with America: The Bold Plan by Rep. Newt Gingrich, Rep. Dick Armey, and the House Republicans to Change the Nation.* New York: Random House, 1994.

Gilligan, Carol. *In a Different Voice: Psychological Theory and Women's Development.* Cambridge, Mass.: Harvard University Press, 1982.

Girth, Marjorie. *Poor People's Lawyers.* Hicksville, N.Y.: Exposition Press, 1976.

Glendon, Mary Ann. *Rights Talk: The Impoverishment of Political Discourse.* New York: The Free Press, 1991.

Goldman, Sheldon, and Jahnige, Thomas P., eds. *The Federal Courts as a Political System.* 2d ed. New York: Harper & Row, 1976.

Goodin, Robert E. *Protecting the Vulnerable: A Reanalysis of Our Social Responsibilities.* Chicago: University of Chicago Press, 1985.

Gordon, Colin. *New Deals: Business, Labor, and Politics in America, 1920–1935.* Cambridge, Eng.: Cambridge University Press, 1994.

Gordon, Linda. *Pitied But Not Entitled: Single Mothers and the History of Welfare, 1890–1935.* New York: The Free Press, 1994.

———. ed. *Women, Welfare, and the State.* Madison: University of Wisconsin Press, 1990.

Grob, Gerald. *Workers and Utopia: A Study of Ideological Conflict in the American Labor Movement, 1865-1900.* Chicago: Quadrangle Books, 1961.

Gunther, Gerald. *Cases and Materials on Constitutional Law.* 10th ed. Mineola, N.Y.: The Foundation Press, 1980.

Gutman, Herbert. *Work, Culture, and Society in Industrializing America: Essays in American Working-Class and Social History.* New York: Vintage Books, 1977.

Gutmann, Amy, ed. *Democracy and the Welfare State.* Princeton, N.J.: Princeton University Press, 1988.

———. *Liberal Equality.* New York: Cambridge University Press, 1980.

Handler, Joel F. *Law and the Search for Community.* Philadelphia: University of Pennsylvania Press, 1990.

———. *Social Movements and the Legal System: A Theory of Law Reform and Social Change.* New York: Academic Press, 1978.

Handler, Joel F., and Hollingsworth, Ellen Jane. *Lawyers and the Pursuit of Legal Rights.* New York: Academic Press, 1978.

———. The "Deserving Poor." Chicago: Markham Publishing Co., 1971.

Hanson, Russell L. *The Democratic Imagination in America: Conversations with our Past.* Princeton, N.J.: Princeton University Press, 1985.

Harrington, Mona. *The Dream of Deliverance in American Politics.* New York: Alfred A. Knopf, 1986.

Harrison, J.F.C. *Robert Owen and the Owenites in Britain and America: The Quest for the New Moral Order*. London: Routledge and Kegan Paul, 1969.

Hartz, Louis. *The Liberal Tradition in America*. New York: Harcourt, Brace and World, 1955.

Hertz, Susan Handley. *The Welfare Mothers Movement: A Decade of Change for Poor Women?* Lanham, Md.: University Press of America, 1981.

Higham, John, and Conkin, Paul K., eds. *The New American Intellectual History*. Baltimore: The Johns Hopkins University Press, 1979.

Himmelfarb, Gertrude. *The Idea of Poverty*. New York: Alfred A. Knopf, 1983.

Hirschmann, Nancy J. *Rethinking Obligation: A Feminist Method for Political Theory*. Ithaca, N.Y.: Cornell University Press, 1992.

Hirshmann, Albert O. *The Passions and the Interests: Political Arguments for Capitalism Before Its Triumph*. Princeton, N.J.: Princeton University Press, 1977.

Hochschild, Jennifer L. *The New American Dilemma: School Desegregation and Liberal Democracy*. New Haven, Conn.: Yale University Press, 1984.

———. *What's Fair?: American Beliefs About Distributive Justice*. Cambridge, Mass.: Harvard University Press, 1981.

Hont, Istvan, and Ignatieff, Michael, eds. *Wealth and Virtue: The Shaping of Political Economy in the Scottish Enlightenment*. New York: Cambridge University Press, 1983.

Horwitz, Morton J. *The Transformation of American Law, 1780–1860*. Cambridge, Mass.: Harvard University Press, 1977.

Howe, Irving, ed. *Beyond the Welfare State*. New York: Schocken Books, 1982.

Hugins, Walter. *Jacksonian Democracy and the Working Class*. Stanford, Calif.: Stanford University Press, 1960.

Ignatieff, Michael. *A Just Measure of Pain: The Penitentiary in the Industrial Revolution, 1750–1850*. New York: Pantheon Books, 1978.

———. *The Needs of Strangers: An Essay on Privacy, Solidarity, and the Politics of Being Human*. New York: Viking Penguin, 1984.

Irons, Peter. *New Deal Lawyers*. Princeton, N.J.: Princeton University Press, 1982.

Irons, Peter, and Guitton, Stephanie, eds. *May It Please the Court: The Most Significant Oral Arguments Made Before the Supreme Court*. New York: The New Press, 1993.

Jackman, Larry R., and Johnson, William A. *Protest By the Poor: The Welfare Rights Movement in New York City*. Lexington, Mass.: D.C. Heath & Co., 1974.

Jackman, Mary R., and Jackman, Robert W. *Class Awareness in the United States*. Berkeley and Los Angeles: University of California Press, 1983.

Jacobsohn, Gary J. *The Supreme Court and the Decline of Constitutional Aspiration*. Totowa, N.J.: Rowman and Littlefield, 1986.

Johnson, Earl, Jr. *Justice and Reform: The Formative Years of the Legal Services Program*. New York: Russell Sage Foundation, 1974.

Jones, Jacqueline. *The Dispossessed: America's Underclasses from the Civil War to the Present.* New York: Basic Books, 1992.

————. *Labor of Love, Labor of Sorrow: Black Women, Work and the Family from Slavery to the Present.* New York: Vintage Books, 1986.

Kairys, David, ed. *The Politics of Law: A Progressive Critique.* New York: Pantheon Books, 1982.

Katz, Jack. *Poor People's Lawyers in Transition.* New Brunswick, N.J.: Rutgers University Press, 1982.

Katz, Michael B. *In the Shadow of the Poorhouse: A Social History of Welfare in America.* New York: Basic Books, 1986.

Kaus, Mickey, *The End of Equality.* New York: Basic Books, 1992.

Kelman, Mark. *A Guide to Critical Legal Studies.* Cambridge, Mass.: Harvard University Press, 1987.

Kerber, Linda K. *Women of the Republic: Intellect and Ideology in Revolutionary America.* Chapel Hill: University of North Carolina Press, 1980.

Kessler, Mark. *Legal Services for the Poor: A Comparative and Contemporary Analysis of Interorganizational Politics.* Westport, Conn.: Greenwood Press, 1987.

Keynes, Edward. *Liberty, Property, and Privacy: Toward a Jurisprudence of Substantive Due Process.* University Park: Pennsylvania State University Press, 1996.

Kipnis, Kenneth, and Meyers, Diana T., eds. *Economic Justice: Private Rights and Public Responsibilities.* Totowa, N.J.: Rowman and Allanheld, 1985.

Kotz, Nick, and Kotz, Mary Lynn. *A Passion for Equality: George A. Wiley and the Movement.* New York: W.W. Norton, 1977.

Koven, Seth, and Michel, Sonya, eds. *Mothers of a New World: Maternalist Politics and the Origins of Welfare States.* New York: Routledge, Inc., 1993.

Kurland, Philip B., and Casper, Gerhard, eds. *Landmark Briefs and Arguments of the Supreme Court of the United States: Constitutional Law.* 234 vols. Arlington, Va., and Bethesda, Md.: University Publications of America, 1975–1995.

Ladd-Taylor, Molly. *Mother-Work: Women, Child Welfare, and the State, 1890–1930.* Urbana: University of Illinois Press, 1994.

La France, Arthur B. *Welfare Law: Structure and Entitlement.* St. Paul: West Publishing Co., 1979.

Lane, Robert E. *Political Ideology: Why the American Common Man Believes What He Does.* New York: The Free Press, 1962.

Lasch, Christopher. *The True and Only Heaven: Progress and Its Critics.* New York: W.W. Norton, 1991.

Laslett, Peter, and Runciman, W.B., eds. *Philosophy, Politics, and Society*, 2d ser. New York: Barnes and Noble, 1962.

Lawrence, Susan E. *The Poor in Court: The Legal Services Program and Supreme Court Decision Making.* Princeton, N.J.: Princeton University Press, 1990.

Leinesch, Michael. *New Order of the Ages: Time, the Constitution, and the Making of Modern Political Thought*. Princeton, N.J.: Princeton University Press, 1988.

Leman, Christopher. *The Collapse of Welfare Reform: Political Institutions, Policy, and the Poor in Canada and the United States*. Cambridge, Mass.: MIT Press, 1980.

Leuchtenburg, William E. *Franklin D. Roosevelt and the New Deal, 1932–1940*. New York: Harper & Row, 1963.

Levy, Frank. *The Logic of Welfare Reform*. Washington, D.C.: The Urban Institute Press, 1980.

Locke, John. *The Two Treatises of Government*. Introduction and Notes by Peter Laslett. New York: New American Library, 1965.

Lowi, Theodore. *The End of Liberalism*. 2d ed. New York: W.W. Norton, 1979.

Lubove, Roy. *The Struggle for Social Security, 1900–1935*. Cambridge, Mass.: Harvard University Press, 1968.

Lucash, Frank S., ed. *Justice and Equality Here and Now*. Ithaca, N.Y.: Cornell University Press, 1986.

Lustig, Jeffrey R. *Corporate Liberalism: The Origins of Modern American Political Theory, 1890–1920*. Berkeley and Los Angeles: University of California Press, 1982.

MacIntyre, Alisdair. *After Virtue*. Notre Dame, Ind.: University of Notre Dame Press, 1981.

MacLean, Douglas, and Mills, Claudia, eds. *Liberalism Reconsidered*. Totowa, N.J.: Rowman and Allanheld Publishers, 1983.

MacPherson, C.B. *The Political Theory of Possessive Individualism: Hobbes to Locke*. New York: Oxford University Press, 1962.

Mansbridge, Jane. *Why We Lost the ERA*. Chicago: University of Chicago Press, 1986.

Marris, Peter, and Rein, Martin. *Dilemmas of Social Reform: Poverty and Community Action in the U.S.* 2d ed. Chicago: Aldine Publishing Co., 1973.

Marshall, T.H. *Class, Citizenship, and Social Development*. Garden City, N.Y.: Doubleday & Co., 1964.

Martin, George T., Jr., and Mayer, Zald N., eds. *Social Welfare in Society*. New York: Columbia University Press, 1981.

McCann, Michael W. *Rights at Work: Pay Equity and the Politics of Legal Mobilization*. Chicago: University of Chicago Press, 1994.

McCann, Michael W., and Houseman, Gerald L. *Judging the Constitution: Critical Essays on Judicial Lawmaking*. Boston, Mass.: Scott, Foresman and Co., 1989.

McClosky, Herbert, and Zaller, John. *The American Ethos: Public Attitudes Towards Capitalism and Democracy*. Cambridge, Mass.: Harvard University Press, 1984.

McJimsey, George. *Harry Hopkins: Ally of the Poor, Defender of Democracy*. Cambridge, Mass.: Harvard University Press, 1987.

Mead, Lawrence M. *Beyond Entitlement: The Social Obligations of Citizenship*. New York: The Free Press, 1985.

Meiklejohn, Alexander. *Free Speech and Its Relation to Self-Government*. New York: Harper and Row, 1948.

———. *Political Freedom*. New York: Harper Brothers, 1960.

Melnick, R. Shep. *Reading Between the Lines: Interpreting Welfare Rights*. Washington, D.C.: The Brookings Institution, 1994.

———. *Regulation and the Courts: The Case of the Clean Air Act*. Washington, D.C.: The Brookings Institution, 1983.

Merry, Sally Engle. *Getting Justice and Getting Even: Legal Consciousness Among Working-Class Americans*. Chicago: University of Chicago Press, 1990.

Meyers, Marvin. *The Jacksonian Persuasion: Politics and Belief*. Stanford, Calif.: Stanford University Press, 1960.

Milkis, Sydney M. *The President and the Parties: The Transformation of the American Party System Since the New Deal*. New York: Oxford University Press, 1993.

Miller, David. *Social Justice*. Oxford: Clarendon Press, 1976.

Mohl, Raymond A. *Poverty in New York, 1783–1825*. New York: Oxford University Press, 1971.

Mollat, Michael. *The Poor in the Middle Ages: An Essay in Social History*. New Haven, Conn.: Yale University Press, 1986.

Monkkonen, Eric H. *The Dangerous Classes: Crime and Poverty in Columbus, Ohio, 1860–1885*. Cambridge, Mass.: Harvard University Press, 1985.

Montgomery, David. *Beyond Equality: Labor and the Radical Republicans, 1862–1872*. New York: Alfred A. Knopf, 1967.

Moon, Donald, ed. *Responsibility, Rights, and Welfare: Essays on the Welfare State*. Boulder, Colo.: Westview Press, 1988.

Morris, Norbal, and Tonry, Michael, eds. *Crime and Justice: An Annual Review of Research*. Vol. 2. Chicago: University of Chicago Press, 1980.

Moynihan, Daniel Patrick. *The Politics of a Guaranteed Income*. New York: Random House, 1973.

Murphy, Walter F. *Elements of Judicial Strategy*. Chicago: University of Chicago Press, 1964.

Nelson, Joel I. *Economic Inequality: Conflict Without Change*. New York: Columbia University Press, 1982.

Nelson, William. *The Americanization of the Common Law*. New York: Cambridge University Press, 1975.

Nightingale, Carl Husemoller. *On the Edge: A History of Poor Black Children and Their American Dreams*. New York: Basic Books, 1993.

Norton, Mary Beth. *Liberty's Daughters: The Revolutionary Experience of American Women, 1750–1800*. Boston: Little, Brown & Co., 1980.

Okin, Susan Moller. *Justice, Gender, and the Family*. New York: Basic Books, 1989.

Osberg, Lars. *Economic Inequality in the United States*. Armonk: M.E. Sharpe, 1984.

Owen, Robert. *The Book of the New Moral World*. New York: Augustus M. Kelly Publishers, 1970.

Pagden, Anthony, ed. *The Languages of Early-Modern Europe*. New York: Cambridge University Press, 1987.

Page, Benjamin I. *Who Gets What from Government?* Berkeley and Los Angeles: University of California Press, 1983.

Paine, Thomas. *The Rights of Man, Part Second*. In *The Complete Writings of Thomas Paine*, edited by Philip S. Foner. Vol. 1. New York: Citadel Press, 1945.

————. *The Writings of Thomas Paine*. Edited by M.D. Conway. New York: AMS Press, 1967.

Patterson, James. *America's Struggle Against Poverty, 1900–1980*. Cambridge, Mass.: Harvard University Press, 1981.

————. *America's Struggle Against Poverty, 1900–1994*. Cambridge, Mass.: Harvard University Press, 1994.

Perkins, Frances. *The Roosevelt I Knew*. New York: Viking Press, 1946.

Pessen, Edward. *Most Uncommon Jacksonians: The Radical Leaders of the Early Labor Movement*. Albany: State University of New York Press, 1967.

————. *Riches, Class, and Power Before the Civil War*. Lexington, Mass.: D.C. Heath & Co., 1973.

Peterson, Paul E., and Rom, Mark C. *Welfare Magnets: A New Case for a National Standard*. Washington, D.C.: The Brookings Institution, 1990.

Piven, Frances Fox, and Cloward, Richard A. *Poor People's Movements: Why They Succeed, How They Fail*. New York: Vintage Books, 1977.

————. *Regulating the Poor: The Functions of Public Welfare*. New York: Pantheon Books, 1971.

Plotnick, Robert D.; and Skidmore, Felicity. *Progress Against Poverty: A Review of the 1964–1974 Decade*. New York: Academic Press, 1975.

Pocock, J.G.A. *The Machiavellian Moment: Florentine Political Thought and the Atlantic Republican Tradition*. Princeton, N.J.: Princeton University Press, 1975.

Polakow, Valerie. *Lives on the Edge: Single Mothers and Their Children in the Other America*. Chicago: University of Chicago Press, 1993.

Pole, J.R. *The Pursuit of Equality in America*. New York: Oxford University Press, 1978.

Quadagno, Jill. *The Color of Welfare: How Racism Undermined the War on Poverty*. New York: Oxford University Press, 1994.

Rae, Douglas, et al., eds. *Equalities*. Cambridge, Mass.: Harvard University Press, 1981.

Rawls, John. *A Theory of Justice*. Cambridge, Mass.: Harvard University Press, 1971.

Richards, David A.J. *Toleration and the Constitution*. New York: Oxford University Press, 1986.

Rochefort, David A. *American Social Welfare Policy: Dynamics of Formulation and Change*. Boulder, Colo.: Westview Press, 1986.

Rohde, David W., and Spaeth, Harold J. *Supreme Court Decision Making*. San Francisco: W.H. Freeman, 1976.

Rothman, David J., advisory ed. *The Jacksonians on the Poor: Collected Pamphlets*. New York: Arno Press & The New York Times, 1971.

Rousseau, Jean-Jacques. *The Social Contract and Discourses*. Translated and introduced by G.D.H. Cole. London: J. M. Dent and Sons, Ltd., 1973.

Sandel, Michael J., ed. *Liberalism and Its Critics*. New York: New York University Press, 1984.

———. *Liberalism and the Limits of Justice*. New York: Cambridge University Press, 1982.

Sarat, Austin, and Kearns, Thomas R., eds. *The Fate of Law*. Ann Arbor: University of Michigan Press, 1993.

Scheingold, Stuart A. *The Politics of Rights: Lawyers, Public Policy, and Political Change*. New Haven, Conn.: Yale University Press, 1974.

Schlesinger, Arthur M., Jr. *The Age of Roosevelt: The Coming of the New Deal*. New York: Houghton Mifflin, 1959.

Schubert, Glendon A. *Human Jurisprudence: Public Law as Political Science*. Honolulu: University of Hawaii Press, 1975.

———. *The Judicial Mind Revisited: Psychometric Analysis of Supreme Court Ideology*. New York: Oxford University Press, 1974.

———, ed. *Judicial Decision Making*. New York: The Free Press, 1963.

Schwartz, Bernard. *The Unpublished Opinions of the Warren Court*. New York: Oxford University Press, 1985.

Schwartz, Robert M. *Policing the Poor in Eighteenth-Century France*. Chapel Hill: University of North Carolina Press, 1988.

Shapiro, Ian. *The Evolution of Rights in Liberal Theory*. New York: Cambridge University Press, 1986.

Shapiro, Martin M. *Law and Politics in the Supreme Court*. New York: The Free Press, 1964.

———. *Who Guards the Guardians?* Athens: University of Georgia Press, 1988.

Sidel, Ruth. *Women and Children Last: The Plight of Poor Women in Affluent America*. New York: Viking Press, 1986.

Sindler, Allan, ed. *Policy and Politics in America*. Boston: Little, Brown & Co., 1973.

Skocpol, Theda. *Protecting Soldiers and Mothers: The Political Origins of Social Policy in the United States*. Cambridge, Mass.: Harvard University Press, 1992.

Smith, Adam. *An Inquiry into the Nature and Causes of the Wealth of Nations*. Edited by Edward Cannan. New York: Random House, 1937.

———. *Lectures on Jurisprudence*. Edited by R.L. Meek, et al. Oxford: Oxford University Press, 1978.

Smith, Reginald Heber. *Justice and the Poor*. New York: Carnegie Foundation, 1919.

Smith, Rogers M. *Liberalism and American Constitutional Law*. Cambridge, Mass.: Harvard University Press, 1985.

Solo, Robert A., and Anderson, Charles W., eds. *Value Judgement and Income Distribution*. New York: Praeger Publishers, 1981.

Spaeth, Harold J. *The Warren Court*. San Francisco: Chandler Publishing Co., 1966.

Spangler, Eve. *Lawyers for Hire: Salaried Professionals at Work*. New Haven, Conn.: Yale University Press, 1986.

Spragens, Thomas A. *The Irony of Liberal Reason*. Chicago: University of Chicago Press, 1981.

Springborg, Patricia. *The Problem of Human Needs and the Critique of Civilization*. London: George Allen and Unwin, 1981.

Stadum, Beverly. *Poor Women and Their Families: Hard-Working Charity Cases, 1900–1930*. Albany: State University of New York Press, 1992.

Stansell, Christine. *City of Women: Sex and Class in New York, 1789–1860*. Urbana: University of Illinois Press, 1987.

Steiner, Gilbert Y. *The State of Welfare*. Washington, D.C.: The Brookings Institution, 1984.

Street, David Martin; George T., Jr.; and Gordon, Laura Kramer. *The Welfare Industry: Functionaries and Recipients in Public Aid*. Beverly Hills, Calif.: Sage Publications, 1979.

Stumpf, Harry. *Community Politics and Legal Services: The Other Side of the Law*. Beverly Hills, Calif.: Sage Publications, 1975.

Sugarman, David, ed. *Legality, Ideology, and the State*. New York: Academic Press, 1983.

Teuber, Gunther, ed. *Dilemmas of Law in the Welfare State*. Berlin: Walter de Gruyter, 1988.

Thompson, E.P. *Whigs and Hunters: The Origin of the Black Act*. New York: Pantheon Books, 1975.

Tomlins, Christopher L. *Law, Labor, and Ideology in the Early American Republic*. New York: Cambridge University Press, 1993.

Tribe, Laurence H. *American Constitutional Law*. Mineola, N.Y.: The Foundation Press, 1978.

Tuck, Richard. *Natural Rights Theories: Their Origin and Development*. New York: Cambridge University Press, 1979.

Turner, Bryan S. *Equality*. London: Tavistock Publications Limited, 1986.

Ulmer, Sidney, ed. *Courts, Law, and the Judicial Process*. New York: The Free Press, 1981.

Unger, Roberto Mangabeira. *Knowledge and Politics*. New York: Basic Books, 1975.

Verba, Sidney, and Orren, Gary R. *Equality in America: The View from the Top*. Cambridge, Mass.: Harvard University Press, 1985.

Walker, Samuel. *Popular Justice: A History of American Criminal Justice*. New York: Oxford University Press, 1980.

Walzer, Michael. *Interpretation and Social Criticism*. Cambridge, Mass.: Harvard University Press, 1987.

———. *Spheres of Justice: A Defense of Pluralism and Equality*. New York: Basic Books, 1983.

Ware, Norman. *The Industrial Workers, 1840–1860.* Chicago and New York: Quadrangle Books and The New York Times, 1964.

Ware, Susan. *Beyond Suffrage: Women in the New Deal.* Cambridge, Mass.: Harvard University Press, 1981.

Weir, Margaret; Orloff, Ann Shola; and Skocpol, Theda, eds. *The Politics of Social Policy in the United States.* Princeton, N.J.: Princeton University Press, 1988.

West, Guida. *The National Welfare Rights Movement: The Social Protest of Poor Women.* New York: Praeger Publishers, 1981.

Wilensky, Harold L., and Lebeaux, Charles N. *Industrial Society and Social Welfare.* New York: Russell Sage Foundation, 1958.

Wilentz, Sean. *Chants Democratic: New York City and the Rise of the American Working Class, 1788–1850.* New York: Oxford University Press, 1984.

Wills, Gary. *Explaining America: The Federalist.* New York: Penguin Books, 1981.

Wisner, Elizabeth. *Social Welfare in the South: From Colonial Times to World War I.* Baton Rouge: Louisiana State University Press, 1970.

Wood, Gordon S. *The Creation of the American Republic, 1776–1787.* New York: W.W. Norton, 1979.

———. *The Radicalization of the American Revolution.* New York: Alfred A. Knopf, 1992.

Young, Iris Marion. *Justice and the Politics of Difference.* Princeton, N.J.: Princeton University Press, 1990.

Articles, Reports, Selected Government Documents and Unpublished Papers.

Abramson, Jeffrey B. "Review—Ronald Dworkin and the Convergence of Law and Political Philosophy." 65 *Texas Law Review* 1201 (May 1987).

Abramson, Jeffrey, and Bussiere, Elizabeth. "Free Speech and Free Press: A Communitarian Perspective." In *New Communitarian Thinking: Persons, Virtues, Institutions, and Communities,* edited by Amitai Etzioni. Charlottesville: University Press of Virginia, 1995. Pp. 218–32.

Allett, John. "New Liberalism and the New Property Doctrine: Welfare Rights as Property Rights." *Polity* 20 (Fall 1987): 57–79.

Altman, Andrew. "Legal Realism, Critical Legal Studies, and Dworkin." *Philosophy and Public Affairs* 15 (Summer 1986): 205–35.

Amanta, Edwin, and Skocpol, Theda. "Redefining the New Deal: World War II and the Revolution of Social Provision in the United States." In *The Politics of Social Policy in the United States,* edited by Margaret Weir, Ann Shola Orloff, and Theda Skocpol. Princeton, N.J.: Princeton University Press, 1988. Pp. 81–122.

American Bar Association. *ABA Code of Professional Ethics.* Chicago: American Bar Association.

Amott, Teresa L. "Black Women and AFDC: Making Entitlement Out of Necessity." In *Women, the State, and Welfare*, edited by Linda Gordon. Madison: University of Wisconsin Press, 1990. Pp. 280–98.

Arendt, Hannah. "The Revolutionary Tradition and Its Lost Treasure." In *Liberalism and Its Critics*, edited by Michael J. Sandel. New York: New York University Press, 1984. Pp. 239–63.

Baker, C. Edwin. "Neutrality, Process, and Rationality: Flawed Interpretations of Equal Protection." 58 *Texas Law Review* 1029 (August 1980).

Ball, Robert M. "The 1939 Amendments to the Social Security Act and What Followed." In *Fiftieth Anniversary Edition: The Report of the Committee on Economic Security of 1935 and Other Documents Relating to the Development of the Social Security Act*, with essays by Wilbur Cohen and Robert Ball; Foreword by Alan Pifer and Forrest Chisman. Washington, D.C.: National Conference on Social Welfare, 1985. Pp. 159–72.

Bane, Mary Jo. "Politics and the Feminization of Poverty." In *The Politics of Social Policy in the United States*, edited by Margaret Weir, Ann Shola Orloff, and Theda Skocpol, Princeton, N.J.: Princeton University Press, 1988. Pp. 381–96.

Beer, John Low. "Perspectives on Social Inequalities." 84 *Yale Law Journal* 1586 (1975).

Beer, Samuel. "Liberalism and the National Idea." *The Public Interest* (Fall 1976), pp. 70–82.

Beitz, Charles. "Procedural Equality in Democratic Theory: A Preliminary Examination." In *Liberal Democracy: Nomos XXV*, edited by J. Roland Pennock and John W. Chapman. New York: New York University Press, 1983. Pp. 69–91.

Benhabib, Seyla. "The Generalized Other and the Concrete Other: The Kohlberg-Gilligan Controversy." In *Feminism as Critique*, edited by Seyla Benhabib and Drucilla Cornell. Minneapolis: University of Minnesota Press, 1987. Pp. 77–95.

Berthoff, Rowland. "Independence and Attachment, Virtue and Interest: From Republican Citizen to Free Enterpriser, 1787–1837." In *Uprooted Americans: Essays to Honor Oscar Handlin*, edited by Richard L. Bushman et al. Boston: Little, Brown & Co., 1979. Pp. 99–124.

Binion, Gayle. "The Disadvantaged Before the Burger Court: The Newest Unequal Protection." 4 *Law and Policy Quarterly* 37 (January 1982).

Blathchly, Cornelius. "Some Causes of Popular Poverty." Printed in *The Pleasures of Contemplation*, by Thomas Branagan. Philadelphia: Eastwick and Stacy, 1817.

Bloch, Frank S. "Cooperative Federalism and the Role of Litigation in the Development of Federal AFDC Eligibility Policy." 1979 *Wisconsin Law Review* 1 (1979).

Blumenthal, Sidney. "The New Something." *The New Yorker Magazine*, May 27, 1996, p. 31.

Boris, Eileen. "The Power of Motherhood: Black and White Activist Women

Redefine the 'Political.' " In *Mothers of a New World: Maternalist Politics and the Origins of Welfare States*, edited by Seth Koven and Sonya Michel. New York: Routledge, Inc., 1993. Pp. 213–45.

Brennan, William J., Jr. "What the Constitution Requires." *New York Times,* April 28, 1996, sec. 4, p. 13.

Brest, Paul. "In Defense of the Anti-Discrimination Principle." 90 *Harvard Law Review* 1 (November 1976).

———. "The Fundamental Rights Controversy: The Essential Contradictions of Normative Constitutional Scholarship." 90 *Yale Law Journal* 1063 (1981).

Brigham, John. "Means Discrimination: An Investigation into the Ideology of Constitutional Equality." 8 *Law and Policy Quarterly* 169 (April 1986).

Brinkley, Alan. "The New Deal and Southern Politics." In *The New Deal and the South*, edited by James C. Cobb and Michael V. Namorato. Jackson: University Press of Mississippi, 1984. Pp. 97–116.

Bussiere, Elizabeth. "The Failure of Constitutional Welfare Rights in the Warren Court." *Political Science Quarterly* 109 (Spring 1994): 105–31.

Cady, Francis C. "The Future of Group Legal Services." 55 *ABA Journal* 420 (May 1969).

Cahn, Edgar S., and Cahn, Jean C. "The War on Poverty: A Civilian Perspective." 73 *Yale Law Review* 1317 (July 1964).

Cain, Maureen. "Gramsci, the State, and the Place of Law." In *Legality, Ideology, and the State*, edited by David Sugarman. New York: Academic Press, 1983. Pp. 95–118.

Carlin, Jerome E.; Howard, Jan; and Messinger, Sheldon L. "Civil Justice and the Poor: Issues for Sociological Research." 1 *Law and Society Review* 9 (November 1966).

Champagne, Anthony. "Legal Services: A Program in Need of Assistance." In *The Attack on the Welfare State*, edited by Anthony Champagne and Edward J. Harpham. Prospect Heights, Ill.: Waveland Press, 1984. Pp. 131–48.

Charvet, John. "The Idea of Equality as a Substantive Principle." *Political Studies* 17 (1969): 1–13.

Clune, William H., III. "Wealth Discriminations Under the Fourteenth Amendment." 1975 *The Supreme Court Review* 289 (1975).

Cohen, Wilbur J. "The Social Security Act of 1935: Reflections Fifty Years Later." In *Fiftieth Anniversary Edition: The Report of the Committee on Economic Security of 1935 and Other Basic Documents Relating to the Development of the Social Security Act*, with essays by Wilbur Cohen and Robert Ball; Foreword by Alan Pifer and Forrest Chisman. Washington, D.C.: National Conference on Social Welfare, 1985. Pp. 5–15.

Connolly, William. "The Dilemma of Legitimacy." In *Legitimacy and the State*, edited by William Connolly. New York: New York University Press, 1984. Pp. 222–49.

———. "Legitimacy in the Modern State." In *Legitimacy and the State*, edited by William Connolly. New York: New York University Press, 1984. Pp. 1–19.

Cox, Archibald. "Constitutional Adjudication and the Promotion of Human Rights." 80 *Harvard Law Review* 91 (1966–67).

Cramton, Roger C. "Promise and Reality in Legal Services." 61 *Cornell Law Review* 670 (1976).

Danelski, David J. "Law from a Political Perspective." *Western Political Quarterly* 36 (December 1983): 548–51.

Daniels, Norman. "Conflicting Objectives and the Priorities Problem." In *Income Support: Conceptual and Policy Issues*, edited by Peter G. Brown, Conrad Johnson, and Paul Vernier. Totowa, N.J.: Rowman and Littlefield, 1981. Pp. 147–64.

Danziger, Sheldon H., and Gottschalk, Peter. "Wanted: Jobs of Last Resort." *New York Times*, February 23, 1996, A31.

Danziger, Sheldon H.; Haveman, Robert H.; and Plotnick, Robert D. "Antipoverty Policy: Effects on the Poor and Nonpoor." In *Fighting Poverty: What Works and What Doesn't*, edited by Sheldon H. Danziger and Daniel H. Weinberg. Cambridge, Mass.: Harvard University Press, 1987. Pp. 50–57.

Danziger, Sheldon H., and Plotnick, Robert. "Can Welfare Reform Eliminate Poverty?" *Social Services Review* 53 (June 1979): 245–60.

David, Laura F. "Public Attitudes Toward Welfare Allocation." Paper presented at the American Political Science Association, Washington, D.C. April 28, 1986.

Davidson, Kenneth M. "Welfare Cases and the 'New Majority': Constitutional Theory and Practice." 10 *Harvard Civil Rights-Civil Liberties Law Review* 513 (Summer 1975).

Dawley, Alan, and Faler, Paul. "Working-Class Culture and Politics in the Industrial Revolution: Sources of Loyalism and Rebellion." *Journal of Social History* 9 (Summer 1976): 466–80.

Dienes, C. Thomas. "To Feed the Hungry: Judicial Retrenchment in Welfare Adjudication." 58 *California Law Review* 555 (May 1970).

Dooley, John A., and Houseman, Alan W. "Legal Services History." Washington, D.C.: Center for Law and Social Policy, November 1985.

Doolittle, Fred C. "State-Imposed Nonfinancial Eligibility Conditions in AFDC: Confusions in Supreme Court Decisions and a Need for Congressional Clarification." 19 *Harvard Journal of Legislation* 1 (1982).

Fineman, Martha L. Albertson "Implementing Equality: Ideology, Contradiction, and Social Change." 1983 *Wisconsin Law Review* 789 (1983).

Fineman, Ted. "OEO Legal Service Programs and the Pursuit of Social Change: The Relationship Between Program Ideology and Program Performance." 1971 *Wisconsin Law Review* 1001 (1971).

Fiss, Owen M. "Groups and the Equal Protection Clause." *Philosophy and Public Affairs* 5 (Winter 1976): 107–77.

Flathman, Richard E. "Rights, Needs, and Liberalism: A Comment on Bay." *Political Theory* 8 (August 1980): 319–30.

Foster, James C. "The Fundamental Continuity of Proprietary Equality in America." In *Elusive Equality: Liberalism, Affirmative Action, and Social Change in America*, edited by James C. Foster and Mary C. Segers. Port Washington, N.Y.: National University Publications, 1983. Pp. 23–41.

Fraser, Nancy. "Struggle over Needs: Outline of a Socialist Feminist Critical Theory of Late-Capitalist Political Culture." In *Women, the State, and Welfare*, edited by Linda Gordon. Madison: University of Wisconsin Press, 1990. Pp. 199–225.

Funston, Richard. "The Supreme Court in Critical Elections." *American Political Science Review* 69 (September 1979): 795–811.

Galanter, Marc. "Why the 'Haves' Come Out Ahead: Speculations on the Limits of Legal Change." 9 *Law and Society Review* 95 (1974).

Gelb, Joyce, and Sardell, Alice. "Organizing the Poor: A Brief Analysis of the Politics of the Welfare Rights Movement." *Policy Studies Journal* 3 (Summer 1975): 346–54.

George, Warren E. "Development of the Legal Services Corporation." 61 *Cornell Law Review* 681 (1976).

Glenn, Gary D. "Inalienable Rights and Positive Government in the Modern World." *Journal of Politics* 41 (November 1979): 1057–80.

Goldman, Sheldon. "Voting Behavior on the U.S. Court of Appeals Revisited." *American Political Science Review* 69 (June 1975): 491–506.

Goodman, Paul. "The Politics of Industrialism: Massachusetts, 1830–1870." In *Uprooted Americans: Essays to Honor Oscar Handlin*, edited by Richard L. Bushman et al. Boston: Little, Brown & Co., 1979. Pp. 163–207.

Gordon, Linda. "The New Feminist Scholarship in the Welfare State." In *Women, the State, and Welfare*, edited by Linda Gordon. Madison: University of Wisconsin Press, 1990. Pp. 9–35.

Gordon, Robert W. "Critical Legal Histories." 36 *Stanford Law Review* 57 (January 1984).

Grbich, Judith E. "The Body in Legal Theory." In *At the Boundaries of Law: Feminism and Legal Theory*, edited by Martha Albertson Fineman and Nancy Sweet Thomadsen. New York, Routledge, Chapman and Hall, Inc., 1991. Pp. 61–76.

Greenberg, Brian. "Worker and Community: The Social Structure of a Nineteenth-Century American City, Albany, New York, 1850–1884." Ph.D. diss.; Princeton University, 1980.

Greenberg, Jack. "Litigation for Social Change: Methods, Limits, and Role in Democracy." 29 *Record of the Association of the Bar of the City of New York* 320 (1974).

Grey, Thomas C. "Property and Need: The Welfare State and Theories of Distributive Justice." 28 *Stanford Law Review* 877 (May 1976).

Gunther, Gerald. "In Search of Evolving Doctrine on a Changing Court: A Model for a Newer Equal Protection." 86 *Harvard Law Review* 1 (1972–73).

Haakensson, Knud. "Natural Law and Moral Realism: The Scottish Synthesis." In *Studies in the Philosophy of the Scottish Enlightenment*, edited by M.A. Steward. Oxford: Clarendon Press, 1990. Pp 61–86.

Habermas, Jurgen. "What Does a Legitimacy Crisis Mean Today?" In *Legitimacy and the State*, edited by William Connolly. New York: New York University Press, 1984. Pp. 134–55.

Hacker, Andrew. "Getting Rough on the Poor." *The New York Review of Books*, October 13, 1988, pp. 12–17.

———. " 'Welfare': The Future of Illusion." *The New York Review of Books*, February 28, 1985, pp. 37–43.

Hannon, Philip J. "From Politics to Reality: A Historical Perspective on the Legal Services Corporation." 25 *Emory Law Journal* 639 (1976).

———. "The Leadership Problem in the Legal Services Program." 4 *Law and Society Review* 235 (November 1969).

Hare, R.M. "Justice and Equality." In *Justice and Economic Distribution*, edited by John Arthur and William H. Shaw. Englewood Cliffs, N.J.: Prentice-Hall, Inc., 1978. Pp. 116–31.

Harvard Law Review editors. "The Concept of Equality: The View from a Wider Perspective." 82 *Harvard Law Review* 1159 (1969).

Hay, Douglas. "Crime and Justice in 18th- and 19th-Century England." In *Crime and Justice: An Annual Review of Research*, edited by Norbal Morris and Michael Tonry. Vol. 2. Chicago: University of Chicago Press, 1980. Pp. 45–84.

Hazard, Geoffrey, Jr. "Social Justice Through Civil Justice." 36 *University of Chicago Law Review* 699 (1969).

Heclo, Hugh. "The Political Foundations of Antipoverty Policy." In *Fighting Poverty: What Works and What Doesn't*, edited by Sheldon H. Danziger and Daniel H. Weinberg. Cambridge: Harvard University Press, 1986. Pp. 312–40.

Herzer, David L. "Federal Jurisdiction Over Statutorily Based Welfare Claims." 6 *Harvard Civil Rights-Civil Liberties Law Review* 1 (December 1970).

Hochschild, Jennifer L. "Dilemmas of Liberal Self-Satisfaction, Civil Liberties, Liberal Theory, and Elite-Mass Differences." *Ethics* 96 (January 1986): 386–99.

———. "The Double-Edged Sword of Equal Opportunity." In *Power, Inequality, and Democratic Institutions: Essays in Honor of Robert Dahl*, edited by Ian Shapiro and Grant Reeher. New Haven, Conn.: Yale University Press, 1988. Pp. 168–200.

———. "Race, Class, Power, and the American Welfare State." In *Democracy and the Welfare State*, edited by Amy Gutmann. Princeton, N.J.: Princeton University Press, 1988. Pp. 157–84.

Hogan, Harry J. "The Supreme Court and Natural Law." 54 *ABA Journal* 570 (June 1968).

Holmes, Stephen. "Liberal Guilt: Some Theoretical Origins of the Welfare

State." In *Responsibility, Rights, and Welfare*, edited by Donald J. Moon. Boulder, Colo.: Westview Press, 1988. Pp. 77–106.

Hont, Istvan, and Ignatieff, Michael. "Needs and Justice in the *Wealth of Nations*: An Introductory Essay." In *Wealth and Virtue: The Shaping of Political Economy in the Scottish Enlightenment*, edited by Istvan Hont and Michael Ignatieff. Cambridge, Eng.: Cambridge University Press, 1983. Pp. 1–44.

Horne, Thomas. "Welfare Rights as Property Rights." In *Rights, Responsibilities and Welfare: The Theory of the Welfare State*, edited by: Donald J. Moon. Boulder, Colo.: Westview Press, 1988. Pp. 107–32.

Horwitz, Morton J. "The Jurisprudence of *Brown* and the Dilemmas of Liberalism." 14 *Harvard Civil Rights-Civil Liberties Law Review* 599 (Fall 1979).

Houseman, Alan. "Legal Services Corporation Funding of National Support Centers—A Cost Effective Approach to the Delivery of Quality Legal Services to the Poor." Washington D.C.: Center for Law and Social Policy, June 1981.

Howard, J. Woodford, Jr. "Role Perceptions and Behavior in Three U.S. Courts of Appeals." *Journal of Politics* 39 (1977): 916–38.

Howe, Daniel Walker. "The Evangelical Movement and Political Culture in the Second Party System." *Journal of American History* 77 (March 1991): 1216–39.

Hunt, Alan. "The Ideology of Law: Advances and Problems in Recent Applications of the Concept of Ideology to the Analysis of Law." 19 *Law and Society Review* 11 (Spring 1985).

Hutchinson, Allan C., and Moynihan, Patrick J. "Law, Politics, and the Critical Legal Scholars: The Unfolding Drama of American Legal Thought." 36 *Stanford Law Review* 199 (January 1984).

Ignatieff, Michael, "State, Civil Society, and Total Institutions: A Critique of Recent Social Histories of Punishment." In *Legality, Ideology, and the State*, edited by David Sugarman. New York: Academic Press, 1983. Pp. 183–211.

Karst, Kenneth L. "Equal Citizenship Under the Fourteenth Amendment." 91 *Harvard Law Review* 1 (November 1977).

Katz, Stanley N. "Thomas Jefferson and the Right to Property in Revolutionary America." *Journal of Law and Economics* 19 (1976): 467–88.

Katznelson, Ira. "Antagonistic Ambiguity: Notes on Reformism and Decentralization." *Politics and Society* 2 (1972): 323–33.

———. "Was the Great Society a Lost Opportunity?" In *The Rise and Fall of the New Deal Order, 1930–1980*, edited by Steve Fraser and Gary Gerstle. Princeton, N.J.: Princeton University Press, 1989. Pp. 185–211.

———. "Working-Class Formation and the State: Nineteenth-Century England in American Perspective." In *Bringing the State Back In*, edited by Peter R. Evans, Dietrich Rueschemeyer, and Theda Skocpal. New York: Cambridge University Press, 1985. Pp. 257–84.

Kelley, Robert. "Ideology and Political Culture from Jefferson to Nixon." *The American Historical Review* 82 (June 1977): 531–62.

Kerber, Linda. "The Republican Ideology of the Revolutionary Generation." *American Quarterly* 37 (1985): 474–95.

Kloppenberg, James, "The Virtues of Liberalism: Christianity, Republicanism, and Ethics in the Early American Political Discourse." *Journal of American History* 74 (June 1987): 9–33.

Kohn, Roger E. "AFDC Eligibility Requirements Unrelated to Need: The impact of *King v. Smith.*" 118 *University of Pennsylvania Law Review* 1219 (1970).

Kramnick, Issac. "Equal Opportunity and 'the Race of Life' " *Dissent* (Spring 1981), pp. 178–87.

Krislov, Samuel. "The OEO Lawyers Try to Constitutionalize a Right to Welfare: A Study in the Limits and Uses of the Judicial Process." 58 *Minnesota Law Review* 211 (1973).

Kritzer, Herbert M. "Political Correlates of the Behavior of Federal District Judges: A 'Best Case' Analysis." *Journal of Politics* 40 (1978): 25–58.

Kurland, Philip B. "The Judicial Road to Social Welfare." *Social Service Review* 48 (December 1974): 481–93.

Lazerow, Jama. "Spokesmen for the Working Class: Protestant Clergy and the Labor Movement in Antebellum New England." *Journal of the Early Republic* 13 (Fall 1993): 323–54.

Leeds, Jeffrey T. "A Life on the Court: A Conversation with Justice Brennan." *The New York Times Magazine* (October 5, 1986), p. 24.

Lemann, Nicholas. "The Origins of the Underclass." *The Atlantic Monthly* (July 1986), pp. 54–68.

Levy, Michael. "Liberty, Property, and Equality: Critical Reflections on the 'New Property.' " In *The Liberal Future in America: Essays in Retrieval,* edited by Phillip Abbott and Michael Levy. Westport, Conn.: Greenwood Press, 1985. Pp. 127–47.

Lipschultz, Sybil. "Social Feminism and Legal Discourse, 1908–1923." In *At the Boundaries of Law: Feminism and Legal Theory,* edited by Martha Albertson Fineman and Nancy Sweet Thomadsen. New York: Routledge, Chapman and Hall, Inc., 1991. Pp. 209–25.

Lowenstein, Daniel H., and Waggoner, Michael J. "Neighborhood Law Offices: The New Wave in Legal Services for the Poor." 80 *Harvard Law Review* 805 (February 1967).

Lowi, Theodore. "The Welfare State: Ethical Foundations and Constitutional Remedies." *Political Science Quarterly* 101 (1986): 197–220.

Lukas, J. Anthony. "Community and Equality in Conflict." *New York Times* (September 8, 1985), sec. 4, p. 25.

Lupu, Ira C. "Welfare and Federalism: AFDC Eligibility Policies and the Scope of State Discretion." 57 *Boston University Law Review* 1 (1977).

March, James G., and Olsen, John P. "The New Institutionalism: Organizational Factors in Political Life." *American Political Science Review* 78 (1984): 734–49.

McCann, Michael W. "Equal Protection for Social Inequality: Race and Class in Constitutional Ideology." In *Judging the Constitution: Critical Essays on Judicial Lawmaking*, edited by Michael W. McCann and Gerald L. Houseman. Boston: Scott, Foresman and Co., 1989. Pp. 231–64.

———. "Resurrection and Reform: Perspectives on Property in the American Constitutional Tradition." *Politics and Society* 13 (1984): 143–76.

McKay, Robert. "Judicial Review in a Liberal Democracy." In *Liberal Democracy: Nomos XXV*, edited by J. Roland Pennock and John W. Chapman. New York: New York University Press, 1983. Pp. 121–44.

McWilliams, Wilson Carey. "On Equality as the Moral Foundation for Community." In *The Moral Foundations of the American Republic*, edited by Wilson Carey McWilliams. 2d ed. Charlottesville: University Press of Virginia, 1979. Pp. 183–213.

Mendelsohn, Wallace. "From Warren to Burger: The Rise and Decline of Substantive Equal Protection." *American Political Science Review* 66 (December 1972): 1226–33.

Michel, Sonya. "The Limits of Maternalism: Policies Toward Wage-Earning Mothers During the Progressive Era." In *Mothers of a New World: Maternalist Politics and the Origins of Welfare States*, edited by Seth Koven and Sonya Michel. New York: Routledge, Inc., 1993. Pp. 277–320.

Michelman, Frank I. "Forward: On Protecting the Poor Through the Fourteenth Amendment." 83 *Harvard Law Review* 7 (1969–70).

———. "In Pursuit of Constitutional Welfare Rights: One View of Rawls' Theory of Justice." 121 *University of Pennsylvania Law Review* 962 (1973).

———. "Welfare Rights in a Constitutional Democracy." 1979 *Washington University Law Review* 659 (1979).

Milkis, Sidney. "The Presidency, Democratic Reform, and Constitutional Change." *Political Science* 20 (Summer 1987): 628–36.

Miller, Arthur Selwyn. "Toward a Concept of Constitutional Duty." 1968 *The Supreme Court Review* 199 (1968).

Mink, Gwendolyn. "The Lady and the Tramp: Gender, Race, and the Origins of the Welfare State." In *Women, the State, and Welfare*, edited by Linda Gordon. Madison: University of Wisconsin Press, 1990. Pp. 92–122.

Minow, Martha. "Adjudicating Differences: Conflicts Among Feminist Lawyers." In *Conflicts in Feminism*, edited by Marianne Hirsch and Evelyn Fox Keller. New York: Routledge, Chapman and Hall, 1990. Pp. 149–63.

Montgomery, David. "The Shuttle and the Cross: Weavers and Artisans in the Kensington Riots of 1844." *Journal of Social History* 5 (Summer 1972): 411–45.

Moon, J. Donald. "The Moral Basis of the Democratic Welfare State." In *Democracy and the Welfare State*, edited by Amy Gutmann. Princeton, N.J.: Princeton University Press, 1988. Pp. 27–32.

———. "Responsibility, Rights, and Welfare." In *Responsibiity, Rights, and*

Welfare: The Theory of the Welfare State, edited by J. Donald Moon. Boulder, Colo.: Westview Press, 1988. Pp. 1–15.

Nagel, Stuart. "Political Party Affiliations and Judges' Decisions." *American Political Science Review* 55 (December 1961): 843–51.

National Conference on Law and Poverty. *Conference Proceedings*. Washington, D.C., June 23–25, 1965.

Navarro, Mireya. "Teenage Mothers Viewed as Abused Prey of Older Men." *New York Times*, May 19, 1996. P. A1.

Nelson, Barbara J. "The Origins of the Two-Channel Welfare State: Workmen's Compensation and Mothers' Aid." In *Women, the State, and Welfare*, edited by Linda Gordon. Madison: University of Wisconsin Press, 1990. Pp. 123–51.

1937–38 Advisory Council on Social Security-Final Report. Reprinted in *Fiftieth Anniversary Edition: The Report of the Committee on Economic Security of 1935 and Other Basic Documents Relating to the Development of the Social Security Act*, with essays by Wilbur Cohen and Robert Ball; Foreword by Alan Pifer and Forrest Chisman. Washington, D.C.: National Conference on Social Welfare, 1985. Pp. 173–202.

Note. "*Shapiro v. Thompson*: Travel, Welfare, and the Constitution." 33 *New York University Law Review* 989 (November 1969).

O'Brien, David M. "Reconsidering Whence and Whither Political Jurisprudence." *Western Political Quarterly* 36 (December 1983): 541–48.

Offe, Claus. "Democracy Against the Welfare State? Structural Foundations of Neoconservative Political Opportunities." *Political Theory* 15 (November 1987): 501–37.

O'Neill, Timothy J. "The Language of Equality in a Constitutional Order." *American Political Science Review* 75 (September 1981): 626–35.

Orloff, Ann Shola. "Gender and the Social Rights of Citizenship: The Comparative Analysis of Gender Relations and Welfare States." *American Sociological Review* 58 (June 1993): 303–28.

———. "The Political Origins of America's Belated Welfare State." In *The Politics of Social Policy in the United States*, edited by Margaret Weir, Ann Shola Orloff, and Theda Skocpol. Princeton, N.J.: Princeton University Press, 1988. Pp. 3–27.

Orren, Karen. "Standing to Sue: Interest Group Conflict in the Federal Courts." *American Political Science Review* 70 (1976): 723–41.

Orwin, Clifford. "Welfare and the New Dignity." *The Public Interest* 71 (Spring 1983): 85–95.

Page, Benjamin. "Why Doesn't the Government Promote Equality?" In *Value Judgement and Income Distribution*, edited by Robert A. Solo and Charles W. Anderson. New York: Praeger Publishers, 1981. Pp. 279–319.

Pateman, Carole. "The Patriarchal Welfare State." In *Democracy and the Welfare State*, edited by Amy Gutmann. Princeton, N.J.: Princeton University Press, 1988. Pp. 231–60.

———. "Problems of Liberalism." *Ethics* 96 (January 1986): 375–85.

Pear, Robert. "Clinton Endorses the Most Radical of Welfare Trials." *New York Times*, May 20, 1996. P. A1.

———. "Clinton Wavers After Backing Welfare Plan." *New York Times*, June 15, 1996. P. 1.

Peterson, Paul E., and Rom, Mark C. "The Case for a National Welfare Standard." *The Brookings Review* (Winter 1988): 24–32.

Phillips, Michael J. "Thomas Hill Green, Positive Freedom, and the United States Supreme Court." *Emory Law Journal* 25 (Winter 1976): 63–114.

Pious, Richard. "Policy and Public Administration: The Legal Services Program and the War on Poverty." *Politics and Society* (May 1971). Pp. 365–91.

Pitkin, Hanna Fenichel. "Justice: On Relating Public and Private." *Political Theory* 9 (August 1981): 327–52.

Piven, Francis Fox. "Ideology and the State: Women, Power, and the Welfare State." In *Women, the State, and Welfare*, edited by Linda Gordon. Madison: University of Wisconsin Press, 1990. Pp. 250–64.

Pocock, J.G.A. "Cambridge Paradigms and Scotch Philosophers: A Study of the Relations Between the Civic Humanist and the Civil Jurisprudential Interpretation of Eighteenth-Century Social Thought." In *Wealth and Virtue: The Shaping of Political Economy in the Scottish Enlightenment*, edited by Istvan Hont and Michael Ignatieff. Cambridge, Eng.: Cambridge University Press, 1983. Pp. 235–52.

———. "The Concept of a Language and the Metier d'historian: Some Considerations on Practice." In *The Languages of Early-Modern Europe*, edited by Anthony Pagden. New York: Cambridge University Press, 1987. Pp. 19–38.

Pollitt, Katha. "Devil Women." *The New Yorker Magazine*, February 26 and March 4, 1996, pp. 58–64.

Pope, Jackie. "Women in the Welfare Rights Struggle: The Brooklyn Welfare Action Council." In *Women and Social Protest*, edited by Guida West and Rhoda Lois Blumberg. New York: Oxford University Press, 1990. Pp. 57–74.

"Poverty Law Developments." *Clearinghouse Review* (1967–77).

Pye, A. Kenneth. "The Role of Legal Services in the Antipoverty Program." 31 *Law and Contemporary Problems* 211 (Winter 1966).

Rabinowitz, Jonathan. "U.S. Opposing Welfare Plan in Connecticut." *New York Times*, December 9, 1995, p. A1.

Reich, Charles. "Individual Rights and Social Welfare: The Emerging Legal Issues." 74 *Yale Law Journal* 1245 (June 1965).

———. "The New Property." 73 *Yale Law Journal* 733 (April 1964).

Rein, Martin. "Equality and Social Policy." *Social Service Review* 51 (December 1977): 565–87.

"Report of the Committee on Economic Security." In *Fiftieth Anniversary Edition: The Report of the Committee on Economic Security of 1935 and*

Other Basic Documents Relating to the Development of the Social Security Act, with essays by Wilbur Cohen and Robert Ball; Foreword by Alan Pifer and Forrest Chisman. Washington, D.C.: National Conference on Social Welfare, 1985. Pp. 21–70.

Robertson, John. "The Scottish Enlightenment at the Limits of the Civic Tradition." In *Wealth and Virtue: The Shaping of the Political Economy in the Scottish Enlightenment*, edited by Istvan Hont and Michael Ignatieff. Cambridge, Eng.: Cambridge University Press 1983. Pp. 137–78.

Roosevelt, Franklin D. "Campaign Address on the 'Economic Bill of Rights.' " October 28, 1944. In *Fiftieth Anniversary Edition: The Report of the Committee on Economic Security of 1935 and Other Basic Documents Relating to the Development of the Social Security Act*, with essays by Wilbur Cohen and Robert Ball; Foreword by Alan Pifer and Forrest Chisman. Washington, D.C.: National Conference on Social Welfare, 1985. Pp. 150–56.

———. "The Initiation of Studies to Achieve a Program of National Security." Executive Order No. 6757. June 29, 1934. In ibid., p. 140.

———. "Message to Congress on Social Security." January 17, 1935. In ibid., pp. 141–44.

———. "Message to Congress Reviewing the Broad Objectives and Accomplishments of the Administration." June 8, 1934. In ibid., pp. 135–39.

———. "Presidential Statement Signing the Social Security Act." August 14, 1935. In ibid., p. 145.

———. "Radio Address on the Third Anniversary of the Social Security Act." August 15, 1938. In ibid., pp. 146–49.

Rosenblatt, Rand. "Legal Entitlement and Welfare Benefits." In *The Politics of Law*, edited by David Kairys. New York: Pantheon Books, 1982. Pp. 262–78.

Rosenheim, Margaret K. "*Shapiro v. Thompson*: 'The Beggars are Coming to Town.' " 1969 *The Supreme Court Review* 303 (1969).

Ross, Dorothy. "The Liberal Tradition Revisited and the Republican Tradition Addressed." In *The New American Intellectual History*, edited by John Higham and Paul K. Conkin. Baltimore: The Johns Hopkins University Press, 1979. Pp. 116–31.

———. "Socialism and American Liberalism: Academic Thought in the 1880s." In *Perspectives in American History II*, edited by Donald Flemming. Pp. 7–79.

Sandel, Michael J. "Democrats and Community." *The New Republic*, February 22, 1988, pp. 20–24.

———. "The Procedural Republic and the Unencumbered Self." *Political Theory* 12 (February 1984): 81–96.

Sanford, Frank P., III. "The Burger Court and Social Welfare Cases." 57 *University of Detroit Journal of Urban Law* 813 (Summer 1980).

Sapiro, Virginia. "The Gender Basis of American Social Policy." In *Women, the State, and Welfare*, edited by Linda Gordon. Madison: University of Wisconsin Press, 1990. Pp. 36–54.

Sarat, Austin. "The Maturation of Political Jurisprudence." *Western Political Quarterly* 36 (December 1983): 551–58.

———. "Studying American Legal Culture: An Assessment of Survey Evidence." 11 *Law and Society Review* 427 (Winter 1977).

Sarvasy, Wendy. "Beyond the Difference Versus Equality Policy Debate: Postsuffrage Feminism, Citizenship, and the Quest for a Feminist Welfare State." *Signs* 17 (Winter 1992): 329–62.

Schaar, John H. "Legitimacy and Modernity." In *Legitimacy and the State*, edited by William Connolly. New York: New York University Press, 1984. Pp. 222–49.

Schauer, Frederick. "An Essay on Constitutional Language." 29 *UCLA Law Review* 797 (1982).

Scheingold, Stuart A. "The Dilemma of Legal Services." 36 *Stanford Law Review* 879 (February 1984).

Schiffrin, Steve. "Liberalism, Radicalism, and Legal Scholarship." 30 *UCLA Law Review* 1175 (1983).

Schneider, Elizabeth M. "The Dialectic of Rights and Politics: Perspectives from the Women's Movement." In *Women, the State, and Welfare*, edited by Linda Gordon. Madison: University of Wisconsin Press, 1990. Pp. 226–49.

Seamon, John W. "Thomas Paine: Ransom, Civil Peace, and the Natural Rights to Welfare." *Political Theory* 16 (February 1988): 120–42.

Segers, Mary C. "Evaluating Affirmative Action: The Limitations of Redistributive Politics in Achieving Equality." In *Elusive Equality: Liberalism, Affirmative Action, and Social Change in America*, edited by James C. Foster and Mary C. Segers. Port Washington, N.Y.: National University Publications, 1983. Pp. 89–97.

Shapiro, Martin. "Fathers and Sons: The Court, the Commentators, and the Search for Values." In *The Burger Court: The Counter-Revolution that Wasn't*, edited by Vincent Blasi. New Haven, Conn.: Yale University Press, 1983. Pp. 218–38.

———. "The Presidency and the Federal Courts." In *Politics and the Oval Office*, edited by Arnold Meltsner. San Francisco: Institute for Contemporary Studies, 1981. Pp. 141–60.

———. "Recent Developments in Political Jurisprudence." *Western Political Quarterly* 36 (December 1983): 541–48.

———. "The Supreme Court: From Warren to Burger." In *The New American Political System*, edited by Anthony King. Washington, D.C.: American Enterprise Institute, 1978. Pp. 179–211.

Shklar, Judith N. "Injustice, Injury, and Inequality: An Introduction." In *Justice and Equality Here and Now*, edited by Frank S. Lucash. Ithaca, N.Y.: Cornell University Press, 1986. Pp. 13–33.

Shriver, Sargent. "Law Reform and the Poor." 17 *American University Law Review* 1 (December 1967).

Silbey, Susan, S. "Ideals and Practices in the Study of Law." 9 *Legal Studies Forum* 7 (1985).

Silver, Carol Ruth. "The Imminent Failure of Legal Services for the Poor: Why and How to Limit Caseload." 46 *Journal of Urban Law* 217 (1969).

Simon, William H. "Rights and Redistribution in the Welfare System." 38 *Stanford Law Review* 1431 (July 1986).

Skidmore, Thomas. "A Plan for Equalizing Property." Excerpt from *The Rights of Man to Property: Being a Proposition to Make it Equal among the Adults of the Present Generation: and to Provide for its Equal Transmission to Every Individual of Each Succeeding Generation* (pub. 1829). Reprinted in *Social Theories of Jacksonian Democaracy, 1825–1850*, edited by Joseph L. Blau. New York: Hafner Publishing Co., 1947. Pp. 355–64.

Skocpol, Theda. "Bringing the State Back In: Strategies of Analysis in Current Research." In *Bringing the State Back In*, edited by Peter P. Evans, Dietrich Rueschemeyer, and Theda Skocpol. New York: Cambridge University Press, 1985. Pp. 3–43.

———. "The Legacies of New Deal Liberalism." In *Liberalism Reconsidered*, edited by Douglas Maclean and Claudia Mills. Totowa, N.J.: Rowman and Allanheld Publishers, 1983. Pp. 87–104.

———. "The Limits of the New Deal System and the Roots of Contemporary Welfare Dilemmas." In *The Politics of Social Policy in the United States*, edited by Margaret Weir, Ann Shola Orloff, and Theda Skocpol. Princeton, N.J.: Princeton University Press, 1988. Pp. 293–311.

Smith, David G. "Liberalism and Judicial Review." In *Liberal Democracy: Nomos XXV*, edited by J. Roland Pennock and John W. Chapman. New York: New York University Press, 1983. Pp. 208–37.

Smith, Rogers M. "Constitutional Interpretation and Political Theory: American Legal Realism's Continuing Search for Standards." *Polity* 15 (Summer 1983): 492–514.

———. "Political Jurisprudence, the 'New Institutionalism,' and the Future of Public Law." *American Political Science Review* 82 (March 1988): 89–108.

Smith, Tom W. "Public Opinion and the Welfare State: A Crossnational Perspective." Paper presented at the American Sociological Association, Chicago, August 1987.

Smolla, Rodney A. "The Reemergence of the Right-Privilege Distinction in Constitutional Law: The Price of Protesting Too Much." 35 *Stanford Law Review* 69 (November 1982).

Social Security Act Amendments of 1939 [Public Law No. 379]. Reprinted in *Fiftieth Anniversary Edition: The Report of the Committee on Economic Security of 1935 and Other Basic Documents Relating to the Development of the Social Security Act*, with essays by Wilbur Cohen and Robert Ball; Foreword by Alan Pifer and Forrest Chisman. Washington, D.C.: National Conference on Social Welfare, 1985. Pp. 205–54.

The Social Security Act of 1935. [Public Law No. 271]. ibid., pp. 73–106.

Sosin, Michael R. "Legal Rights and Welfare Change, 1960–1980." In *Fighting Poverty: What Works and What Doesn't*, edited by Sheldon H. Danziger and Daniel H. Weinberg. Cambridge, Mass.: Harvard University Press, 1986. Pp. 260–83.

Sparer, Edward. "The New Legal Aid as an Instrument of Social Change." Address Before the Midwestern Conference of the Law Students Civil Rights Research Council. The University of Illinois, April 24, 1965.

——. "The Right to Welfare." In *The Rights of Americans: What They Are—What They Should Be*, edited by Norman Dorsen. New York: Random House, 1971. Pp. 65–93.

——. "The Role of the Welfare Client's Lawyer." 12 *UCLA Law Review* 279 (January 1965).

Strauber, Ira L. "Transforming Political Rights into Legal Ones." *Polity* 16 (Fall 1983): 72–95.

Stumpf, Harry P., and Janowitz, Robert J. "Judges and the Poor: Bench Responses to Federally Financed Legal Services." 21 *Stanford Law Review* 1058 (May 1969).

Stumpf, Harry P.; Schroerluke, Henry P.; and Dill, Forrest D. "The Legal Profession and Legal Services: Exploration in Local Bar Politics." 6 *Law and Society Review* 47 (August 1971).

Stumpf, Harry P.; Shapiro, Martin; and Sarat, Austin et al. "Whither Political Jurisprudence: A Symposium." *Western Political Quarterly* 36 (December 1983): 533–69.

Sugarman, David. "Law, Economy, and the State in England, 1750–1914: Some Major Issues." In *Legality, Ideology, and the State*, edited by David Sugarman. New York: Academic Press, 1983. Pp. 213–66.

Sumner, Colin. "Law, Legitimization, and the Advanced Capitalist State: The Jurisprudential and Social Theory of Juergen Habermas." In *Legality, Ideology and the State*, edited by David Sugarman. New York: Academic Press, 1983. Pp. 119–58.

Tate, C. Neal. "Personal Attribute Models of the Voting Behavior of U.S. Supreme Court Justices." *American Political Science Review* 75 (1981): 355–67.

Taylor, Charles. "The Nature and Scope of Distributive Justice." In *Justice and Equality Here and Now*, edited by Frank S. Lucash. Ithaca, N.Y.: Cornell University Press, 1986. Pp. 34–67.

Tushnet, Mark. "Departing from the Framer's Construct and the Rule of Law: The Critical Legal Scholars' Quest for Intrinsic Justice." *Cogitations* (Winter 1984), pp. 19–21.

——. "Following the Rules Laid Down: A Critique of Interpretivism and Neutral Principles." 96 *Harvard Law Review* 781 (1983).

Unger, Roberto. "The Critical Legal Studies Movement." 96 *Harvard Law Review* 563 (1983).

Van Alstyne, William. "Cracks in 'The New Property': Adjudicative Due

Process and the Administrative State." 62 *Cornell Law Review* 445 (1977).

Vandevelde, Kenneth J. "The New Property of the 19th Century: The Development of the Modern Concept of Property." 29 *Buffalo Law Review* 325 (1980).

Vernier, Paul. "Rights to Welfare as an Issue in Income Support Policy." In *Income Support: Conceptual and Policy Issues*, edited by Peter G. Brown, Conrad Johnson, and Paul Vernier. Totowa, N.J.: Rowman and Littlefield, 1981. Pp. 219–32.

Walkowitz, Daniel J. "Working-Class Women in the Gilded Age: Factory, Community, and Family Life Among Cohoes, New York Cotton Workers." *Journal of Social History* 5 (Summer 1972): 464–90.

Walzer, Michael. "The Agenda After Reagan." *The New Republic*, March 31, 1982, pp. 11–14.

———. "Welfare, Membership, and Need." In *Liberalism and Its Critics*, edited by Michael J. Sandel. New York: New York University Press, 1984. Pp. 200–218.

Weir, Margaret. "The Federal Government and Unemployment: The Frustration of Policy Innovation from the New Deal to the Great Society." In *The Politics of Social Policy in the United States*, edited by Margaret Weir, Ann Shola Orloff, and Theda Skocpol. Princeton, N.J.: Princeton University Press, 1988. Pp. 149–97.

Weir, Margaret; Orloff, Ann Shola; and Skocpol, Theda. "The Future of Social Policy in the United States: Political Constraints and Possibilities." In *The Politics of Social Policy in the United States*, edited by Margaret Weir, Ann Shola Orloff, and Theda Skocpol. Princeton, N.J.: Princeton University Press, 1988. Pp. 421–45.

Wertheimer, Alan. "The Equalization of Legal Resources." *Philosophy and Public Affairs* 17 (Fall 1988): 303–22.

West, Robin L. "The Difference in Women's Hedonic Lives: A Phenomenological Critique of Feminist Theory," In *At the Boundaries of Law: Feminism and Legal Theory*, edited by Martha Albertson Fineman and Nancy Sweet Thomadsen. New York: Routledge, Chapman, and Hall, 1991. Pp. 115–34.

Westwood, Howard C. "Legal Aid's Economic Opportunity." 52 *ABA Journal* 127 (February 1966).

Wexler, Stephen. "Practicing Law for Poor People." 79 *Yale Law Journal* 962 (1970).

Whitaker, William Howard. "The Determinants of Social Movement Success: A Study of the National Welfare Rights Organization." Ph.D. diss., Brandeis University, 1970.

Wiedner, Paul A. "The Equal Protection Clause: The Continuing Search for Judicial Standards." 57 *University of Detroit Journal of Urban Law* 867 (Summer 1980).

Wilkinson, J. Harvie, III. "The Supreme Court, The Equal Protection Clause, and the Three Faces of Equality." 61 *Virginia Law Review* 945 (June 1975).

Williams, Bernard O. "The Idea of Equality." In *Philosophy, Politics, and Society*, edited by Peter Laslett and W.G. Runciman. 2d ser. New York: Barnes and Noble, 1962. Pp. 110–31.

Winter, Ralph K., Jr. "Poverty, Economic Equality, and the Equal Protection Clause." 1972 *The Supreme Court Review* 41 (1972).

Withorn, Ann. "The Politics of Welfare." *Radical America* 16 (September 1982): 67–73.

Wolin, Sheldon. "Democracy and the Welfare State: The Political and Theoretical Connections Between *Staatsrason* and *Wohlfahrtsstaatsrason*." *Political Theory* 15 (November 1987): 467–500.

Yale Law School editors. "The New Public Interest Lawyers." 79 *Yale Law Journal* 1069 (1970).

Young, Iris M. "Toward a Critical Theory of Justice." *Social Theory and Practice* 7 (Fall 1981): 279–302.

Zetterbaum, Marvin. "Self and Subjectivity in Political Theory." *Review of Politics* 44 (January 1982): 59–82.

Archival Sources

The William J. Brennan Papers, The Library of Congress, Manuscript Division.

The Earl Warren Papers, The Library of Congress, Manuscript Division.

Case documents contained in Philip B. Kurland and Gerhard Casper, eds. *Landmark Briefs and Arguments of the Supreme Court of the United States: Constitutional Law*. Arlington, Va., and Bethesda, Md.: University Publications of America, 1975–1995. Vols. 50, 59, 61–62, 68–69, 76, 84.

Documents held by the library at the Center on Social Welfare Policy and Law, New York City.

Index